Alison is a mum to fou
to two older kids who
the time of writing were
trained teacher who runs a Taekwon-do business with
her partner and has been teaching for over twenty
years. When she can she blogs about life with four
teenage girls, two dogs, two cats and her partner, at
www.madhousemum.com. The mad house is situated
in Edenbridge, Kent.

www.facebook.com/MHouseMum
@MHouseMum

Raising *Girls* who can BOSS IT

MADHOUSEMUM

Published in 2017 by MadHouse Mum

www.madhousemum.com

Copyright © Alison Longhurst 2017

Designed and Typeset by Simon Hadlow

ISBN 978-1-9998997-0-7

For Mollie, Emily, Josie, Lily and Tasha
Without you as my guinea pigs this book
would not exist

Acknowledgements

Firstly I have to say a huge thank you to my girls: Mollie, Emily, Josie, Lily and Tasha, for allowing me to write about you and post photos of you, with fairly minimal fuss. You have been and continue to be my inspiration and my motivation. We're all surviving, often succeeding, sometimes screaming, always supporting and I am proud to be your mum and stepmum. Go out and boss it girls!

Thank you to my partner, Simon. For your never-ending encouragement in writing and publishing this book. For your belief in me. For all your work designing it – you are a creative genius and we make a great team.

To my friends, Jo Oranje and Natalie Dodd, to Jane Hadlow and to Simon Greaves, all of whom spent their precious time reading drafts of the book and editing it. Pointing out my shite grammar, whilst bigging up the book. I appreciate your time, your advice and your love.

To everyone who reads and supports my blog. Thank you for giving me the belief that I can actually write!

To Mike Hadlow, who told me to "just do it!"

Thanks to you all, I did!

Contents

Preface

If you've come here looking for top psychological information from an expert on how to raise your daughter, then you may want to ask for a refund, or just move to another shelf. I would by no means call myself an expert, more a work in progress: muddling through and failing regularly. I have five girls: four who are bona fide mine and one stepdaughter. I do have a stepson, but he only lasted living with us for 6 months before escaping and his current location is India. I'm not sure how much that reflects my parenting of boys. I teach boys, I love boys, I find boys fascinating, but my area of non-expertise is most certainly girls. Partly, because I am one and I was brought up with two sisters and no brothers. My sisters had mainly daughters: my Dad has 13 grandchildren, 11 of whom are girls. I couldn't go as far as to say that girls are my comfort zone - they are quite complicated creatures, who have to be 'worked out' before you can approach, sometimes with caution. My girls push me to my limits, but, as crazy as it sounds, I want them to. I want to raise girls who have a voice. I want to raise girls who have great self-esteem and are confident about who they are. I want to raise girls who can boss it.

This book is my thoughts on bringing up girls: getting through the minefield to raise daughters to be strong and sassy and how we as parents can potentially stay sane in the process. If you, like me, find parenting manuals a bit scary, slightly too officious and definitely too long, then you may find a connection here. This book is from the coalface of parenting girls. Psychologists tell us what we should be doing to bring up our daughters to be strong and independent beings. I am giving an insight into what it's really like putting it all into practice, with a healthy dose of going with the gut. It can be daunting. Women are still struggling for equality and as a parent to a girl, the responsibility to get it right can seem huge.

When my eldest daughter was three years old, I bought a notebook made by the company, 'Felicity Wishes', who at that time, made lots of products aimed at girls. On the front of the book it said, 'Wishes and Dreams', with a picture of a fairy leaping over a bright star and holding a wand up high in front of her, from which little stars were coming. I wrote to my girls in this notebook, thinking that it would be something they could read when they were older. At various points in the book there are pictures of different fairies, accompanied by a comment. I added to the comments with my own thoughts. Each chapter of this book is named after one of the wishes from my notebook.

Fairies are mistresses of magic. They symbolise power and the limitless quality of the imagination. They are the embodiment of the feeling that anything is possible and this is the legacy that I want for my daughters.

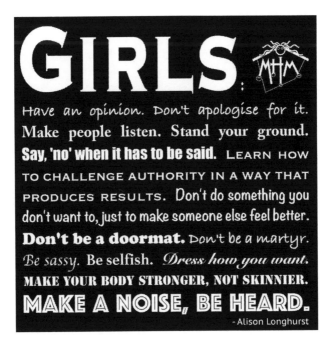

GIRLS: Have an opinion. Don't apologise for it. Make people listen. Stand your ground. Say, 'no' when it has to be said. LEARN HOW TO CHALLENGE AUTHORITY IN A WAY THAT PRODUCES RESULTS. Don't do something you don't want to, just to make someone else feel better. **Don't be a doormat.** Don't be a martyr. *Be sassy.* Be selfish. *Dress how you want.* MAKE YOUR BODY STRONGER, NOT SKINNIER. MAKE A NOISE, BE HEARD.
- Alison Longhurst

Decisions...decisions

I got the distinct impression, when I was pregnant with daughter 1, that people expected my then husband to want the bump to be a boy. Maybe it was the, "what are you hoping for - a girl or a boy? A boy?" that gave their inner thoughts away. This was compounded when I was pregnant with daughter 2: "I expect you're hoping it's a boy?" and then sealed with daughter 3's pregnancy: "surely it's going to be a boy?" By this time, I was getting a little irritated and had ammunition to fire back, a hand grenade in the form of statistics: "actually, it's 80% likely to be another girl" and a machine gun fire of, "I'm hoping it's a girl, because I've got a shed load of girls' clothes and I know how to wipe a girl's bum." By pregnancy four I was battle scarred and couldn't even be arsed to reply.

It did leave me wondering, however, whether people are a little bit afraid of girls. By 'people' I mean society and by 'society' I mean men. I do

❝*people are a little bit afraid of girls* ❞

wonder whether men have a subconscious fear of more women entering the world, because they know that we are just so bloody good at bossing it. To be fair, I think women are pretty freaked out by girls too; they have a reputation of complexity that goes ahead of them and once daughter 4 had appeared on the scene, people's comments quickly changed to: how will you cope when they are all teenagers?

Until I was eleven, I was essentially a boy. Women would try to direct me to men's toilets and I would regularly beat my chest in the hope that it would prevent anything from appearing. I never wore skirts or dresses and other girls in my school (I went to an all girls school) would often ask if I was going to have a sex change when I was older. I always found this a strange question, as in my mind there was no confusion as to who I was: a girl who didn't want to act like a girl and this certainly didn't mean that I wanted to be a boy. It was as if I knew that it was a phase and sure enough, by age 13 I was ready to sniff out the boys.

Because I was pretty confident about who I was when I was young, I think that I just presumed that my girls would be confident too. It wasn't until I had my own children and started mixing with other mums that

I realised that, when it comes to bringing up kids, there is a lot of anxiety around. While other parents were worrying about potty training and weaning, I was blindly stomping my way through each different stage, relying on gut instinct to ensure that we all survived. We did...just. Meanwhile, I found myself thinking about other things, things that seemed to be far more important to me than whether they could pee in a pot at one or three, or whether controlled crying or co-sleeping were good ideas. I turned my attention to how the hell I was going to bring up the girls so that they could boss life.

Despite having only girls, I didn't really give gender stereotypes a thought when they were young and I certainly didn't read any manuals on the subject. I think that I was far too busy surviving with small children who were born very close together: daughter 2 was born when daughter 1 was sixteen months old, and daughter 3 was born when daughter 2 was fifteen months old. I had a respectable age gap of two years between daughters 3 and 4. Everything I did came from my gut, which would of course have been influenced by my own upbringing. Nowadays, gut instinct is lost amidst the vastness of the Internet. Parenting forums are full of anxious exchanges between highly-strung

"Nowadays, gut instinct is lost amidst the vastness of the Internet"

parents, who quite honestly can't see through the fog of exhaustion and conflicting advice. It's no longer just the mums at your baby group who you are turning to; it's Mandy from Iowa, and Debs from Australia who are putting their oar in, along with hundreds of others from all different places. You end up swamped with opinions and advice that may also be loaded with cultural differences that muddy your own natural waters.

Then there's nature and nurture and where exactly do these two fit into this epic task of bringing up a girl who can boss it? That moment when two cells collide. In ecstasy. In desperation. In denial. In hope. In disbelief. The DNA is now the writing on your wall. Its destiny is already partially decided, but the way you

"how much will the social aspects that we have less control over, spray paint graffiti over our good work?"

nurture your creation will give it shape and substance. How much can we actually influence that DNA and how much will the social aspects that we have less control over, spray paint graffiti over our good work?

Doesn't it really piss you off when you have a baby and people say, "oh she looks so like her dad! I can't see you in her at all", and you're left thinking, 'I've just spent 48 hours pushing this little fucker out, at least tell me she's got my eyes'. Ah, nature. When you find out that you're pregnant and your first thought is: 'I hope she doesn't inherit my partner's OCD'. You then spend the first 6 years of her life, suspiciously watching the way she arranges her toys and deliberately push a teddy out of a line up to see if she melts down. How much should we be worrying about this and how much should we be concerned about who her friends at nursery are and what she is watching on TV?

Looking at my Wishes and Dreams notebook now that my girls are teenagers, is really interesting and throws some light on this whole debate. So many of their characteristics now, were written in that notebook 15 or so years before: the sporty one who is now a footballer and cricketer, as well as loving basketball, volleyball and hockey, loved balls from 18 months and never went anywhere without one. My daughter who is musical made up her own songs and sang them constantly in the back of the car from when she could talk. I referred to one of my daughters as a 'pickle' and 'cheeky' in the notebook and when I think of her now as a sassy 16-year-old, I wonder how much her hearing this made her live up to her labels, or how much was conceived in the womb. Naturally, any of their positive characteristics, I always attribute to myself and any negative ones are inherited from their father, but to what extent are they there at all? From the writings in my book, I would say that many of them are already there from birth.

Of course, we'll never know exactly to what extent. We do know that they are heavily influenced by the world around them, meaning our job as parents is tough. We also know that we must nurture their natural interests, even if, perhaps especially if, they don't fit into a stereotypical female role. By five years old, gender stereotypes become more set in a child's mind, so as parents we need to be pretty quick off the mark to influence them. There may be some elements of their natural character that we want to nurture and some that we want to eliminate entirely. We also need to be aware of our own preconceptions and how this will influence how we nurture our girls.

My friend has two boys and a girl. Her daughter is the middle child. I asked her whether there are ways that she treats her daughter any differently to her brothers. She told me that she folds the boys' clothes and puts them away in their drawers, but she leaves her daughter's clothes out for her to put away herself. I asked her whether this was because she'd shown her daughter how to fold clothes, but not her sons and she said "no". She just knows that her sons wouldn't put them away properly and so does it for them. Nature or nurture? Are boys naturally less able to fold clothes, and so need that bit of extra help and if so, by giving that, are we just nurturing an element of their nature that we should be trying to change by making them do it themselves? Is this sort of behaviour giving our daughters the idea that they are more capable at domestic chores and so this a role they continue when they are in a relationship?

Complicated stuff, isn't it?

Instinct told me that with my ever-increasing brood, I wasn't going to be able to take any shit from them and friends used to joke that I ran my house like an army boot camp. Whether they'd been girls or boys, I don't think that it would have mattered a jot. As my health visitor once said to me, they can wind you around their little finger

"they can wind you around their little finger from newborn"

from newborn and I have to say that I totally agree.
I sincerely believe that with bundles of joy it is vital
that you start as you mean to go on: firmly. You need
to set boundaries for their little legs to kick against
from birth and if your partner and you both agree, it's
a huge bonus. Just bear in mind that daddies may look
at their little girl and feel an overwhelming desire to
protect her, making him easier to manipulate. Dads –
don't be a push over and mums neither! Protecting our
daughters doesn't teach them resilience and if there is
one thing she is going to need in life that is it.

"a little less indulgence goes a long way"

Our daughters do not need to
be bubble wrapped. When they
fall over, I don't think we should
be too quick to rush and scoop
them up. A brisk, "come on,
you're fine!" works wonders
for diverting a potential meltdown. I have a rule: unless
there is blood, you're ok. There are exceptions, like
the time I dislocated daughter 4's elbow, by taking her
coat off at a slightly odd angle and the time she drank
white spirit because she was thirsty and a friend had
left it out. But for many of our daughter's scrapes and
bruises, I find that a little less indulgence goes a long
way to making her robust.

We know that a girl's self esteem drops at puberty, so we need to do everything in our power to give our daughters the best chance for it to be rocking by then.

Girls often feel pressure to be people pleasers and as parents we must be careful not to feed in to this gender stereotype. Daughter 1 was definitely like this from a very young age and

"Girls often feel pressure to be people pleasers"

I have to admit it's tempting as a parent to indulge in it, particularly as in our case she is the eldest of a large brood. Even now we refer to her as, 'Mummy Mollie' as she certainly carved out this role for herself and I'm not going to lie, it has been a huge help to me over the years. We have to be careful though, as we don't want our daughters' focus to constantly be outward looking. If she is always pleasing others, she won't have much energy left for herself. This is why I now teach my daughters to be selfish.

"Selfish" has very negative connotations and because of this I think that as parents we may shy away from uttering it. The last thing we want other parents to think is that we are telling our children to push to the front of the lunch queue, or grab at a favourite toy.

Yet, if you listen to the safety talk given on a plane, it sums up for me the need to look out for number 1 first: 'place your oxygen mask on yourself, before your child.' If we don't see to our own well-being before that of others, we've actually got less to give and therefore less to share.

I want my daughters to understand what makes them tick. To know what makes them feel really alive, to learn what energises them. I feel this will give them the skills to energise others.

"*Let's face it, there's always someone who is pissed off with us***"**

Another benefit of teaching our daughters to be selfish is that they are less likely to need reassurance from others that they are doing a good job. Let's face it, there's always someone who is pissed off with us, however hard we're trying. We're never good enough in someone's eyes. When we are selfish and inwardly connected we can feel positive about ourselves, whatever other people think. This is a skill that I really want to develop in my girls. If they see that I take time for myself, as well as looking after them, they will learn how important this is and they will benefit from having a recharged mum!

People can be cruel. Selfishness builds resilience and inner confidence and paradoxically this will make our daughters better placed to share.

People pleasers can also get the impression that they must be perfect at everything and so become risk averse, as they don't want to make a mistake. To combat this, we need to praise her efforts and not just her ability, whilst at the same time tell her that it's fine

"*praise effort not ability* "

to make mistakes. I point out to her that we learn more from mistakes than successes, so happy days! Let's be honest here, as parents we get a lot of practice very early on in our daughter's life to praise effort not ability, as a never-ending supply of indistinguishable pictures our cherub has drawn, appear from nursery. "That's a lovely bus you've drawn today, darling!" "It's not a bus, mummy, it's you!" I can't be the only one who has stared blankly at a 3-year old's masterpiece and thought to myself, 'what the fuck is it?'

On top of this, I think we should encourage her to take risks. Gulp, yes I know. Don't worry, I'm not suggesting that you do what my dad did. He decided to use me as a guinea pig after doing a rock-climbing course in

Wales. Before I knew it, I had a rope around my waist with the other end attached to the leg of my bed. I was standing on the ledge of my bedroom window, sobbing my heart out, while my mum and sisters were looking on with a mixture of bemusement and terror. Dad and Bear Grylls would say that it was character building. I say, know your daughter's limits and then push her a tiny bit further – in this case, off the ledge. Because of the way a female's brain works, we are more likely to get out of a stressful situation than fight it, which makes risk-taking harder for girls than for boys. I try to encourage my daughters to assert themselves in challenging situations and not to shy away from them. Having said that, I've yet to chuck them out of a bedroom window.

"Too much praise will actually serve to lower her self-esteem"

One important lesson that I have learnt is not to praise everything our daughter does, as if it's never been done before: "That's a brilliant picture of me, sweetheart and don't listen to anyone who tells you it looks like a bus!" It certainly pays to be selective and save high praise for when she really achieves. Too much praise will actually serve to lower her self-esteem:

giving a medal for coming last, devalues the medal for coming first and she will know it.

Everything nowadays is so immediate and when your daughter doesn't accomplish something straight away, she may well get easily frustrated and give up. I see this a lot in my work as a Taekwon-do instructor. We must teach our daughters the dying art of patience – her future employers and any children she may have will thank us for it, as will she. The trouble is, it's us against today's culture of instant gratification. Kids are growing up now without having to wait for anything. But if they don't get something straight away, we need to try to sit on our hands and zip up our mouths.

We shouldn't be too quick to help, because yes, you guessed it – we will fuck up her self-esteem. She needs to learn how to work things out for herself. A culture seems to be growing where parents aren't happy with standing on the sidelines. At my daughter's football club, parents have been reprimanded for coaching during matches. We try to encourage parents of our Taekwon-do students to sit outside the room, thus denying them the temptation to help their child from the side. We are teaching the students the art of perseverance, whilst the parents are honing their own self-control!

"We need to tell our girls that they can achieve anything"

At this point, we could all be forgiven for wondering how on earth our daughters are going to get to puberty with their self-esteem intact, but as parents we can only do our best. We need to be the best role models there can be – yes mum, why the hell weren't you hanging off that bedroom ledge with me? We need to tell our girls that they can achieve anything, because gender stereotypes may try to hinder this view. Because of this, we mustn't assume anything: she can boss maths and she can boss science and we need to encourage her to try all sorts of things and to take seriously the things she is interested in. Let her figure it out.

Daughter 3 was doing ballet classes for a year from the age of 2. She seemed to be enjoying it, until one day she said to me, "I want to do football". Bearing in mind neither her dad nor I played football and she had no brothers who were watching and playing football, this came as a complete surprise. So, aged 3, I signed her up for the local classes. Now aged 15, she has been signed with clubs Chelsea and Millwall since she was 9-years-old and plays for Wales. A couple of years ago she asked me to find her a cricket club. I had a vague look – I don't like cricket. My partner, a cricket fan, did some research and the following season she got in to the Kent team.

What I am saying here is don't be hoodwinked by gender stereotypes. Your daughter has the potential to boss anything and you need to be right behind her, even if it's not your bag!

To raise a girl who can boss it, we are going to have to allow her to! This takes courage and earplugs. We need our daughters to have a voice and this is yet another gender stereotype that we need to smash. We have to allow her to disagree with us and allow her to become angry. It isn't easy when you're tired and have lost the will and you'd rather she just gave up on her convictions in order to keep the peace.

I am very aware that it's important that we encourage our daughters' assertiveness, because fast forward a few years - yes, I know you don't want to, but bear with me - and she may be being told what to do in a situation that really does require her to take control, such as with a beguiling crush or a dodgy stranger. She also needs to be able to stand her ground with a bossy friend. We can teach her how to do it, with phrases such as, "I don't like the way you are talking to me".

Daughter 4 is the bossy one in our house (am I feeding a gender stereotype by referring to her as 'bossy'?) I have often listened in on a play date and wanted to say to her friend, "stand up to her!" At her year 7 parents' evening, her teachers kept telling me how assertive she was. "Bossy?" I said to each one in turn. "No", they all replied, "she's a natural leader". I think that it is really important that we teach our girls how to express themselves so that people will listen. Earplugs at the ready and get your daughter to make herself heard! It is also probably really important that we don't refer to our daughters as 'bossy'. She's not bossy, she has good leadership skills. I find that I have to retrain my own brain when it comes to gender stereotypes.

"I have to retrain my own brain when it comes to gender stereotypes"

Having gone through a divorce, I am acutely aware of the need for us to develop our daughters' communication skills in all areas, so that they can say how they feel. This way they will hopefully understand their own feelings better and be better equipped to deal with them. I have tried to encourage my daughters to focus on their own feelings and not just on the feelings of others.

One of the easiest ways of doing this is by expressing how we feel about something, such as excitement about a holiday or a family outing. If one of them says something is 'good', then I try to ask her what she means. Of course, to a teenager this simply feels like interrogation, so I have to tentatively try to explore her feelings, by asking her, for example, what was the best bit? And, what are you most looking forward to? Daughter 3 would answer every question she could with, 'good' and when we tried to 'explore her feelings' she would say, "good and great". It has become a family joke: "how was football training? Good and great?"

Daughter 1 is pretty chilled out, until all of a sudden, she is prone to complete meltdown. I have worked out that these meltdowns occur when she doesn't fully understand her own feelings. Perhaps she can't recognise whether she is sad, angry, frustrated or disappointed and doesn't always know how to manage them. She is 18, but it is the same for a toddler.

My advice would be, suss out communication early on, to save teenage toddler tantrums. I have also learnt that it is really important that you empathise

"*it is really important that you empathise with your daughter***"**

with your daughter, so that she knows that she matters and that her feelings are important – whatever her age.

Girls get so bombarded by mixed messages, that it is up to us as parents to cut through the crap: bodies, rights, abilities… it's complicated being a girl and they will rely on us to navigate. When they are teenagers, you are literally a taxi driver. You've seen the signs in the back of people's cars: Mum's/Dad's taxi. But all through their lives we are metaphorical taxi drivers, taking them to a place where they are in control. We need to steer them around the gender stereotypes. Or just get them to drive straight over them. For example, sexism is one area that parents can give their daughters some clarity from a young age. Children recognise brand names from 2 years old, so I guess it's never too early to start. When we are watching TV with our daughters we can give them a balanced view, although don't be surprised if your 4-year-old just croons, "she's so beautiful" at every Disney princess. We can certainly highlight positive female role models in their lives, be it on screen, in the family, in the books they are reading, or we are reading to them.

"We can certainly highlight positive female role models"

According to some experts, dressing our daughters in pink is limiting their social and economic potential, as well as maintaining the gender pay gap. No wonder people seemed concerned that I would be having yet another girl, as they seem to come fraught with issues. Yet ask a little girl what her favourite colour is and the chances are, she will say, "pink". Shit. What the hell are we supposed to do? It may stunt my daughter's personality and drastically limits choices and decisions!

> **"***ask a little girl what her favourite colour is and the chances are, she will say, "pink"* **"**

I'm going to be honest here, I didn't give the colour of their clothes a thought. That was until one Christmas when my dad and stepmum bought daughter 1 a baby pink, sparkly, fluffy coat and I immediately realised it objectified everything I hated about dressing girls in pink. I actually remember thinking that it was vulgar. I was confident that she would hate it and we could just bring it out on the odd occasion that we all got together. Of course, she absolutely loved that damn coat. She loved the sparkles, she loved its fluffiness, but most of all, she loved the colour pink. At first, I was embarrassed by the coat. Strangers would admire it and I would mutter that it was a gift and not my style.

Other coats would come and go, but that coat stayed and because she didn't grow very fast, it was with us for a long time. Long enough, in fact for me to realise that it wasn't vulgar and in fact, it didn't matter. She had decided that she liked it and I couldn't think of a good reason to argue.

So, what is it with the colour pink? Pink is just another colour. A colour that has been hijacked and shoe horned into a box by marketeers and now we live in fear of it. We give stickers to our youngest Taekwon-do students at the end of each class. The stickers are red, blue, yellow, green and dark pink. They can't choose their own stickers, because it would be carnage, but I dread a boy getting the pink sticker, because more often than not the bottom lip goes out, the arms cross and the head shakes, particularly if they are nearer the older age in the class, four or five, rather than three.

Pink has been sabotaged by toy and clothes manufacturers and we are all conditioned like Pavlov's dogs to think of it as a girl's colour. Then, bam! As simply as that, girls' choices are limited as gender stereotyping gets its grip around them. Pink doll's houses, pink doll's clothes, pink tea sets and before we know it girls are putting themselves into stereotypically feminine roles.

Do girls like pink because it's 'girly' and makes them feel 'pretty' or just because they like the colour? Is it even possible to distinguish between the two once she is exposed to the cultural view that pink is the colour for a girl?

I think it's one of those chicken and egg situations. What came first, girls born preferring pink or girls born gender neutral and have pink thrust upon them? Psychologists argue amongst themselves over this one, as some say that the innate differences in male and female

"What came first, girls born preferring pink or girls born gender neutral and have pink thrust upon them?"

brains are so malleable that tiny differences are easily amplified over time. Others say that under two years of age they don't seem to show a preference and then they are quite literally bombarded and there goes a hope in hell. It's probably a bit of the chicken and a bit of the egg, but whatever the answer is, the pressure is on us as parents to be aware and we really are up against it. Allowing my daughter to wear that pink, sparkly coat, was certainly feeding the stereotype.

Friends who had boys would bemoan the fact that they couldn't dress them up. Girls are definitely brought

> **"***Girls are definitely brought up with the expectation of dressing up***"**

up with the expectation of dressing up put upon them. I was expected to dress up for the theatre and dress up for a party. When daughter 1 was 3, I was taking her to a party in a party dress and, of course, that goddamn pink coat. As we left the house, I saw her put a little tinted lip salve in her pocket, which someone had obviously given her. "Why are you putting that in your pocket?" I asked. "So that I can put it on again after I've eaten," she replied. I was shocked. I was still at the stage of looking like a bag of shit. You know that stage, when it's been all about babies and you've not got around to reconnecting with your pre-baby self. In fact, I only got reconnected by my younger sister, who went through my underwear drawer and threw out all but two pairs of knickers, telling me that I should be ashamed of myself. She then took me on a shopping spree and convinced me to buy plastic, black patent, knee-high boots. I was outwardly reconnected, inwardly still a shitbag mother.

Daughter 1 would clip clop around in any pair of high-heeled shoes she could get her hands on. She earned the title, 'princess' and everything in her room became pink. Was this because I wanted to dress up my little girl? Not at all! In me there was still a tomboy somewhere, who didn't need a mannequin to fulfil her own needs. It was all coming from her...although a part of me blames the coat.

Let's cut the over-analysis and get to the point: girls enjoy dressing up. Once, at nursery, daughter 2 climbed in to the suitcase filled with dressing up clothes and pulled down the lid. When her teacher came to tidy up, my daughter opened the lid suddenly and stood up beaming. The teacher nearly jumped out of her skin and was never the same again. My daughters loved their Disney Princess outfits and one day dressed my friend's son as Ariel. My friend was horrified and I seem to remember her saying, "get him out of that, before his dad sees him!" It's lucky he didn't see the nail polish the girls would paint on him.

I think that we need to understand that some things are just in-built and not worry. Perhaps not push things onto our girls either, if they are clearly uneasy about it. I mean, plastic, black patent, knee-high boots. What was my sister thinking? Whether our daughters wear pink, blue or any colour of the rainbow, there are two things that are certain: they will still never have enough money for all the clothes they want to buy when they are teenagers and they will never forgive you for the crap clothes you dressed them in as a kid. Oh, and my friend's son – there were no long-term effects (although he does have a part time job as a drag queen. No, I'm joking, but really, so what if he does?)

One of my bugbears is sexualised clothing for little girls: 3-inch heels on shoes for an 8-year-old, really? T-shirts with the slogan, 'Future WAG' and a top for a toddler with a bikini stuck on the front? Let's let little girls be just that: little girls. I have teenagers and trust me, they wear what the hell they want. If you tell them to take it off, they will stuff it in a carrier bag and put it on when they get there. So please, no padded bikini tops for 7-year-olds. Early sexualisation is damaging the aspirations of our daughters and it also affects how boys and men view them.

"Let's let little girls be just that: little girls "

There is no doubt about it, as parents of girls we are constantly battling against stereotypes and one place this is extremely prevalent is with toys. When I was growing up, I played with Barbies and Action Men.

This had nothing to do with my parents; this is what I chose to do. My youngest daughter loved dolls. The way she left them at bath time, with one token Action Man surrounded by eight naked Barbies, made it look like an orgy was taking place every night. When she asked for a doll for Christmas aged 9, I was a little concerned. Surely she should be growing out of them by now? At 10 she moved onto those china Victorian dolls. These ones really freak me out. I always feel as if they should be part of a horror film, with those intense, staring eyes. Psychologists probably have a field day on the effects of girls playing with dolls: taking on the role of carer and fulfilling their own stereotype. Well, you know what? I think that's rubbish. None of my other daughters gave a toss about dolls and yet the youngest that did is the most selfish, single-minded of all of them. She'll be the one with the full-time job, unable to bear the thought of not having time to herself in the day.

I think as parents we should encourage our girls to enjoy a range of toys, but not to get uptight if they seem drawn to the gender stereotype. Encourage them with construction toys, science experiments, cars on a track, but don't be disappointed if they enjoy pushing a pram. They could still be a doctor or a mathematician.

"as parents we can only do so much to influence them"

I think that they find their own way and just like when they are teenagers, as parents we can only do so much to influence them; I think that this starts at a very young age.

The first comment in the Wishes and Dreams notebook is, 'Decisions...decisions'. Parenting is all about decision-making and one thing I have learnt is not to over-analyse anything, because then we lose what is real for our daughters. Life is so full of 'ifs' and 'buts', but we need to lead by example and show our girls how to be confident and decisive. We need to make decisions about what is worth tackling and we need to teach our daughters how to take responsibility for making their own decisions. If the shit hits the fan, then we show them how anything can be dealt with. Literally, anything.

Treat yourself!

There's an excerpt from 'Wishes and Dreams' that reads, 'you already have bright pink nail polish on your fingers and toes. You love shoes and looking pretty'. Shoot me now! For, according to psychologists, I have committed the cardinal sin: I have referred to my daughter as 'pretty'! We are damaging girls psychologically by calling them 'pretty'. This is apparently undermining their self-esteem, as they grow up feeling that they are ultimately defined by their looks. Shit –

> **"We are damaging girls psychologically by calling them 'pretty'"**

rewind! I'm thinking about all the other times I have referred to my daughters as 'pretty'. What the hell have I done to them? Is that why they can't stop taking selfies? It's my fault (again!).

Deep breaths and perspective here. I can see their point. I have never just defined my daughters by their looks. I am not a mum who feels the need to constantly tell them how beautiful they are. But you know what? If I want to tell them they are beautiful, I will. I am sure that mums tell sons that they are looking good. This is just a small part of the way in which I talk to them. My complimenting their clothes and their looks is not defining who they are, it is simply complimenting them on their clothes and their looks.

People also get very hot and bothered about the different ways girls and boys are spoken to. For example, strangers tell little girls that they are pretty, while their brothers are told that they are smart. Is this really true? I mean, I am constantly telling people that all their children are gorgeous. There I go again. I must stop before I set any more children up for failure.

The point is, however, that if we are always referring to girls as 'pretty' first off, then it is telling them that appearance is the first thing we notice, which gives them the message that their looks are their most important quality. We don't want our daughter to grow up thinking that her looks are more important than being strong or independent. We don't want her to apologise for having an opinion. Girls must have a voice.

> **"**We don't want our daughter to grow up thinking that her looks are more important than being strong or independent**"**

As parents of girls, I think that it is important that we tell them what they can achieve and show them what they can do. I think that we must be specific with our daughter when we praise her smartness, for example, "You know a lot about the planets, don't you?" rather than just, "You're such a clever girl". I don't think that we need to be fearful of complimenting them on their looks, if that's not all we are telling them. I do think that we need to think about what we say, so that they grow into confident adults.

The thing is, that even if we don't define them by their looks, the chances are that they will grow up obsessing about how they look anyway. Girls often link happiness to body image. It's important that as parents we divert attention to what interests them, big-up how we love that they can express themselves and regularly ask what they are doing. However, given the fact that there is a media fire burning so hot on body image that it is impossible for girls to grow up unaffected by it, I don't think the blame

"there is a media fire burning so hot on body image"

for the pressures our daughters may feel as they are growing up can be laid squarely at our feet. Although, we certainly don't want to add fuel to the fire.

I feel as if I am walking a tightrope. Body confusion is rife among women and it's all too easy for us to pass this confusion on to our daughters. We may admire a size 16 model in a magazine, celebrating the fact that she is owning her curves, whilst at the same time looking at our own bodies in the mirror and despising our fat. If we genuinely think that the model looks amazing, then why are so many of us dissatisfied with our own body image? I think that as women we don't really know what we want to be. I don't think that we know what to do with our bodies and who we are doing it for. I think that from a young age girls are bombarded with such mixed messages about female body shape, that by the time they are teenagers, they are totally confused and this is pretty much how they remain throughout their adult lives.

> **"I don't think that we know what to do with our bodies"**

Having a positive body image means that our daughter sees herself accurately and she probably feels pretty good about how she looks. Of course, there are always going to be things she doesn't like about her body. If our daughter raises a concern with us about her image, then we should be sympathetic. We should listen, acknowledge and perhaps let her know that we have wrestled with the same problems. However, we need to reiterate that it didn't get in the way of our life, or what we wanted to do. It is not insurmountable and she can get over it. Daughter 1 was looking in the mirror. "I hate my nose," she said. Then looking over at me, she added, "It's like yours, but at least I've got nice eye lashes." "Well," I replied. "Evidently I am managing to survive life even with the burden of a wonky nose and crap lashes, so you needn't worry!"

Severe negative body image can lead to serious eating and exercise disorders. We all take our cues from the world around us, and friends and family can be highly influential. I can remember being told that my bum looked big in a pair of leggings. I thought for years that I had a big bum. Until several boyfriends and a fair few compliments later, I decided that actually my arse was rather bloody amazing. Negative comments stick and as parents we need to be careful how we talk to our daughters.

Sometimes I feel as if I am on a knife edge between criticising something my daughter is wearing and encouraging her to change it, without sounding overly critical. For example, if a cropped top is revealing a belly of puppy fat, how do you get her to change the top to one that doesn't accentuate her tummy without sounding critical of her body shape? I am frequently pretty terrified of saying the wrong thing. That one comment that may stay with her for years. That one negative thought that could trigger an eating disorder.

"I am frequently pretty terrified of saying the wrong thing"

Indeed, what do we say to our daughters if we think that they are overweight? I mean, on the one hand we are told categorically never to talk about weight with them, as this can lead to mental issues such as anorexia nervosa, and yet on the other hand we are told that children are getting fatter and we need to do something about it. Have you ever tried suggesting to your daughter that she is overweight, without mentioning the words 'fat' and 'diet'? It's impossible. You can encourage her to exercise more and of course extol the virtues of healthy eating. You can lead by example, but she will probably suss you out and bring you back to one of those words. It's a minefield, because these are words you just can't highlight. On top of this, we are told that everyone is beautiful just the way they are, and on the other hand we mustn't refer to our girls as beautiful.

How do you get it right?

Well, I know that if my girls don't see me constantly trying to diet, this will help them not to obsess. We are our kid's role models. Kitchen shelves all over the world, are heaving under the weight of low carb diet cook books. My Instagram feed is full of photos of shredded veg. Photos of every meal, meticulously prepared under Slim Fast rules. Mum wants to lose weight. Nothing wrong with that. Mum is obsessed with losing weight. Every pound lost gives rise to an exuberant shout out in her Facebook news feed. We all know that losing weight is bloody hard work and making the ordeal public helps keep the momentum going. Meanwhile, her daughter is taking all this on board. Her mum's desperation to change her body shape. Her daughter can see that it's not about who her mum is: a hardworking, amazing person who is always there for her family and who gave birth to wonderful human beings. No, her daughter is seeing through her mum's eyes that it isn't, in reality, about who you are, it's about what you look like. Because ultimately, for many, this does go quite some way to defining who they are.

"*it's not what you look like, it's who you are***"**

We should be telling our girls that it's not what you look like, it's who you are. It's easy to fall in to these traps though: feeding our own insecurities to our daughters. Perhaps we need to tell ourselves that we don't need to change our body shape to conform.

We certainly need to talk to them about nutrition, so that they will understand what is good for them. It is important that they understand the difference between health and appearance. My younger sister was always stick thin. She would eat all sorts of crap and still be as thin as a pencil. Being a different body shape to her and someone whose body would visibly show a packet of biscuits after consumption, I used to tell her that although she wasn't putting on weight, she was 'fat inside'. This comment always made me feel better and although it was a sibling jibe, it contained an element of truth.

Our daughters need to understand the importance of eating a healthy balanced diet, over appearance. The truth is, however, that you cannot be watching them all the time, so there is an element of trust and a prayer involved here. I used to find receipts for packets of doughnuts in my stepdaughter's room. Pancakes and bagels were hidden in her drawer. I find biscuit wrappers under daughters' duvets and when I tackle them they reply, "we are hungry!"

We must also remind ourselves that it is usual for girls to gain weight before hitting puberty, so we mustn't become too fat phobic. When one of my daughters was 7-years-old, I noticed that she had steadily put on weight. Family members were beginning to comment and she would look at her tummy and say it was big. I didn't want to put her on a diet and I certainly didn't want to single her out from her sisters. I decided to make changes to our diet and lifestyle that benefited the whole family. Within a few weeks she herself could notice a difference in her body shape and it was really interesting to see what a positive effect this had on her, even at such a young age. With this part of bringing up our daughters I think we can educate, we can demonstrate, we can hope.

"*we can educate, we can demonstrate, we can hope*"

We can also try not to fall in to the traps that the media set for us, such as telling us to get 'beach body ready!' In my Ladies' Taekwon-do class, I make motivational comments through gruelling exercises. Before a

Summer break, I was shouting, "come on ladies, not long until we'll be getting in to our bikinis!" I suddenly found myself questioning whether this is perhaps the wrong thing to say? I work in the fitness industry. Part of my job is to get people fitter. It matters not what size or shape they are, my goal is to make them stronger. Yet by making the comment about the 'bikini body', I was projecting the wrong image. We need to keep our focus on our strength and our health and not feed the media led obsession with striving for a certain look.

A negative body image develops when someone feels that his or her body just doesn't measure up. They will measure themselves against family and friends' ideals and against images in the media. As parents, we have a huge responsibility to get this right, because media images are a powerful force on our daughters. It is important that we point out that models are photo-shopped and that therefore the images aren't real. There are the models who are starving themselves to within an inch of their lives, only to have curves photo-shopped on to their bodies. Oh, the irony of it! Meanwhile, our daughters are lapping up the images. Images that are reinforced by celebrities, who

"*Girls are obsessed with their image***"**

further feed the obsession with looks. In a warped kind of way, they make it all seem more real than the photos of models, because their whole business is built around making people connect with them.

Girls are obsessed with their image. They are obsessed with other girls' images. They are hypercritical of both. I can remember hearing that a friend had bought her daughter expensive make-up for Christmas, when she was eight years old. I saw this as feeding her daughter's obsession with her looks. Then there's the social media obsession with make-up. Driven at high speed forwards by beauty bloggers, who are telling our impressionable daughters that it is vital to have a different make up brush for each part of your face. Trust me, I know. I know because my daughters are keeping Chinese factories in business. There is often great debate amongst parents on what age is suitable for their daughter to have her ears pierced. Is there a right and a wrong? Does this constitute early sexualisation of our daughters? It's all a matter of perception and how our own parents brought us up.

I was recently shocked by what I perceived to be a highly sexualised, derogatory image of a woman dressed as a super hero, on the back of the school bus, accompanied by the words: Super Service. The image made me really angry: the huge cleavaged, short-skirted, high-booted, sexually posturing female made me wonder what message it was sending our kids. I felt that it was somehow normalising a certain look and the connotations of the juxtaposition of the image and the words undermined everything I was teaching my daughters. I also felt that it undermined the message that parents are hopefully trying to teach their sons about the difference between women on screen and real women. When I voiced my concerns to other mums, I was really surprised by some of their responses. Some agreed, others couldn't see a problem with it. They looked at the image and saw an empowered female heroine. One lady even said how the cartoon resembled her daughter and went on to list her daughter's vital statistics. My brain began to whirr. Many who disagreed with me felt that we have bigger issues to worry about and that this is the least of our worries. But is it?

"Young girls are bombarded with highly sexualised images "

You see, ours is the adult perspective. Whilst some mums may only see power and strength represented in the cartoon, what their 13-year-old daughters are seeing may well be very different. Young girls are bombarded with highly sexualised images of females online, in magazines and on the TV and research shows it affects them. It undermines their self-confidence and is detrimental to their mental health. A 13-year-old girl may look at that cartoon and see yet another image that she feels unable to emulate: huge boobs, a tiny waist, full lips and a thigh gap to die for. These girls won't necessarily see the superhero that their mum is seeing. Their daughters are at an age when they can look at an image and form a critique, but that critique may very well be detrimental to them.

My brain continues to whirr. Perception: one mum watches her 4-year-old daughter gyrating to Beyoncé with pride, whilst another wonders with bewilderment and sadness where on earth she learnt those moves. One mum will buy make-up for her 7-year-old daughter, while another will look at her 16-year-old go off to school with her face caked in make-up and shake her head. How many of us have watched documentaries on American beauty queens and thought, wtf? We need to be aware of perception to understand that what we perhaps think is ok, because of our adult perception, may mean something very different to our children. Whilst as parents we may well think there are more important things to worry about, a young, impressionable girl has worries that are very different to ours.

> **"***I want my daughters to be comfortable in their own skins***"**

I want my daughters to be comfortable in their own skins and not just at the service of others. I want them to understand that the images the media portrays aren't real. I also want them to know that in most situations they aren't the subjects of scrutiny, so they don't need to be too self-conscious.

I am constantly telling my daughters that they look far nicer with less make-up, but they just don't get it. They don't get it because the images they are seeing on social media are telling them otherwise. My daughters own so many make-up brushes, they are at risk of them taking over their rooms. I swear the brushes are having babies. I asked daughter 1 what they were all for and she tried to explain. By her explanation of the fourth brush, I was lost in a different language. "This is for the crease of my eyelid," she said, by which point I really had decided that I was faced with an alien. No wonder it takes them so bloody long to get ready in the mornings – there's a brush for every inch of their face!

The obsession is down to the eyebrows, which even get their own word: on fleek. Thigh gaps are talked about, the size of a bum. Celebrities are their role models and it is all about the look: girls comment, 'hot' and 'cute' on their friends' Instagram photos. These are not words that as a parent we want to see written about our daughters, but see it you will and this is their world. It all really matters now to our girls and, as their parent, it is pointless telling them that it doesn't. Yes, we must keep asking them what they like doing. Yes, we must keep telling them that we love that they can express themselves, but don't be deluded: to them, looks matter.

We need our daughter to know that we love her no matter what she looks like. We need to encourage acceptance of what she has and get her to focus on all her positive qualities that have nothing to do with what she looks like. We need to encourage her to surround herself with people who make her feel good. Above all, the message I think we want to give to our daughters is: treat yourself kindly. Love yourself, look after yourself, because you are worth it.

"You are already what you are looking for"

Believe in your dreams!

As I started to mix with more and more mums, I became acutely aware that there are a lot of women out there suffering with low self-esteem, which, I began to realise, has a huge effect, not only on their lives, but also on their daughters. It's funny that it hadn't occurred to me before. I went to an all girls' school that was full of privileged, confident young ladies. My sisters and I had huge stability at home with a stay at home mum and a dad who taught us the importance of independent thinking from a young age.

I remember a time when all the girls in my year were in emotional meltdown at school, due to a decision that had been made by the headmistress that really rocked the boat. I was explaining what had happened to my dad and started crying as I was talking to him. He firmly told me that all this emotional crap wasn't going to get any of us anywhere and that I needed to take control of the situation by meeting with the head and calmly and clearly outlining the argument against her decision. So, I did and guess what, it worked! It was a defining moment for me and one that I often find myself thinking about in relation to bringing up my girls. As parents, it is so important that we give our daughters the tools to be able to hit the ground running. Unfortunately, it's a tightrope and it just seems so easy to fuck up. I think that there are certain principles that we should be trying to follow, to give them the best possible chance and I think that my dad showed me one of them early on.

> **"it is so important that we give our daughters the tools to be able to hit the ground running "**

There's no two ways about it: girls get upset. We are emotional creatures and fairly prone to showing it, often quite hysterically. This is not the time for us as parents to break open the Kleenex and work our way through the box with them. Now is the time for us to support and to advise. We mustn't show them that their problem is worrying us. As long as my dad wasn't worried, I always felt that everything was going to be ok. Equally, we mustn't solve their problems for them. My dad gave me the confidence to talk to the headmistress, but he certainly wasn't going to go and see her himself. From that moment on, I knew that I had the ability to make things change and this made me feel empowered.

That's how parents should deal with their daughters' worries, but what about our own worries? Should we be hiding these from them to protect them from anxiety? Well, I know from my own experience that the answer is, no. Girls are particularly nosey and they have an uncanny sixth sense. If you are hiding something from her then one of two things will happen: either she will find out by overhearing a conversation, or without knowing exactly what is wrong, she will blame herself. This is what I did and as a teenager that was really hard. I think that it's important to share our worries with our daughters and through our honesty with them, they will learn strategies for coping with it.

One of the traps that I fall in to as a parent is focussing on what my daughters are struggling with. It's easy to get drawn in to this by comments made by teachers and by the child themselves worrying about something that they can't do. The trouble is, the more time spent on this, the more time we are spending focussing on their negatives. I am beginning to realise how important it is to focus on things they are good at and this will develop their confidence, which will then have a positive impact on their weaker areas.

Daughter 2 is dyslexic and I spent a great deal of time focussing on the fact that she never read. It would start as a discussion, move in to a shouting match and end up with both of us in tears. Did it actually make her read more? No. It just made us both feel miserable and it probably left her feeling even worse about her struggles. I have to keep reminding myself to highlight the good stuff, which often seems to get overlooked.

❝I have to keep reminding myself to highlight the good stuff❞

It is all very well having values, but sometimes as parents I think that we make them just a little bit too high. Our girls need to know that these values exist, but they also need to know that we understand that they will fuck up, just as we did at their age (and still do!) If we create expectations that are too high, they turn in to pressures. I sometimes find myself responding to a comment from one of my daughters of, "I got a B" with, "why didn't you get an A?" Or, "next time you should try for an A". We need to be careful not to make their achievements a reason to constantly expect more, thus making something that they may actually really enjoy, highly pressurised.

One area in which there is huge potential to boost a girl's self-esteem and confidence is sport. As a Taekwon-do instructor, I teach over 500 students the Korean art of self-defence. We start teaching this from the age of two and a half and find that, up to the age of about 7, the girls are more confident than the boys. When girls join us who are older, they often seem to lack the confidence that boys of a similar age are starting to show. Of course, there are many exceptions, but unfortunately, as girls get older they do drop out of sport. In fact, the majority of teenage girls in the UK don't do sport at all.

Teenage girls don't do sweat. They see sport as unfeminine and this, coupled with a drop in self-esteem when they reach puberty, makes the drop out rate high.

"*the majority of teenage girls in the UK don't do sport at all***"**

You may have heard about the campaign run by Always (of sanitary pad fame): Like a Girl. The phrase 'like a girl' is often used derogatorily and the campaign seeks to change this. They discovered that girls don't regain their pre-puberty level of self-esteem, partly because of the impact of gender stereotyping at this highly influential time. When girls are constantly getting the message that leadership, power and strength are mainly associated with men, it affects how girls start to see themselves. They begin to define themselves through their looks and submissive behaviour and their relationship with sport dies. The campaign asked people to run or throw a ball like a girl. Adults responded meekly, but young girls did it with athletic vigour, as they had yet to be conditioned.

We need to recondition. We need female role models and varied PE lessons. We need to make sure as parents we are not favouring boys when it comes to sport. Quite often girls feel that it is only the most athletic girls in the school who get all the attention – you remember that pretty, blonde girl in year 10 who was captain of every sports team and really popular?

It is also suggested that girls like to connect with other girls and form relationships and they don't want to jeopardise this with ruthless competition.

In fact, sport is an environment where looks don't matter. No make-up is required – no mask (unless your sport is fencing). Whenever a teenage girl comes in to my Taekwon-do class, I whoop with joy. In this environment males and females are equal. There's no need to conform to an athletic stereotype; they can just be themselves. They can perform like the girl that they are. This is empowering in itself. Their self-confidence grows while at the same time they are learning self-defence. There is no 'like a girl' negativity associated with Taekwon-do.

All five of my daughters are black belts in Taekwon-do. When my stepdaughter was young, she was extremely shy. She started Taekwon-do when she was 6 and gradually her confidence grew. By 16 she was in the junior England squad and she is now a confident instructor. She attributes overcoming her shyness to Taekwon-do. Of course, it can be any sport. We need to encourage girls to ignore stereotypes, embrace the sweat and to smash it like a girl.

"*We need to encourage girls to ignore stereotypes***"**

Shyness is not a problem per se. In fact, often shy people are extremely thoughtful and empathic. It is only a problem if it stops our daughter from doing something she wants to do. Encouraging her to participate in a sport is a great way to build her confidence and parents can also help by practising situations with her. For example, we can encourage her to practise her smile, even in front of the mirror. This will have the additional bonus of standing her in good stead for the teenage selfie-obsessed years! Get her to try initiating conversations with people she is comfortable with, such as family and then ease her into situations outside, such as paying for something in a shop. We can tell her that giving a compliment to someone goes a long way in making a social situation easier. Our shy daughters need plenty of encouragement and we must emphasise to her that we don't want to change her, we just want her to feel more comfortable. Shyness can be overcome.

> **"make sure that our daughters have a voice"**

It is so important that we make sure that our daughters have a voice. There are ongoing gender inequalities: women still get paid less than men in some sectors and are still subject to high levels of gender-based violence and sexual abuse. There is inequality in sport and often discrimination and harassment in the work place. Why aren't women's voices being heard? I want my daughters to be heard. I know that sometimes at home we want a quiet life, but it is up to us as parents to put in the hard graft and get it right.

Feminists who speak in the media are telling us how much women struggle in the face of men. Even these wonderfully intelligent and incredibly strong women are telling us that they must fight because of men, again and again. I use the word 'fight', because from where I'm sitting it sounds as if it is a daily battle to deal with the overbearing strength of the males in our society. Women's voices aren't heard, they tell us. We have to shout, but men don't like us shouting because we are supposed to be happy and when we shout we don't appear happy, and when we don't appear happy the foundations of society are rocked. Shouts of complaint are referred to as 'moans'. Venus and Mars are still miles apart.

I feel a huge responsibility as I have five daughters I can influence. I question whether I am doing enough to make them realise the task that lies ahead for them. How can I best equip them to be able to fight these battles? I don't want them to be afraid of what the future holds, but I want them to be aware of these divides: forewarned is forearmed. Yet teenagers don't seem ready for this fight, or particularly interested or bothered. This worries me. There is a palpable apathy that comes from their attentions being drawn online to other things: to a celebrity, selfie, and body-obsessed culture. A culture where fighting male dominance is irrelevant, but rather, grabbing their attention is key. Just getting attention, anyone's. It's less about supporting other girls than comparing. It's less about ignoring the haters, than letting them affect you and allowing them to drive you to being someone you are not.

Thinking about my own teenage years, I remember the abuse I got from male friends through banter and how I didn't know how to deal with it, so I took it. Harmless, right? But it hurt. It confused me. Because I never learnt how to deal with it, I carried this confusion through my 20's and 30's – accepting that the male voice is louder. Expecting to be talked over. Expecting my voice to be the smallest in the company of men.

"*Loud, deliberate, intelligent and strong*"

Loud, deliberate, intelligent and strong. This is how I want our daughters to be and it is my responsibility as their mother and their most influential voice, to get it right. I want my daughters to be strong and sassy girls, who know how to challenge authority in a way that produces results. I want them to have the confidence to make waves. Sometimes girls are expected to be 'nice'. 'Nice' girls don't make waves. Being nice is curtailing their potential and limiting their superpowers. I am trying to teach my daughters to have an opinion, but also to listen to others. I want them to accept that they aren't always right, but that their opinion counts (almost as much as mine.) We must tell our daughters: believe in yourself first and then you will believe in your dreams!

A little love
goes a long way

What words would spring to mind if I were to say to you, *girlfriends*? You may say, *love*, *sharing* and *being close*, but you're just as likely to say, *bitch* and *cow*. Girls really can be bitchy cows and because of this, these words are a part of our female lingo. The thing is, women, and some men, can be bitchy cows too and this isn't providing good role models for our children. My Facebook feed is full of nasty, sarcastic comments from mums to other mums. It's like a full-on catfight that is being played out on screen. The thing that surprises me the most, is that they don't even seem aware that they are doing it. They are constantly judging their fellow species and don't give a thought for the other woman's feelings. What is it that makes people so unkind? What can we do to help our daughters through the quagmire of friendships and not grow up to be the on-line bitch?

It starts young – very young. It could start at the school post box at Christmas time. Do you think it's there to weed out the most unpopular kids in the class? No – it's there to promote friendship and sharing. It is so important that we use this opportunity to talk to our kids about kindness. We need to lead by example. Do we buy them one pack of cards and let them choose who they will send them to? No! We must grab this moment to show them a lesson

"show them a lesson in how to be kind"

in how to be kind. This is a golden opportunity to get this message across. We buy enough cards for the whole class (the cheap, crappy ones are fine) and we make sure they write one to everybody. Inevitably, as they are writing a card they will turn to you and say, "but I don't like her. I don't want to send one to her". If they are saying this at 4-years-old then it is our job as parents to make sure they are not saying it at 5. Because we must turn to our child when they say this and we must tell them that it is very important that they send that person a card. We must tell them that the naughty kid, the loud kid, the boisterous one, the one who isn't very nice, is probably the one who needs their card the most. Children understand the spirit of Christmas and this will make our message all the stronger and easier to understand. So that on our child's birthday, when they turn to us and say, "I don't want to invite him", when they are inviting everyone else in the class, we are able to build on what our children already know about being kind.

My daughter was once the only child in an entire group at primary school who wasn't invited to a party. I don't blame the child for not inviting her – they didn't always see eye-to-eye and so given a choice, she chose to exclude her – a childish punishment for not always getting on. It is the parents who must see past this childish behaviour, because we are not seeing the world through a child's eyes. We know that this is unkind. Sometimes, even on their birthday, we must force our children to be kind. Then, as they grow up and move in to secondary school, they will have an inbuilt sense of what is right and what is wrong, what is kind and what is unkind behaviour.

Arguably the most psychologically damaging thing is leaving people out and ignoring them. Humans long for human affection and as parents we are responsible for teaching our children to be kind. Not just to people they see on the news, such as refugees, who they may

"*the most psychologically damaging thing is leaving people out***"**

be encouraged to send some toys to. It's actually very easy to show kindness this way. We must firstly teach them to be kind to the child whose name they know, whose class they are in. Be kind to the child who is different. Be kind to the child who craves it. Those children don't really know what kindness is and over time, that will really, really hurt. We need to educate ourselves and see that this is bullying.

"Bullying isn't always obvious"

Bullying isn't always obvious. It isn't always a punch in the face or calling someone names, it can be small things: little incidents that build up and the layering of the small things can cause the mind to warp and the mental state to turn. Because of this, as parents we don't always notice. We may not even give a second thought to our daughter excluding a child from a party, an outing or a play date, when that child normally feels a part of her friendship group. We may put it down to them having 'a typical girl' fallout. Yet this is bullying. The child may not even be aware that they are being a bully, so we parents must be the vigilant ones. We must talk to our daughters about kindness and we must be the ones who scream and shout to get our voices heard if we suspect that something is wrong, to prevent a person's mind being so warped and twisted and turned so many times that they no longer know how to unravel it.

As one mum of a 17-year-old boy who took his own life after suffering daily taunts from bullies said, we must teach our children to think and to ask themselves, is it true? Is it necessary? Is it kind? before they write anything on social media. Cyber bullying doesn't stop at the school gates; it

"is it true? Is it necessary? Is it kind? "

carries on into the victim's home, their usual safe place. If your daughter is a victim of it she needs to know that there is help available. She should screenshot the proof and report it to the social media network, if that's where it occurred. Tell the police and encourage her to speak to a teacher at school.

I tell my daughters that actions and words have consequences. I have watched as they scroll through their phones, questioning what someone has posted, even laughing with their sisters and friends about it. I've heard mums do the same. We need to explain to them that when we are nasty about people we end up feeling bad about ourselves. It lowers our self-esteem, while being kind to others makes us feel better about ourselves. We all need to remember to be kind and as parents, we must lead by example. If our daughters hear us bitching about someone at the school gate, they will think that it is ok to do the same. Equally, if they see us backing down in situations, so as not to create a scene, they may model this behaviour too.

I don't think that the deluge of reality TV shows help with example setting, as the contestants bitch and back stab their way through. They do, however, offer a good opportunity to talk to older daughters about how human beings get along and how the people who are being mean are often the ones with the lowest self-esteem and probably the unhappiest. We can explain to them that they might not be able to change the way other people treat them, but they can change the way they react.

I hate cliques. Coming from an all girls' school, I had plenty of experience of them. From this, I learned that I actually preferred to be friends with girls from different groups, rather than sticking to one. This way I found that I kept my individuality, as I didn't have to conform to a type. I think that we can use our own examples of how we fitted in at school to help our daughters.

There's always the clique that is too cool for school and I tell my girls that they don't need to aspire to be in it. In fact, I suggest that they steer well clear and I tell them that it's no reflection of their own worth if they aren't in that group. In my experience those groups are full of girls who are vying for attention and who are constantly worried about how they can stay popular – all way too high maintenance for my liking and there's rarely a winner. These girls are always thinking about themselves, and the 'friendships' within the group are less genuine. It's not about friends, it's about group membership.

Another characteristic of girl friendships is what I call, push me, pull me. You know the scenario, when someone tells you that you are her best friend and simply can't get enough of you and the next minute, for absolutely no apparent reason, she is pushing you away. We need to be explaining to our daughters that a real friend is one who makes her feel good and who doesn't try to keep her to themselves. We want our daughters to remain in control.

"**a real friend is one who makes her feel good**"

Has someone ever told you, "it's only banter"? I really hate that. It's usually said just as you've finally plucked up the courage to stand up to someone who continuously teases you. Often they have latched on to one small thing and won't stop going on. They are trying to excuse their behaviour and often get others on side, so it becomes like a gang who are laughing at you. I can remember this happening to me. It would make me feel sick in the stomach and lonely. I felt as if my control had been stripped away. You tell yourself that they are only joking, but you have become the joke and you begin to believe what they are telling you. I tell my girls that real banter isn't one way, but bullying is. If someone isn't joining in the joke, then they are being targeted. It's personal and it is bullying.

"real banter isn't one way, but bullying is"

We teach 'Bully Awareness' as part of our Taekwon-do programme from age 2 and a half. It's never too young to teach our kids how to recognise when they are being bullied and how to deal with it, as bullying quite often starts at nursery or playgroup. We do role-plays with our students and this is something that you can do at home in order to teach your daughter what she can do to stop herself being the victim. Explain to her that bullying is an abuse of power and she needs strategies to readdress the balance of power. Tell her that it's ok to feel angry, but not to physically retaliate nor be verbally aggressive. It's also extremely important that their anger doesn't end up with them crying or looking upset; after all, the bully is looking for that sort of reaction. She needs to make the bully aware that she is not going to stand for their behaviour. This can be done with eye contact and a simple, "Stop it!" or the use of humour when they are older can work well: "Tell me when you get to the funny part" shows strength of character. She could reply with a non-defensive question such as, "Why would you say that?" or agree with the bully. For example, if they say, "You're stupid", reply, "Yes, but I'm good at it." She could also respond with sentences that begin with 'I want': "I want you to stop." Her voice needs to be strong so that she sounds self-assured, even when she is most probably feeling anything but. She needs to 'fake it 'til she makes it' and practising with you will help her confidence to grow.

Explain to your daughter the importance of using her body to assert herself: shoulders back and head up are simple and effective ways of standing up to a bully. Tell your daughter to walk away and talk to someone they can trust. They should then ignore the bully, who will probably eventually get bored and leave them alone. When she can, make sure she avoids places she knows the bully will be and gather a friendship group, or as one of my daughters calls it 'her squad', around her.

Sometimes it can be hard to find out from your daughter exactly what is going on, especially if she isn't showing any physical signs of abuse. Some warning signs could be that she is acting differently, she seems anxious, she isn't eating or sleeping. She may be moodier than usual and easily upset. You may also notice that she doesn't want to take her usual route somewhere.

Even if you suspect that she is being bullied, she may not want to admit it. Your daughter may not want to feel that she is somehow disappointing you. She may even feel that it's her fault and she may be afraid that the bully will be worse if they find out she's told on them. You may have to use your crafty parenting techniques to find out in a roundabout way. Asking her opinion on something you are watching on TV where there is a situation of conflict is often a good way of getting her to open up. Once she begins to talk then make sure you remain calm. Our first reaction as a parent may well be to confront the bully, but we must concentrate on comforting our daughter and reassuring her that it isn't her fault and that she has done the right thing by telling us. Talk to the school first and I would avoid approaching the bully's parents; no one wants to think of their child as a bully and they may well just get very defensive. All schools have an anti-bullying policy, so make sure that they implement it.

It may take some time for your daughter to get over an episode of being bullied and unfortunately it is something that can scar her for the rest of her life. It's important that she understands that although she can't stop people from saying nasty things, she can have some control over how she reacts to it.

Ultimately, even if they aren't the victims of bullying, girls will fall in and out of friendships and it is never going to be easy. Leading by example is certainly the most important step to our daughters developing healthy relationships with other girls, teaching them that a little love goes a long way and quite simply, to be kind.

Have a silly, funny, hippy, happy day!

Is it just me, or are girls getting older, younger? I mean, I was still wearing a pink pinafore age 13, but now for a 10-year-old, only (see through) leggings will cut it. It is a scientific fact, I believe, that girls are hitting puberty earlier these days, so 10 is quite normal to start the nightmare that is periods. It seems unfair, but then again, girls are used to that concept and are extremely adept at just dealing with it. How do we deal with them, when they are dealing with it? Well, in my experience their hormones are raging for about 6 months to a year before they actually start and when they arrive, things calm down a little. Thank God, because by that time the rest of the family are running for the hills.

"the rest of the family are running for the hills"

When my youngest daughter was 12-years-old she was talented and wonderful and lovely in many ways, and often angry. When I talk to other parents about their pre-teens and they often comment that they feel the tweenie stage starts at 8 or so years old. Being the youngest of five girls, whose changes I have observed, I knew what was coming and so one day we had this conversation:

"Why does everyone keep telling me I'm so angry all the time? I'M NOT ANGRY!!!" (Said as a yell)

I sat down on her bed, wrapped my arms around her and pulled her close to me. Her head rested on my lap.

"You see, darling, it's because you are angry. Every time you answer a question, you sound angry. Whenever I ask you to do something, you look angry. Your hormones are raging around your body. You are at a difficult and at times horrible, angry age. You may not realise how very angry you sound, because those nasty hormones make you think that it is everyone else who is having a go and getting at you, but we're not. We are just being us and you are just being you and in a few months' time that 'you' will be a slightly calmer person. You will be a teenager. You may still be horrible and angry, but slightly less so. You will still think that everyone else is unfairly having a go, but you will gradually begin to see it from our point of view too. Then, not too long after this you will occasionally be pleasant. Just often enough that I see glimpses of how things might be one day, when we might go for a coffee and chat.

"Until this time sweetheart, we will take deep breaths back at you, but this will not make us feel too good. We will love you with every bone in our bodies and we know that this time will, as it has done before, pass".

Of course, there can be many reasons for a child's anger. We can't blame everything on hormones, but they make a plausible scapegoat when nothing else is entirely obvious, and the reason may not even be obvious to her. In fact, she may well be shocked by her own anger! I know that now isn't the time to get angry back. Now is the time to be her sounding board. If she's held it in all day at school, then she's fit to burst by the time she sees me. I try not to take it too personally, as this is the way I stay just about sane and can be more of a support to her. I remember that her friends are no help, as they are just as erratic as she is right now! It's all down to me to weather the storm. At this point, even a response from me worthy of an Oscar will be scornfully rejected. (I save my Oscar performances for when I'm recharging my batteries and recounting the episode to partner or bestie over a bottle of wine). No, I know that right now I just need to let her vent - although if it's going to ruin everyone's evening then of course she needs to be told. My role may even extend to owning the reason for her anger for a while, in order to give her a break (this often involves a door slam), giving me a chance to work out whether it really requires action. By then she has probably figured it out for herself and we can all breathe again until the next time. Sometimes with tweens and teens, a crisis one day is all but forgotten the next.

One thing that I have learnt living with five girls, is that things are never obvious. For example:

"Morning!" I say cheerily to daughter 2. "Why are you all annoying me so much, this morning?" is the reply. Ah ok, it's a morning when the floor is strewn with eggshells.

In the kitchen, I am making their lunches. Daughter 2 is stomping around and declaring, loudly, everything that is currently disgusting her: "there is dog hair everywhere, I hate beetroot in my salad, there is nothing I like for breakfast, why is there never anything I like...?" We're all zoning out, including the dogs, who are flat out on the floor, ignoring the hormonal fuss. She trips over dog 1. It sets her off again: "why is he there, why isn't our kitchen bigger, why are you all ganging up on me?!"

I contemplate voicing my irritation at her early morning ranting, but there just isn't room for two of us going on, so I resort to the breathing techniques I learnt in my NCT classes 16 years ago, when one of the drama queens was but a cute little package, surrounded by calming amniotic fluid.

She's flounced off upstairs, where her grievances are continuing to be aired to her sisters: "why do you have to use my hairbrush, why don't you get your own moisturiser, why are you wearing my tights?!"

She's back downstairs. I brace myself. "Muuum". I know that voice. That voice can only ever mean one thing. "Can I have a friend over for a sleepover on Friday night?" I look into her pleading eyes. "Well, the thing is", I reply, "I wouldn't want you to be embarrassed bringing your friend to such an awful place, filled with such irritating people..." and before she has a chance to respond, I gently ease her out the door to school.

This is why men have sheds! Partner generally hides upstairs in the mornings, until the storm that hits every weekday at 6.30am, has dispersed out of the front door by 7.35am. I'm on a huge learning curve with teenagers. Stepdaughter was my guinea pig. I thought, who is this creature who texts us from her bedroom, rather than walking downstairs? Who is this person who, when I'm asking her a question, doesn't respond? Who is this alien who stays in her room when we come in, having not seen her all day? I put it down to the fact that she was my stepdaughter and not 'one of my own', however precious she still was. And now I have 'my own' teenagers and, guess what? They behave in exactly the same way. Teenagers are a species, just as babies and toddlers are. They are a group with predictable behaviours and who follow regular patterns, dictated by nature even more than nurture. Their brains are hard-wired to wind parents up.

"Who is this alien who stays in her room "

I am learning that just because they aren't responding, doesn't mean that they aren't listening. Just because they can sound cruel, doesn't mean they don't love. Just because they prefer spending time with friends, doesn't mean they don't like their family. Just because they can't stand seeing you naked – even in your own bedroom – doesn't mean that, deep down, they don't think that you are beautiful. I am definitely still

> **"***Just because they can sound cruel, doesn't mean they don't love* **"**

learning. Here are a few things that I have learnt so far:

- You will get to know the postman extremely well, as he or she will be delivering ASOS products and packages from China to your door weekly, possibly daily.

- The Ikea shoe rack you bought when your kids were toddlers, no longer caters for one, let alone any more teenagers. Shoes will take over your house. Shoes and boots. Teenage girls will continue to buy shoes and boots that look exactly like the shoes and boots they already own.

- Despite duplicating shoes and boots regularly, they will constantly tell you that they have no money.

- They shave their thighs. I was so shocked when I learnt this on holiday in Spain this year, I almost spat out my sangria. Yes, you heard me: their thighs...or perhaps I'm the last to know?

- Contrary to popular belief, they don't initially like to shower. It requires way too much effort. Once they hit 16ish, showering suddenly becomes very important.

- They will quite happily take shit photos of you to feed their Snapchat story, but will demand that you delete even the nicest shots of them. They will threaten to report you for child abuse if you don't.

- They will not take off their school jumper, even in a heat wave.

- They will not wear a coat, even in a monsoon. Unless it is a coat they have bought – which won't keep the rain out anyway.

- They have a very different concept of appropriate clothing to their parents. They will quite happily let their arse hang out of a pair of shorts and wear see-through leggings. This is very normal behaviour for a teenage girl and to suggest otherwise simply shows how ignorant you are.

- They will bake cakes. Quite a lot.

- They will pout. I never wanted to believe that my girls would ever pout. I honestly didn't think they had the pouting gene. They are not even embarrassed by their pouting.

- As already discussed, they will have friend issues. You will never quite get to the bottom of it. Just as you think you have nailed the friend that is being the little bitch, bam – that one is the bestie. Stand well back. Be there for them when they allow you onto their hallowed turf, otherwise keep a safe distance. That way, you are doing everyone a favour.

- They will wear fake nails. You will find fake nails in odd places. The dog will shit fake nails.

- Your house will smell like a whore's boudoir all the time.

- Teenage girls can never have too many bags.

- They may talk of getting an eyebrow tattoo…this does not mean they want their boyfriend's name across their temple.

- They can make you feel like the most unfashionable/unkempt/ignorant idiot with a mere look. If the phrase 'on fleek' was invented by teenage girls to describe eyebrows, I think the word 'disdain' was actually invented by teenage girls to describe how they feel when they look at their parents.

When our daughters are young, the words 'silly', 'funny' and 'happy' are adjectives that we would almost certainly readily use to describe them. As puberty hits, these characteristics sometimes drown a little bit, as they are engulfed by a tsunami of hormones. We need to keep telling ourselves that they will come through and so will we! All with our silly sense of humour intact. Contrary to popular belief, teenagers can show many moments of happiness. Above all, teenage girls are vivacious, loving, astute and savvy and I feel extremely privileged to have the terrifying task of bringing them up as single-minded individuals. You get this far... then what?

Every cloud has a sparkly lining

For me, there are several elements that make being a parent to teenage girls a challenge: their withdrawal from you, your lack of control, their need for independence and, of course, all these elements are interrelated. The transition from your little girl, who needs you and openly shows her love for you, to your teenage daughter, can be a difficult time.

Every girl is different and I have gone through a different transition period with each of mine. Daughter 4 isn't quite yet there. With daughter 1 it was a breeze (of course she's still high maintenance in other ways!) Daughter 3 is so into her sport, that there is little time to notice anything between school and ferrying her to practices and matches. I am sure that focus has eased the transition though. With daughter 2, I feel that we're going through exactly the sort of transition that you might expect to go through as a parent of a teenager and I wrote this to her to express how it made me feel:

I don't expect your thanks, but I want your respect.

When you were on the cusp of hitting these teenage years, I read that your brain was going to change. I was in denial. I didn't want to believe a word of it. Not my child, I smugly thought. My little girl, who is ever growing. My child who is thoughtful and thankful and who, I honestly feel, everyday, adores me. She thinks that I am funny and I know that because we laugh together – we catch each other's eye and we get a bit hysterical. We don't care that those around us don't get it, all that matters to us is that we do.

I don't expect your thanks, but I want your respect.

It crept up on me. I was too relaxed, too content that we were 'cool' together. You didn't want to seek me out in a room. You didn't need to rest your gaze on me. Moments together became fleeting and tense. Every interaction became a possibility for a battle. Anger made you put up a defence, from where you hid, sharing your woes by text, escaping from them through Snapchat.

I don't expect your thanks, but I want your respect.

I tried to stay close by – within reach, where you had always been happy for me to be. Your coldness pushed me away. I eased forward like a pawn in a game of chess, one square at a time and like the queen you pushed passed me, taking my now fragile mummy ego with you and discarding it at your will. That hurt and stupidly, I let it show.

I don't expect your thanks, but I want your respect.

So, like a sailing boat forced by the wind, I changed my tack. I sailed away. Not too far: I dropped the anchor where I could see you and I moved with the waves. I reached occasional highs and I crashed back to the surface many times, but the anchor prevented me from drifting away and the curves of the boat's hull meant I didn't sink. I no longer sought your laughter. I no longer sought your thanks. I did things for you out of love.

I don't expect your thanks, but I want your respect.

Then one day, when I had sorted through your wardrobe – a job that you were intending to do, but the task had seemed too huge – you came home to that task complete and you said, 'thank you'. I didn't let you see me whoop for joy. You didn't see me smile. You heard me reply with a nonchalant, 'no problem'. I am happy with a little distance. I am quietly smug that I've worked us out.

I know I get your thanks and your respect and in return, you know that you get mine.

"Quite often I am just a pain in their arse"

Of course, you don't always get your teenage daughter's respect. Quite often I am just a pain in their arse. A typical scenario is when the pain in the arse returns from the daily dog walk. I enter the kitchen that I had left an hour ago issuing strict instructions on how I wanted to find it on my return. "Can I have bacon for breakfast, Mum?" "If you wipe the hob down afterwards. Make sure you wash up, wipe the table, sweep away the crumbs". The pain in the arse drones on to deaf ears, but continues undeterred. It makes me feel better. It makes me feel as if I might be achieving something by giving orders. That maybe, just maybe, someone will be listening. One out of four? Perhaps there is a chance that one out of four may hear a small part of what I am saying and fulfil my expectations.

I scan the kitchen on re-entering. It's not so bad that I can rant, it's not good enough that I can't comment loudly. So, I grab the dishcloth and shout my way around the worktops. Moan a little over the splashing washing up water and grumble loudly about the state of the floor.

Silence.

I shout a little louder. No response. I'm muttering to myself, how I imagine Old Mother Hubbard would have done, when she went to her cupboard and found it bare.

Partner comes in and asks whom I am talking to. "The girls", I reply. "They didn't leave the kitchen to my standards".

"They're all out", he says. "You're talking to yourself".

Always, I thought to myself. Regardless of whether they are in or out, I feel as if I'm always talking to myself...myself and the dogs. To rectify this, I asked daughter 2 to start a group text chat, which she has named: 'Family chat jobby.' This has improved communication no end. Now while I am on the dog walk I can get straight to where their attention is hiding behind their screens and send them texts such as: make sure the kitchen is tidy when I get home. Whereas I used to question why the hell my stepdaughter texted us when from her bedroom, when we were sitting just downstairs, Family chat jobby is the go-to place for me when I require my daughters' undivided attention. If you can't beat 'em, join 'em!

Quite often I see threads on my local mums' Facebook page about how to discipline a teenager. I read these threads that are detailing the issues they are having and I nod along going yup, yup, yup, like some kind of nodding dog. They are usually asking for advice, and although I don't always jump in and give it as I don't necessarily feel equipped to, I do find myself questioning what I do, or how I think I would react.

With each teenager, I am experiencing new things and coming up against new issues. The issues that existed with my stepdaughter are now different for my daughters and so on. Life changes and evolves in all sorts of ways and as parents, we must be prepared to move with it. Here are a few nuggets I have picked up that have worked and are working for me on my journey:

- Sometimes against every gut feeling in your body, show them and tell them that you trust them. If someone feels they aren't trusted, they are more inclined to stray. It builds up a huge amount of resentment. Trust is an essential part of any relationship and it is certainly important with teens.

- Equally, make them aware of your expectations surrounding this trust. This gives them boundaries to push against, and therefore the security that you care and that what they do matters to you.

- Communicate with them. Try to get them out of the house and on neutral ground. A walk is perfect, whether it's a dog walk, a walk around town, even a trip to the supermarket. Stepping into their bedroom with the words 'we need to talk', is guaranteed to switch them off.

- When a teenager wants to talk to you, rather than the other way around, you must be available. Even if (when) it's in the middle of your favourite programme, or you're engrossed in Facebook and it's the first time you've sat down all week. Tv off. Phone down. You are now emotionally there.

- Don't be afraid to thrash things out. You cannot avoid confrontation for an easier life. If you haven't got the energy to deal with it, put it on hold until you have. Sometimes it's good to let the dust settle.

- Don't set unrealistic rules and be prepared to be flexible. Don't see this as backing down. Often if you listen to your teen they are making valid points about something that you may have previously dismissed. Not listening to their point of view will push them away and closer to their friends who will always agree with them.

- Try to keep them close. You will feel that you are losing them, but you are not. Don't smother them; let them go and ironically this will keep them closer to you. As they start to seek independence, to spend more time in their rooms and less time on family activities don't panic – this is normal. At about the age of 15, they will probably stop bothering to come downstairs to say goodnight. Don't hold it against them; it's nothing serious.

- Don't use cutting off their lifelines as punishments: their friends, their phones, and social media. They quite literally are their lifelines. By doing this you are simply making them feel even more isolated and less likely to cooperate. If they see that you are listening to them and trying to understand, then they are far more likely to play ball.

- Acceptance is so important. Accept that they are going to push against you. Accept that they are going to break some rules. Pick your battles. It is not a reflection on your inability to parent, it is a sign that they are growing up.

- Embrace their noise! Be happy that they have a voice. Teach them how to argue effectively and to put their point of view across. Then sit back and listen to World War 3 erupting amongst the siblings. Don't get drawn in. These are the battlegrounds where their characters are formed.

- Throw comments into conversations. Snatched moments are all you may get with a teenager, so use them in a way that you haven't perhaps before. Don't see it as futile and worry that you're not getting time with your teen to get a message across. If you sit down at a table and talk to them for 10 minutes, they will only be listening to a tiny part of the conversation anyway and will actually remember even less of it. Think back to those throwaway comments people have said to you in the past that you remember. Sound bites have a place – be a parent politician.

All these nuggets should help to get you through the minefield, but I have identified a problem with being the mother of teenage girls – I am a control freak

> **"***I am a control freak and teenagers don't like being controlled***"**

and teenagers don't like being controlled. Sometimes they will humour me and then, free from my clutches, carry on their way regardless. Other times they will dig their unhealthily high heels in and refuse to budge.

I am a professional snooper. So far my snooping has averted a large gathering taking place in our house whilst we were away, an inappropriate one night stand, use of a hip flask and late night doughnut eating. And that is just one – I have four more to go.

Sometimes, however, my snooping simply leads to frustration and worry, such as when I overhear a snippet of conversation that leaves me desperate to know more, but unable to find out. God knows I try. First, I start subtly: "are you ok?" "Yes, mum". I leave it an hour or so: "everything ok?" "Yup". Later in the evening: "school ok?" "Yes". The next morning I'm haranguing other daughters to find out what's going on. If they don't seem worried, then this worries me even more. At this point I think they are all in this together and paranoia sets in. By the evening I can't stand it any longer and I go for the direct approach:

"is it a boy? Are you gay? Are you wondering whether you might be gay?" "No, I'm not gay". "Has someone touched you inappropriately?" "I don't know what that means, so I presume not mum". "Are you pregnant?" "No!" An exclamation of true incredulity will leave me momentarily relieved, but I will soon go to start again. Now I would be gently pushed out of the room and the door would be shut on me. I'd be left standing outside the frontier, debating the rights of teenage privacy over a parent's need-to-know and would still be none the wiser. With persistence and dogged determination, I might be given a clue when I promise to stop going on, which always seems like a fair starting point, so I agree. But just one little "it's not about me" and that's it – I'm off again: "is it about your sisters? Is it about your friend; is it about your friend's friend? Is it..." Cue being screamed at and even I know that it is time to let it go.

I suddenly realised why teenagers are so difficult and why letting go is anything but straightforward. It's because they are half way between being under our control and us relinquishing all control. It's not always their fault that they are such bloody hard work sometimes, and it's not our fault as parents either. For example: they can't drive until they are almost adults. This means that they may be proactive in getting a job and thus allowing us to relinquish some monetary control, but then they can't very easily get there so we still have to have some control. This causes stress, because the part that is in their control contains information that is useful to the person who is in control of getting them there, but being teenagers they only really think about themselves. The result is that as a parent you are expected to suddenly be available to assist in their independence, without having full control of the facts.

This is just one example of hundreds. Sometimes I just want to scream at them: you take full control of your lives then! You organise everything – I don't have the headspace for these snippets of your life that you are expecting and/or needing me to dip in and out of. Then I remember that I am their parent and they are still a child.

> **"I am their parent and they are still a child"**

I've always drawn comparisons between toddlers and teenagers and I think that one of the only real differences between them is this issue of control. As a parent, you have total control over a toddler. They'll push against the boundaries you are setting, but ultimately you control their whole world. As a parent of a teenager you are gradually releasing your control to prepare them for the world outside, however the control you are giving over to them is still not entirely theirs, but it is also no longer yours. This blurring of the boundaries of control causes a great deal of the stress involved with bringing up our teens.

Once your daughter gets to about 13, that period of full parental control is over. That time you think you will spend time together going to museums, to the beach, on shopping sprees and baking has gone and you suddenly realise that you didn't do as much as you thought you would. You see, the time to do all these things is while you are in total control of your children. You think you will. You say you will. Then all of a sudden your youngest child is a teenager and all you have is the memories of when you did.

Parenting a teenager often feels as if you are both on two separate aeroplanes, going through the same storm cloud. There is no denying the fact that there is lots of turbulence. Yet, even for a control freak like me, there is a sparkly lining to this cloud you find yourselves going through: if we get it right then the turbulence will make her stronger. She will be growing in confidence with her newfound independence and you will have developed a mutual respect.

Girls just want to have fun

I came to the conclusion a little while back, that in order to retain my sanity through the teenage years there comes a point in our children's lives, when you have to step back and trust and hope. Instinctively, I think that I had known this for a while, before I allowed myself to openly admit it. You see the thing is, shit will happen. Whether you are a parent who hovers or a parent who doesn't have the time and/or the inclination to, shit will still go down.

Daughter 2 is sixteen. She's the third 16-year-old I have parented. It's taken me this long to acknowledge that sometimes their take on life is ok. Sometimes, when I judge their perspective on things, I am wrong to do so. Not always, but sometimes and probably a lot more than I ever thought. Having said that, there's

> **"Sometimes, when I judge their perspective on things, I am wrong to do so"**

nothing quite like a conversation with your mum to make you think that you have fucked up as a parent... again.

One such fuck up was allowing daughter 2 to watch a band in Camden.

"What! On a school night? How old is she? 15?" Yes mum, you know that already (and actually she was 3 weeks off being 16, which didn't sound nearly as bad). "I would never have let you do that on a school night!" Erm, well actually you did – remember, I went to see 'The Bolshoi' and when I told my teachers the next day, they all thought I'd been to see a ballet. "I don't remember that."

No, I sighed. You never do.

The thing is, I had felt as if I'd fucked up when daughter 2 had reminded me two nights previously that she was going. "You're doing what?" I'd asked incredulously, confident that I would never have agreed to such a thing – especially on a school night. "Yes, you remember Mum. I bought the tickets ages ago." I searched my brain for a glimpse of a recollection... nothing. "I thought it was tomorrow, but actually it's the day after." Ah, now the penny dropped. She had told me that it was on the night she stays with her Dad, so I had relinquished all responsibility for the decision. Now, with two days to go, she told me it's on my watch. Shit. Suddenly it was left to me to explain to the police, if anything were to go wrong, that I allowed my 15 but nearly 16-year-old daughter out on a school night, with only her 15-year-old friend as a chaperone. I faltered. I was stuck. I remember partner shooting me one of 'those' looks, which says: she's taking the piss. I can remember thinking: she can't let her friend down now. It's too late to stop her. What's the worst that can happen? At which point I just switched off.

Until the morning of the night of the concert, when I suddenly panicked that I didn't know the name of the band she was going to see, let alone the name of the club. I marched into her room and demanded details. She was too busy getting ready for school to be able to pay me much attention; she just waved her hand towards her bag where the tickets were. I took a photo of the ticket. This made me feel a bit better. What I actually achieved by this, I have no idea, but it did make me feel a little more responsible.

I spent all morning worrying that I was a really bad mother, and then her friend's mum rang me and reassured me that they'll be ok. I felt fine again. Anyway, I had other things to worry about, so I was more than happy to put this one to bed. I texted daughter 2 to tell her that I'd spoken to her friend's mum and she was to ring me when she leaves the venue. "I haven't got any credit", she texted back. Shit, I thought to myself and started worrying all over again. I rang her, "you can't go to London with no credit on your phone. What if you get lost? Separated from your friend?" I was back to imagining various scenarios that involved young males and police. "I'll be fine mum", she said, adding reassuringly, "I can still text".

She sent me a photo, "we're right at the front". The text didn't serve to reassure. I could see the barrier. I envisaged her getting squashed up against it. "You're in the mosh pit", I texted back. "Don't get trampled on". "Hahahaha we won't it will be fine", was her text back.

And with that, I let go of my worry. I cooked, I blogged, I stared mindlessly at Facebook. I periodically told the kids to get on with homework and I watched TV. Then I went to bed.

Shit! I woke-up at midnight. I'd forgotten to worry. I grabbed for my phone – nothing. I did a quick calculation of timings. How could I have forgotten she was travelling home? How the bloody hell could I have forgotten to worry? I sent a text, "you back yet?" and waited...

"Yeah. It was soooo good xxxxxx".

Another worry put to bed, until the next one. For example: desks. Teenagers don't use desks. Some do, of course, but many don't. It is quite normal for you to come home and find your teenager wrapped up in their fluffiest of dressing gowns, in bed, duvet pulled up with a laptop positioned precariously on their knees... at 2pm on a Sunday. No, they are not still in bed from the previous night. Under their dressing gown they are fully clothed and have been for a while. This used to make me mad. "What are you doing in bed?" I'd holler. Then I noticed a sister was doing it and then a cousin. Now, it may well be that it's genetic, but I suspect it's a teenage 'thing'. I don't like it, because it seems slovenly. They do it because it makes them feel comfortable and cosy. Does it affect whether they get that required level 6 in GCSE Maths? Probably not. Perhaps I should step back and let it go.

> **"You certainly have to pick your battles with the teens"**

You certainly have to pick your battles with the teens. You can't be a one-man army, firing shots in all directions at every thing you don't like or agree with. Those teens will be off like a shot – jumping into the nearest fluffy dressing gown and diving under the duvet for cover.

When daughter 1 was revising for her GCSEs, she announced that she was going to revise with a friend – on FaceTime. "No way!" I responded. "You will never get any work done!" She dismissed my worry and did it anyway. I decided to step back and observe, rather than to keep piling in. It's not how I could ever have imagined revising, but she's not me. She got fantastic grades. She attributes this partly to her working with her friend. I couldn't argue.

Music was blaring out of her bedroom one night. I went to investigate and there was daughter 1 at her desk. The only reason being, that daughter 3 was on her bed, surrounded by maths books. "Why aren't you working?" I shouted (over the noise of Will Joseph Cook). They both looked at me incredulously. "We are!" they chorused, as a Snapchat buzzed through. I was sceptical. I hovered. Do I turf daughter 3 out? Or, do I trust them? Do I step back and tell myself that their world isn't my world, or do I take the hard-parental line? I left them to it. Because you know what? They know what my expectations of them are. I've laid the ground rules over the years. I continue to be interested in their grades and their progress at school. I make sure that I still involve myself with how the personal statement for university is shaping up and how the maths test went. But at the end of the day a large part of being a teenager is learning how to do things their way. Yes, shit will happen. It will happen at some point whether we are there or not and this is the step to independence, resilience and ultimately, success.

"Yes, shit will happen"

So, my new parent mantra is: don't worry, hope. Stand back, take a breath and hope. Because you will all survive. You get through the night feeds and the nappies and the relentless grind. Getting up in the night AGAIN and not even having the energy to feel sorry for yourself. You survive the lines of snot and the tantrums, the far too early mornings and monotony of toys out, tidy away, toys out, tidy away. You rock bath time and

"Stand back, take a breath and hope"

story time, because the end, for just a few hours, may possibly be in sight (or not). You might even get a chance to eat dinner with another adult and have a glass of wine to toast/drown the day and to tell each other: we will survive. You do survive. You are in control. It may not feel that way, but you are controlling your world and that of the little people who live in it. Whilst you spend many days feeling out of control and feeling as if you are hostage to a band of toddlers, ultimately you are the superhero.

When your little girl grows in to a teenager, you become an observer. You are detached and no longer have complete control. They have a phone and then a key. They have freedom, to a degree. Their world is no longer your world and you struggle to understand it, or to keep up. Yes, you are now an incredulous voyeur, who is looking at the number of make-up brushes and phone cases that make their way from China, with surprise. They have bankcards and money from their work. Clothes appear in the wash that you have not bought. Perhaps, that

"Their world is no longer your world"

you don't like. 'Like' becomes a loaded word. 'Like for a like', 'gorge', 'stunning', 'hotty', 'beaut', 'get ugly' on your 12-year-old's Instagram account. You are at an arm's length in disbelief. At first you are astonished at their selfies. How can they possibly keep it up? It's relentless. Every time you look at your daughter her phone is out and a Snapchat story is being written. You worry – is there actually enough time in their day for them to get their grades that will lead them to their goals and to their dreams? Do they have sight of goals? Do they dream?

You are a spectator. You are not totally in control. Control is now an art form and you must become a master of negotiation. You can't slip up or you will now be found out. Gone are the days when you could lie and bribe. You have entered the realms of Secret Service tactics and so have they. It is now a battle of wits, where both sides have the ability to see the bigger picture and to fight for control of their territory and as you don't fully understand this territory that you are now in, you struggle.

You do survive. Through unconditional love. With tears of laughter and of heartache and with the help of tissues and of hugs. You get through the differences with understanding, communicating and by a bit of letting go. You are an observer. Sometimes, you even feel appreciated.

When my kids were younger, there were times that I was incredibly proud of my parenting. I wanted recognition. I wanted a boss and an appraisal scheme. I wanted to be called into HR and told by a lovely person with a huge smile what an amazing job everyone thinks I am doing. I wanted to get employee of the month and get taken out for drinks on a Friday night to celebrate the week I'd just had. I wanted to stand at the bar, getting back slaps and high fives. I was desperate for all my hard work and achievements of that week to be acknowledged.

Now the girls are teenagers, whether I like it or not, they are my HR personnel. They are the vocal judges of my parenting skills. They are the ones who very occasionally will tell me with a big smile that I am getting it right, but will also make me feel and quite often tell me that I am getting it wrong.

One day we were sitting having a family meal, when their uncle asked them directly, "is she a good mum?" They squirmed with discomfort and didn't seem to know what to say. I was metaphorically kicking them under the table, say yes goddamn it, please say yes.

"Sometimes", daughter 1 replied.

"Like when?" Their uncle continued.

"Erm, I can't think of any examples", she said.

I was crushed by her words. Gone were my hopes of celebratory drinks. No pats on the back or high fives for me. All my hard work: my taxi driving, my hugs, my support, my cooking, the cleaning and the washing on a 24 hour turn around – none of this really seemed, in that instant, to matter.

A couple of days later, it was raining and I thought I would swing by the station on my way home from work to pick the girls up, as I was almost passing and I knew that they didn't have coats. (Why would any teenager ever need a coat...ever? I mean, really mum!) In the car daughter 1 said to me, "you see this is what I meant when I said 'sometimes'. You never normally pick us up, but today you did and I'm surprised, but this is the kind of lovely thing you do, sometimes".

"*it just feels so incredibly good to get something right***"**

She gave me the biggest smile. I smiled back. I think that I know what she meant and I took it as a great, big high five. In the uncertain world of bringing up girls, it just feels so incredibly good to get something right.

There is no denying that my stepdaughter was my guinea pig for bringing up a teenage girl, but when she graduated from university and had an amazingly enriching time in the process, I felt that as parents we must have done something right. Although, of course she must take a great deal of the credit, I like to think that we set her on the right road. The thing is though, there were so many times when I felt what we were doing was harsh – she certainly thought so and it would have been so easy to take another path.

I remember a time when she was 15 and she wanted to go to her friend's house, but her dad and I were both busy at home and didn't want to trek over there. We told her to get the train and buses and then walk the final leg. She told us that her friends could not believe that we were asking her to do this. I wavered slightly and questioned whether we were indeed asking too much. Don't you find yourself doing this a lot as a parent? Questioning yourself and your decisions? Analysing whether it is correct and fair. I feel that this is one of the hardest things about parenting a teenager.

The day she had to move in to her university halls of residence was on a Tuesday. Both her dad and I were working, so we told her that we had to take her up on the Sunday. She wasn't allowed to move in early and so we deposited her and all her belongings in a motel, that we had got her to locate and book, and said goodbye in the car park. Due to work, we didn't visit her again in the three years she was there. On her moving in day, she got a taxi to her halls and moved herself in. Harsh? Necessary – and I am glad that it was, because as parents we need to pull back. By over parenting, we haven't taught our teenagers to survive by themselves in the world. This lack of skills of independence is at the heart of the rise of stress and anxiety among students. As the warden of a university halls of residence told me: her job used to be breaking up parties and confiscating drugs, now it's being a counsellor to homesick students.

"*By over parenting, we haven't taught our teenagers to survive by themselves in the world***"**

The evening we left my stepdaughter in the motel was the first time she had ever left home, but we knew that we had paved the way for her to be able to cope with the situation. When we got home later that evening, I saw she had posted on Facebook a photo of her bonsai tree, sitting on the windowsill of her motel room. I could easily have seen it as a symbol of her being alone.

My partner and I make sure that our children work, cook, travel independently wherever possible and they have all had their fair share of disappointment. We try to let them experience it, rather than protect them from it. So when I saw my stepdaughter's photo of the bonsai, I didn't see it as an image of loneliness, I saw it as her saying to the world that she is ready for a new life: the roots were firmly established and she was ready to grow.

I don't think for a moment that we are doing everything right, but sometimes it's easy to think that you are being too harsh. Your teenager may feel hard done by, but it is our job as parents to stand firm and then they will flourish. When our girls just want to have fun, we must embrace their need for independence and show them that for them to have it, parents sometimes have to seem cruel to be kind.

Lose yourself
in sparkly bubbles

Girls on screen: every parent's nightmare and it starts so young. Your little girl is hardly out of baby grows and she knows what a tablet is. The Internet is like a bubble machine, churning out endless sparkly bubbles to keep us all mesmerised and entertained. Parents use tablets as the perfect babysitter. Parents who don't allow their toddlers much time on the iPad are then worrying about whether their little one will be behind when she starts nursery. It's the familiar scenario to a parent: you're damned if you do and you're damned if you don't.

Most parents do and with the best will in the world, your daughter is going to be vulnerable. Her vulnerability will come partly from us as parents not fully understanding our daughters' online world. It will also come from the lack

"with the best will in the world, your daughter is going to be vulnerable"

of accessible 'digital citizenship' - Internet education - being available for our girls and partly because we cannot police our daughters 24/7.

There is a huge amount of naivety among parents. I had a friend request on Facebook from a 10-year-old boy who was at my daughter's primary school. I was about to ring the mum and tell her what he'd done, when I saw that she was his first Facebook friend. First in line to give the seal of approval to her son, who was 3 years under the age limit to have an account. A family friend came up as a suggestion to follow on my Twitter account – he was 8 years old at the time and had set his account up himself. A friend's 9-year-old daughter spammed my Instagram feed one night when her mum was out with me and the babysitter was in charge.

Young girls who are friends with parents' friends are opening themselves up to adult content on their social media feeds. Aunty Doris may be sweetness and light at the family do's, but her social media may paint a different picture. Our daughters are entering an adult world, where censorship is minimal. Despite our best efforts.

I have been to numerous talks by the police on Internet safety. After a few, they became repetitive and I had heard it all before. I felt that I was pretty savvy and was teaching my girls to be the same. Daughter 4 was using an app called Musical.ly on her iPod, or on the family iPad, where you can create an instant musical video. Apart from the fact that I felt it was all a bit ridiculous, it appeared to be totally harmless and recently she has grown out of it. Then a post came up on my Facebook feed warning parents about a girl who had been groomed on the Musical.ly app through the messaging part of it. I was really shocked, because I had no idea that there was messaging available. I talked to my daughter who told me that her account was private and that she only messaged her cousin. How could I not have known? Young girls are using this app. As I said, with the best will in the world, they are at risk.

A mum posted a warning on a parenting forum about an app called 'Roblox'. Her daughter told her that someone was messaging her and asking her to call him 'daddy'. The mum had not realised there was a chat feature to this app. Reading the comments that followed, it was clear that hundreds of parents were not aware of this chat feature. These parents aren't all being wilfully negligent, they just aren't keeping up.

> **"***parents aren't all being wilfully negligent, they just aren't keeping up***"**

I have always found the parental controls fairly ineffective and if you have savvy daughters, where there's a will, there's a way. If they don't know the latest trick, then you can bet they have a friend who does and they will always be one step ahead of the parents.

We are always told to only allow our children to use the Internet where we can see them. This was slightly easier when their only access to it was via a family computer. Now we are giving them iPods for their 8th birthdays. We are actually buying our daughters a potential lethal weapon and not only that, we are giving it to them as a gift. Our actions are normalised by the fact that all their friends have them too and in just a couple of years they will all have smart phones and their iPods will be resigned to the back of a drawer. We will have unwittingly upped the ante. We almost have no choice but to keep up with their mates, otherwise they are the odd ones out and no one wants that for their child.

Technology moves at such a pace, that we oldies don't have a hope in techno hell of keeping up with the latest 'thing'. This is why digital citizenship is so vital in schools; regular lessons on how to be savvy and safe. Unfortunately, the government thinks they are doing enough. Enough isn't even enough! The Internet is impossible to police and so the best we can hope for is educating our daughters and then hope. Hope that she will not venture where many have gone before and still go. Hope that she doesn't unwittingly come across any nasties, although statistically it is highly likely that she will, and hope that Aunty Doris doesn't post too many drunken selfies or photos of scalped animals. Because our daughters will not know how to deal with some of the shit they come across online. When she's old enough (and don't leave it too late), it's worth talking through with her what she might see. Remember, it's not 'if' she'll see nasties but 'when'. The Internet was never designed for kids and yet they are the biggest users.

> **"The Internet was never designed for kids and yet they are the biggest users"**

Then there's what they are posting, without knowing they are building up a history of themselves. I paid for a post I had written to be sent to Instagram accounts. I gave the age range as 13-50 years, as it was a quote I had written about empowering girls. It gained 1000's of likes, many of them from 13-year-old girls. Out of interest, I clicked on some of their accounts and it horrified me how many of their accounts were public. As I scrolled through their photos, I was quickly able to build up a picture of them: school uniforms would be visible, recurring locations and so on. It's the same story on other social media platforms; reading through people's news feeds they are often easy to locate. You think your daughters know this, because you have told them a hundred times, but scary things still happen. Make sure that you are checking your daughter's online activity as much as you can. Be a detective and don't give it a second thought. Don't feel guilty that you aren't respecting her privacy, as I have heard some mums say.

"Be a detective and don't give it a second thought"

Then back to hope. Hope that our daughter won't be the one sending tit pics to a boy, that then get distributed around all his mates. Hope that they won't say nasty things about others. Hope that they won't look at something online that you wouldn't want them to see.

When I asked one of my daughters about tit pics she told me that lots of people do it, but she doesn't. I can only hope. I see tits displayed over Facebook and Instagram like a badge of misplaced honour. Friends 'like' and comment 'so beautiful' and 'hot', while I'm bumping into their mothers in the supermarket in a moral dilemma: do I mention the fact that your daughter's tits are currently gathering 'likes' on Instagram faster than holes in tights? How do I approach the subject? Now I'm in no way, shape or form criticising you, your daughter, nor her beautiful tits, but while I can safely admire that she is growing into a lovely young lady, so can all the stalking 55-year-old perverts, who are slathering over them as we are choosing our veg.

I don't consider myself to be easily shocked and I certainly don't want to be that person who tuts and says: it's all changed since I was young, because historically girls have always got their tits out – look at the Tudors and their heaving, corseted bosoms. The difference is that back then it wasn't friends, friends' dads, their teachers, their prospective employers, old uncles and all who got to lust. I'm no prude, but I am a great believer in more is less: more clothes (and I'm not talking a nun's habit) means less unwanted attention.

At the end of the day, the message we parents want to get across to our daughters, is that it isn't her tits that define her as a woman, however bloody amazing they are; they are just one part of her and if her tits are stealing the show, then the rest of her sure is missing out on a whole lot of 'likes'.

Nothing can prepare you as a parent of a teenage girl, for quite how much time she will spend on her phone. I've come to a conclusion on something: I wouldn't want to be a teenager today. I realised this having spent nearly two weeks in the company of all four of my daughters on holiday – something that never normally happens due to a mixture of work, their clubs and divorce. It made me realise the constant, unrepentant pressure they are under in their lives. Social media – they cannot get away from it. It is all-consuming. It sucks them in and changes them in the process. It turns them into highly-strung, short-tempered individuals, who would otherwise be perfectly pleasant. In fact, who are perfectly pleasant to other people; they save their stress outs for their parents.

"Social media – they cannot get away from it. It is all-consuming"

Social media changes them. It's a bit like someone who is having an affair. They have to get their next contact hit or a sick feeling builds up inside, as the stress of separation becomes almost unbearable. It's as addictive as a drug and it also has side effects: paranoia, fear of missing out, depression. They are only the start: body image is distorted, as are people's lives. Everything is just so perfect on screen: happy photos of happy groups, photo-shopped photos and photos that have been whittled down from a million selfies to one. Imagine the pressure for 'likes' on that one selfie. That one selfie that is literally one in a million. It is this pressure that creates stress and it is this stress that induces mental health issues in many teenagers.

Let's talk about sex baby and specifically online porn. It's setting the benchmark for my girls' experiences and that really bothers me. You see, I want them to feel empowered when it comes to sex – mentally as much as physically. I want them, not only to say 'no' if they don't want it, but to say what they do want too. Porn is making their future sex lives so much harder. It's setting completely unrealistic expectations and I know that this isn't good for the boys either. We need to talk to our daughters about the difference between the sexualised images they see in the media and on their screens, where sex is portrayed without love or emotion and healthy sexuality, as part of a meaningful relationship.

When I ask my daughters about the pressures they face, they shrug their shoulders and quite rightly say that it is all they have ever known. They cannot imagine life without social media – of course they can't, but we parents can't understand why they can't put their phones down for a minute without feeling horribly alienated from their world. Their world isn't our world. They have to learn how to cope with it and we can't help them with this one. That is why, as parents we get so frustrated with their world. The best we can do is try to understand and deal with the inevitable fallouts: low self esteem, paranoia, depression to name but a few. What we can't do is try to enter their world. I made that mistake once.

A bit tipsy on 2 Euros fizz one afternoon after a day in the sun on holiday, I gave selfie-taking a go. I don't think that I was exactly inspired by my daughters, as most of their selfies seemed to be a series of gurns for Snapchat. However, I was curious. Did I have what it takes to nail a selfie? I've never been able to pout, I just have the wrong sort of lips, but pumped on wine I thought I'd give it a go. I locked myself in the toilet, having noted all summer that a great deal of teenage selfies are taken in front of a sink. Plus, there's the added advantage of no one seeing you. I snapped away. I felt like a complete twat, but I carried on regardless.

I exited the loo quite pleased with my results. Yes, I felt like a sad old cow who was trying to keep up with her teenage daughters, but I was safe in the knowledge that no one was ever going to see the photos except me and it was something I wanted to experience. It's a bit like the shot on the beach or the photo of the sunset, it's what everyone (teenagers) seemed to be doing on holiday and I wondered what it felt like to do it – to be so self-indulgent.

That night we were sitting outside a café enjoying a drink, when one of my daughters asked if they could look at my phone. Knowing that I never have anything to hide, I passed it over.

"What the hell!" came the first cry.
"Oh-my-god-mum!" came the second.

The cries came fast and furious after that. Yes, they had found my selfies.

At first I tried to front it out.

"They're not bad, are they? For an oldish person?"

"Mum, they are awful. Why? I mean... what the...?"

"Well, this one's ok...isn't it?"

"NO!" (A four-part chorus)

They made me promise that I would never, ever lock myself in a toilet alone again. I was put on a month's probation, during which time the toilet door had to be kept ajar.

God forbid if you're on holiday and the place you are staying doesn't have WiFi. This means that catching up on Snapchat streaks, Instagram and Facebook has to be done in cafés. Teens work fast when a streak is at stake: break a streak and you'd think it was the end of the world. "I must tell my streakers so that they can keep up the streaks while I'm away", daughter 2 had once said before we embarked on a camping trip. My parental voice of concern kicked into action: "streakers?" I asked. "What the hell are you talking about?" I don't want to think about it too hard. "On Snapchat mum, don't worry about it." Oh, great, I thought to myself at the time. Another thing one of my teenagers tells me I don't need to worry about, which always makes me worried. Now I am an expert on streaks and know that it is when two people send photos on Snapchat for several consecutive days. Your teenagers will quickly have the WiFi password to every café in the local area and once they realise that they can actually sit on the public bench next to the café and still get the WiFi, they won't even need to embarrass themselves by sitting with you.

If there is, however, the occasional time when you want them to join you - without their phones, it will probably prove to be pretty much an impossibility. One lunchtime over tapas on our recent holiday in Spain, I sat at the top of the table, large glass of Rioja in hand and surveyed the scene: four teenagers, heads down, incommunicado.

"We've bought you this meal," I announced, taking matters into my own hands, "the least you lot can have the decency to do is put down your phones while you're eating."

They vaguely looked up and very slowly, very reluctantly put their phones on the table - screens still clearly on view to catch any notifications that may appear. My eldest daughter was still hanging on to hers. "I just have to reply to this streak quickly". "Why?" I questioned, with the stupidity of a parent. "Because

"you will spend your entire holiday watching your teens pouting and gurning into their screens"

otherwise my friend will think I'm really rude!" Oh, the irony.

So, instead you will spend your entire holiday watching your teens pouting and gurning into their screens, whilst at the same time rugby tackling you to the floor whenever you take a photo of them. They will zoom in and check every feature at close range, only to announce that they look disgusting, that there is no way that is getting posted on Facebook and if you do they will report you.

There is no getting away from the fact that your daughter's screen will rule her life and parenting forums are full of how, as a parent, you should deal with it. Some say limit their screen time. Others take their phones away at night. Personally, I think that denying them access to their lifeline simply causes huge amounts of resentment and makes life with your teenage daughter (even more of) a daily hell. I think that they need to understand your expectations and respect them, but be realistic and bear in mind it is like denying an addict their drug: the withdrawal symptoms may not be worth the battle.

To help any parents with younger children who are reading this, who are blissfully in a state of denial as to the creature their little angel is going to turn in to and just so that parents of teenagers can nod along, I have summarised some thoughts on your daughter's relationship with her screen:

- Don't be fooled into thinking that when she has a phone, you will be able to keep track/get hold of her. I regularly ring all four of my daughters' phones and no-one answers. It is probably a conspiracy.

- Don't get a phone contract without being very sure that there is a cut off to spending. However much you trust your angel and with the best will in the world, they click on an app that costs a shed load of money, which they don't have a hope in hell of ever paying off and so you have to. I don't let the girls have contracts. Ever.

- You will get totally and utterly confused with top ups – especially if you have more than one child. They will all be topping up on a different day and on different networks. They will run out of credit a week before this day. They will then try and tell you that you topped them up a month ago. They are lying.

- If you bought the phone for your child to be safe, bear in mind the above. No credit = back to the olden days pre-mobiles, when we were all at the mercy of paedophiles at every turn. Or, just relax until teatime, when they are sure to appear.

- If you buy a phone from the Internet for your child, be aware that if it is reconditioned it could be full of porn. This happened to my best friend. She sent the phone back after a couple of days...

- Teenagers lose things. Teenagers lose their phones. This causes two things to happen: firstly, a complete and utter meltdown of proportions you have never previously witnessed, and secondly a bill for someone. Make sure that bill is theirs, to teach them responsibility. At least you may get your toilets cleaned for a year.

- You will frequently be sharing your house with extras – FaceTime extras. This creates more noise and just don't enter their bedroom naked – I have had one or two close encounters with this one...or rather, their FaceTime friends have.

- Expect the phone to be used for selfies. These selfies will also include you – probably when you are looking at your most shit and they will stick a pair of dog's ears and a nose on you, then refuse to delete it until you up their pocket money.

- You will take a photo of them, it will be heavily scrutinized and then they will refuse to let you keep it. Your only revenge is to photo bomb their selfies.

- They will take photos of inanimate objects for the purposes of keeping a streak going. Do not question why they are taking a photo of their bedside table – you will be ridiculed, when you thought it would be the other way around.

- Expect to find them on their phone first thing in the morning and last thing at night. Unless you take it away from them an hour before bedtime, just as all the experts agree you should. In which case just expect an ongoing battle, in which part of their argument will contain the phrase: but I'm only listening to my music...Ha, yeah...just like I never read your texts.

- They will constantly be on the hunt for your/aunt's/ uncle's/friend's/neighbour's upgrade. They have no shame. They will ask the checkout assistant in the supermarket if they have to.

- Everyone has a better phone than them. Woe betide you if you have a better phone than them. When their granny has a better phone than them there is total humour failure, until the situation is rectified (either they have a birthday, or granny dies).

As much as we all have a way in which we want to parent, rules that we want to enforce and strict behaviours that we want our children to exhibit, we are all real people. We are all living in the real world. The world in which we are living is ever changing and if, as parents, we don't keep our ears to the ground, observe, listen and be willing to change, then our relationship with our children and their development into mature, rational human beings will be compromised. The pressure nearly kills me sometimes. The desperate want and need to get it right. We read books and listen to experts on the radio. We are terrified by newspaper headlines and articles and weighed down by our own parents' expectations of us. Through all this, however, when all's said and done, as parents we must hit the ground running and learn on the job. Because nothing can prepare you for the impact of the screen on our children at each different stage of their lives.

"nothing can prepare you for the impact of the screen on our children"

Screen use will always be a hot topic of conversation: do we let our primary school kid get a mobile phone because her friends have all got one – justifying it with the fact that she needs it to be safe? Do we allow our 12-year-old to get a smart phone, in the knowledge that once we do we effectively are giving them a free, uncontrolled rein on the world-wide web and all the shit that lies within? Do we happily relinquish control of everything that up until the moment we were faced with these dilemmas, we had a pretty good handle on? Do we let our teenagers have a smart phone, but take it away from them from 9pm-7am? As this chapter has shown, such is the mountain of issues we face as parents when our child utters those words: I want a mobile phone.

As parents, we can all harp on about the fact that back in the day we didn't have mobile phones and we never got lost and we actually communicated with each other. We weren't all narcissistic, selfie-obsessed Snapchatters and we used Eye Spy books to get us through long car journeys. But then you become the voice of experience and you begin to realise that this is their world and you realise that all the ideals you held when your child was an embryo are actually worth jack shit, because we are living in this world that we are creating now! Add to this the fact that as parents we can hardly put our phones down, because it's our world too.

I don't think we should abandon all our ideals and just give up, or give in. We must remember that we are all living and getting lost in this world of sparkly bubbles that is the Internet. I think we need to listen to our daughters, observe them, communicate with them and ultimately learn with them and from them.

"*communicate with them and ultimately learn with them* **"**

Beautiful wishes

When it comes to sex, I want my girls to be in control. I want them to understand the importance of consent, respect, rights and equality, as well as the importance of safe sex and STDs. I want them to have the confidence to say no when they don't want it and to enjoy it when they do.

The aspect of our daughters being in control during sexual activity is a subject very close to my heart. So, when my stepdaughter had a steady boyfriend at 16, I turned to Google for advice. I typed in: 'sex and girls being in control'. Here is a sample of the advice I was offered: 'Hot, hot, hot women-in-charge sex positions', 'sexy girl control sex – sexy teacher controlled by student – You Tube', 'sex tips from a Guy: 10 ways he wants you to take control in bed'. It quickly dawned on me that the control I was talking about and the advice I had found on control were both very different.

I want my girls to be in control of the situation and to have the confidence to say "no" if they don't want to do something. I want all our kids, sons and daughters, to know that 'no' means 'no'. I don't want this message to get diluted in the pool of porn or the 'banter'. I don't want it to be misunderstood by alcohol, naivety or uncontrollable desire. Because none of these factors are excuses: NO means NO! This is such an important issue and one that we must make sure teenagers understand. 'No' can be whispered, it can be a kick in the balls or a shake of the head. We must teach our children to recognise the signs and to take control.

We bring our kids up with the notion that consent isn't always required, for example relatives kiss and hug them whether they like it or not. I remember hating being kissed by an uncle because of his prickly beard, but it would never have occurred to me that I could say "no". Yet as they grow up, consent is an important skill for our children to learn. We need to make them aware that nobody can force them to do anything they don't want them to. It's such a tricky one though, because when we want them to do something we have asked, such as tidy their bedroom, there may have to be an element of force applied to the request. Because of the mixed messages we give our children surrounding consent, it is even more vital that we talk to them about it in relation to their bodies and sex.

Of course, I hate the thought of them having sex. It's actually very strange when you suddenly find yourself faced with that thought. Teenagers are far more open about sex than we were and the thinking among teens these days is that sex is a normal part of their lives and that it is their right to have it if they want to. This attitude would make their grandparents shudder, but as parents, we need to adapt our thinking to the changing times. Your little girl has a boyfriend, or quite possibly a girlfriend, who they are shagging and if they aren't now, they will be soon. The question is, have you done your bit in educating them about sex?

"The question is, have you done your bit in educating them about sex?"

All parents find this bit awkward, but if I can offer any advice it would be get in there quite early, because if you have ever tried to talk to a teenager about sex you will know that talking about it openly brings awkwardness and shut down, making exploring the issues surrounding it a whole lot trickier. We can bring our girls up to be savvy and confident females in many areas of their lives, but the world of sex is different. Their sexual experiences are hidden so far away from us parents, that getting an understanding of their views on it is virtually impossible. "Don't ever send tit pics," I lamely told my eldest daughters. They both looked at me as if I was a freak. The disdain in their faces made me feel uncomfortable, when I thought it would be the other way around. I am parenting in the dark here. This is why parents need help from schools. I really appreciate a bit of help from teachers who have an element of detachment. People who can give out the facts to kids who can't walk away with eyeballs rolling towards the ceiling. Kids who must listen, even if they think that they know it all. My daughters may not want to sit and chat to me about sending naked images of themselves online and the implications of it, but they may feel grateful if it came up in an organised discussion at school.

"*parents can't always be the Internet police*"

Kids are accessing porn younger and younger. Kids own mobile phones younger and younger. My stepdaughter didn't have a smart phone until she was 17. My 13-year-old had one at 11. With the best will in the world, parents can't always be the Internet police. Primary age children are being exposed to violent and graphic pornographic images and common sense tells us that many of them will normalise what they see, to try to understand it. The porn industry's core target is boys aged 12-17. As author Mark Kastlemann said, "Giving porn to a teenage boy is like giving crack to a baby. Addiction is almost guaranteed."

Schools are a hot bed of risk for our girls and so it's good that they share the responsibility of sex education. Apparently, almost a third of girls aged 16-18 say they have been groped at school. I'm sorry? You what? It is also commonplace for girls to be slapped on their bums and for naked pictures of girls to be circulated among boys. I worry about teenage boys' attitudes to girls. I worry because I know how influenced boys are now by online porn. I know that this gives the boys unrealistic expectations of what girls will do and do the boys care what the girls want? Nearly three quarters of girls in their late teens said that they heard names such as 'slut', 'bitch' and 'slag' used several times a week. Boys call it banter; I call it harassment. I call it undermining females and taking away their control.

Fear and shame allow sexual harassment to perpetuate. We need our girls to be shouting out when they are being harassed and never to accept it as normal behaviour. I can remember a boy my sister's age, 16, groping her bum at a party and she immediately swung around, slapped him in the face and told him never to do that again. Observing this at 14, I found it so empowering to see her react like that, and I want my daughters to feel able to do the same. We need to talk to them about what situations they may encounter and make it clear that they can, and must, react loudly.

"*I don't want my girls to grow up feeling powerless*"

I'm not sure that we, their mums, are the best role models here. How many of us have whispered about sexual harassment, or kept it buried under shame? We are supposed to be the epitome of calm and control and really shouldn't lose our shit. Society brings us up knowing this and it's seemingly better that way. Well I want our daughters to stand up to this bullshit! Yes, there are so many reasons for our fear: fear of losing or not getting a job, fear of being disbelieved, fear of being ignored... perfectly legitimate reasons for fear. Then the shame – shame that we didn't leave/shout/retaliate/say 'no' more forcefully. This is why I was empowered by my sister's reaction to the hand on her bum. We must bring our daughters up to have a voice. They mustn't feel shame. They must face their fear and not keep the peace like 'good girls'. Our girls must be in control.

I wonder whether girls and boys know how to communicate with each other any more. I know that boys can be hard to drag off their Xboxes. My stepdaughter told me that most of her friends at university were using Tinder. At uni?! I nearly fell off my chair! If there was one place you could always guarantee to pick someone up it was in the Student Union Bar. What's the world coming to?

There has definitely been a huge cultural shift since I was a teenager and I just don't get it. I'm not saying that I should, or that I want to, but equally I don't want my girls to grow up feeling powerless. Wolf whistling is to become a crime. Well, good. It's not just a bit of a laff. It's not funny. It's not harmless. The reason that I can say this with such certainty is because I am a woman. I'll tell you how it has made me feel in the past: frightened to leave the house, hugely intimidated and incredibly embarrassed. It is undoubtedly worse for teenagers. As I got older, they no longer intimidated me, they just irritated the hell out of me.

I never want my girls to feel intimidated. I want them to be empowered. They are all black belts in Taekwon-do and through the martial art we are teaching them how to be strong and fit and how to use their bodies and their strength in the most effective way to keep control in any given situation. However, even with this knowledge, I know that as females they are still incredibly vulnerable.

We must talk to our daughters about what is acceptable behaviour, both in and out of the bedroom. We can be far more direct than our parents ever were. We must tell our girls in no uncertain terms that their actions now can have long-lasting effects and we're not just talking pregnancy. We're talking about inappropriate photos and videos posted on line and not being in control of their thoughts and their actions. We must tell our girls to take control and to know that their wishes count.

Follow your dreams

Driving whilst under the influence of parenting, I've decided that I've passed my test. I've got four girls to teenagers and one has successfully and happily flown the nest. None of this experience makes me anywhere near an expert, but I feel like I've earned my P plates.

I still fuck up, a lot. I still feel guilty a lot of the time. I still feel like there are many roads I am yet to travel with my kids and some will be full of pot holes, some will just be a little bit bumpy and others will be smooth, and we'll fly along those roads with the wind in our hair. But whatever road I travel, those P plates are staying on. We are always learning. There isn't always a right or a wrong answer to a problem or a question; I've learned that it can depend on the child and the situation. I've learned that it is good to be honest with our children, especially if we feel that we have failed them in some way, and I've also learned that they

> **"There isn't always a right or a wrong answer to a problem or a question"**

are capable of an awful lot more than we, as parents, often give them credit for.

Some time ago, I bought myself a hammock. Ever since I can remember I have wanted a hammock. Its swaying and lulling represents relaxation and holidays and it gave me the thought that I'm beginning to parent from my hammock. It's partly because of the girls' ages: daughter 1 will quite often cook the family meal and daughters 2 and 3 are both very capable and willing cooks too, time permitting. So, I let them. I don't hover over them; I get on with something else. If they need ingredients that we haven't got, they go to the shop to get them. I leave them to it.

My three eldest daughters have all done their DofE Bronze awards. This involves going on a weekend camping trip. When daughter 1 went on her DofE weekend, I sat on her bed, clutching the kit list and methodically going through it with her. It felt wrong. I kept saying to her, do you really need me here? And then promptly felt guilty for asking.

Armed with my P plates, I parented the others from my hammock for their trips, metaphorically speaking. They did all the packing themselves, everything. I didn't get involved at all. They even talked to me about needing new walking boots and head torches and I just brushed off their requests with comments like: 'use your sister's' and, 'you don't need a head torch, use any torch'. To some, this may appear unkind, because they think that they need these things and they won't want to feel uncomfortable not having exactly what is on the list. And yes, my hammock parenting did cause them to fuck up: a groundsheet was forgotten and the night before daughter 2's trip she discovered that the tent had neither poles, nor pegs. However, they sorted out these problems themselves. I didn't rescue them, because if we always rescue our children, how will they ever learn to spread their wings and fly?

"if we always rescue our children, how will they ever learn to spread their wings and fly?"

Many times, when I've taken daughter 3 to her football training, I have sat in my car and watched parents arriving, struggling to get their reluctant daughter out of the car and then promptly carrying their bag to the training ground for them. I hate seeing this. It represents for me the parent carrying their child through life, when the child needs to use their own legs to walk. I saw the same the morning we dropped daughter 4 at camp. Parents carrying rucksacks and sleeping bags for their children, while the child trots along, happily bag free at their side. Then parents standing and watching at the fence, while their child is in a field, with 60 of their friends, playing a game with their young and fun team leaders, but the parent is finding it hard to let go. Desperate for their child to turn and make eye contact; to seek them out from among all the desperate parents standing at the fence, who should all just be walking away and letting go.

"We are our children's role models and with this comes a huge responsibility"

We are our children's role models and with this comes a huge responsibility. As a mum of girls, I feel that to bring them up as powerful, independent women, I have to do so much deconstructing of language that it's pretty daunting. Gender stereotypes are deep-seated and they are so much a part of our society and culture as well as our upbringing, I worry that I sometimes perpetuate them without thinking.

Don't call her 'beautiful' because it will teach her to place more value on her looks, than their ambition.

Don't tell her to be 'nice' because it limits her potential and leaves her open to abuse. Not only that, it sets a high standard that she may never feel she can reach and she will spend her entire life hampered by self-criticism. Don't tell her that the clothes she is wearing are too revealing, because that is implying that she must adapt what she wears to be safe from men. Don't tell her to be 'non-judgmental' because she may think she shouldn't have an opinion. Don't let her think of herself as 'special' to be a girl, because this is patronising and girls and boys should be equal. Don't call her a 'princess' as it has connotations of neediness and requiring a prince. Don't stop her being angry because she needs that anger to fire her beliefs. Don't talk about her in terms of 'liking boy's things' if she enjoys building models and playing football, as you will condition her to think that she isn't just being herself. Don't just praise her ability, praise her efforts or she will only ever strive for perfection and will never feel good enough, nor take a risk. (But for God's sake, don't praise everything she does.) Don't call her 'bossy' when she actually has good leadership skills. Don't call her 'clever' as you must give her specifics. Don't tell her an 'A' should be an A*, because the

> **"Don't call her 'bossy' when she actually has good leadership skills"**

pressure will turn a love in to a hate. Don't tell her that she's doing something 'like a girl' because she must learn there's no such thing.

You see what I mean?

Do tell her to remember who she is and that she matters in the world, equally. Do tell her to have her own voice and to use it confidently. Do let her develop her independence. Do tell her that she can be anything she wants to be. Do tell her that kindness is the best form of communication and to surround herself by people who make her feel good. Do tell her that the images in the media aren't real. Do tell her to follow her instinct. Do tell her to be in control. Do tell her to make her body strong. Do show her positive female role models and be one yourself. Do encourage acceptance.

"*Give her space to breathe in her own air and exhale her own thoughts***"**

Give her space to breathe in her own air and exhale her own thoughts. We are doing far too much 'helicopter parenting', where we hover over our children like an irritating mosquito, swooping in if our child needs rescuing. Keeping a close eye on proceedings, ready to throw the rope down for them to grab hold of and get taken back to the safety of the home at the slightest whiff of potential conflict or danger.

I would even take it a step further in my analogy of how we're bringing up our kids. Modern parenting is more like drone parenting: even more intrusive, with its ability to get in closer and to gather the necessary information required to control our children. This is my definition of a parent drone: a 24-hour 'eye in the sky', seven days a week, loitering over an area and sending back real-time imagery of activities on the ground. Piloted by parents who analyse the images which the cameras send back, who then act on what they see. Information from teachers, tutors and sports coaches, to name but three. Parents are incessantly requiring feedback on their offspring, to use to remain firmly involved at every decision-making process. Drones can spy, and as parents we are encouraged to spy on our kids: check their internet activity, read their texts, always be on the lookout for clues to them entering the dark side, from where we will immediately rescue them.

We'll rescue them by droning on to teachers when our child is even slightly struggling. Droning on at the side of the pitch, telling a child how to play a game that the parent probably knows little about. This isn't just words of support, this is telling them what to do and even worse, telling them what they should have done. This is apparently one of the main reasons kids, particularly girls, give up sport in their droves as they approach the teenage years – they are embarrassed and made to feel even more self-conscious by well-meaning drones.

Drones, unlike helicopters, can swoop right in. They are on the PTA, on the school trips, on the school reading rota, they are constantly at school. Then the next thing they know they are traipsing around university open days where frustrated Deans are prising their child away from them and telling them to go and do something else for a couple of hours. They are writing the personal statement, sorting out their child's work experience and attending their interviews with them.

"well-meaning drone parenting is creating children who are more likely to develop low self-worth"

Drones are doing everything they can to prevent risk: risk of injury, risk of failure and risk of boredom. But this well-meaning drone parenting is creating children who are more likely to develop low self-worth, who are stressed and anxious and who are more likely to engage in risky behaviour, such as binge drinking.

I'm not the parent who drones on at the side of the pitch – I leave that to the coaches. Nor am I the parent drone, hovering in the school. But I am a drone. When one of my teenage daughters became a little more withdrawn than usual, I worried. I worried that she had lost her spark and so I asked her, "what's wrong?" "Nothing", came her reply. But I asked again and over the months again and again: are you sure? No wonder she withdrew. She was doing well at school, she had good friends, but I still worried too much. When parents drone on, anxiously asking "are you ok?" they can make the child anxious because they sense that we're worried and, of course, it can make them pull away. I was over-analysing, when I should have been giving her the space to breathe.

The other time that I drone on is about chores. That constant, can you do this? Have you done that? I asked you to tidy up and so on, doesn't teach them to notice for themselves when things need doing. I repeat myself too frequently. I am not raising robots, I am bringing up independent human beings, whom I want to be self-aware.

Parent drones are well meaning, because not being a drone can feel detached and alienating; hands off parenting can make you feel extremely guilty. Ironically, to develop our children's confidence, we need to develop our own. Do you think our own parents ever felt guilty when they told us to "go and play"? No, because they weren't surrounded by other parents who were hovering over their offspring and they weren't being constantly fed horror stories in the media about paedophiles who lurk on every corner. They don't. But they do exist. They exist in places where you cannot always be: it could be your child's friend's dad, or a family member. All we can do is to develop our children's confidence and self-esteem; let go and trust.

> **"**to develop our children's confidence, we need to develop our own**"**

So, next time I'm sick of my own voice droning on I might just shut up and see what happens. I might be pleasantly surprised.

We want to raise powerful girls. 'Power' is a word that is more readily associated with males. It is time to redress the balance and it is our job as parents to do so. Powerful girls feel secure in themselves and they know who they are. They make things happen rather than waiting for others to take control and they make positive choices about their own lives, as well as having a positive impact on

"Powerful girls feel secure in themselves and they know who they are"

others. Of course, they will still make mistakes and sometimes feel insecure, but this won't stop them from getting on and bossing life.

We must show her values and behaviours that are important to us and lead by example. I sometimes hear parents blaming themselves for their children's foibles and behaviour. As parents, we can feel that we are being harsh on our children, possibly even cruel, and when we compare ourselves to other parents, we feel even guiltier at the way we treat our own. I feel we need to step back from judging ourselves so harshly. Because

so often, it is when we are being harsh on our children that we are being the kindest. When we are being what they and others may call 'cruel' we are doing the best possible thing that we

"it is when we are being harsh on our children that we are being the kindest"

can for them and when we are letting them go, we are allowing them to spread their fairy wings and fly.

We must remember that living with a powerful girl is not necessarily going to be easy. We are encouraging her to have a voice and an opinion, to be independent and to take risks. We must be prepared to listen to her, to embrace her characteristics and, above all, to enjoy her.

I have this quote on my toilet door and for me, it sums it all up:

"There are two things
we should give our children:
roots and wings"

As parents, we give our children direction to make strong roots. We do our best. We guide them, teach them right from wrong, instil in them courtesy and respect for others. However, ultimately we must let go a little: test their independence and resilience, which in the future they are going to need, and give them the confidence, from our hammocks, to follow their dreams and to fly.

To Mothers of Daughters

Tell your daughter that you love her every day

But expect a few, 'I hate you's in return

Tell her that she is beautiful just the way she is

But let her dye her hair anyway

*Tell her that it doesn't matter whether she is tall
or short*

But if she is short, accept that she will use fake ID

Tell her that it doesn't matter if her hips are wide

But still support her periodic healthy eating campaigns
by buying quinoa and dates

*Tell her that what really makes her beautiful cannot
be seen in the hundreds of selfies that she takes every
day*

But 'like' them anyway

Tell her that what is important is in her heart

But expect it to be broken several times and be there
to piece it together again and again and again.

Wishes and Dreams

The comments taken from the notebook

With the thoughts I added when my daughters were little:

Decisions...decisions

Use your instinct. It will get you through some tricky situations. If you make the wrong decision, admit it and make amends.

Girls just want to have fun – we do have fun – lots

of fun! Don't take life too seriously – remember – life goes on. Survive and move forward. You will succeed.

A little love goes a long way

When I tell you off, I do it because I love you. You will grow in to wonderful human beings, who embrace all things and all people with love.

Listen to what people say but always *follow your dreams...*

Don't have regrets. Work hard to make dreams happen. Be proactive.

Treat yourself! Kindly

Lose yourself in sparkly bubbles
Embrace freedom, but always be aware. Stay safe.

Believe in your dreams!
Just because something hasn't been done before, doesn't mean it can't be done. Just because people are negative about something, doesn't mean you can't be positive about it.

Beautiful wishes
Act on your wishes – you can make them in to realities.

Have a silly, funny, hippy, happy day!
An open, smiley face makes people notice you. It makes people warm to you and you will spread happiness.

Every cloud has a sparkly lining
So often, from bad comes good. Look for the good in people and situations. Be positive.

Dear Daughters,

Don't worry, this isn't one of those schmoozy letters, where I tell you how beautiful you all are – apparently, that would damage you for life, as it would eat away at your self esteem (and anyway, you already know you are). No, this is just me wanting to tell you what I really love about you. Because let's be honest, we have to deal with a lot of crap on a daily basis – some yours, some mine and I really don't want the good times to get buried. So here is a celebration of what I love.

I love it when I can lean on you – not emotionally – you have enough of your own stuff to deal with – I mean physically lean on you. Drape my arm casually around you and lean in close. It's more subtle than a hug and I love it when you don't pull away and even more when you rest your head on my shoulder.

I love it when you say, 'oh mum' in a tone of pity drenched in love, when I don't understand something in your world. Or when you say: I haven't given you a hug in ages and you wrap your arms around me tight. Or when one who doesn't often hug me, does.

I love it when you help each other with your homework, because I can't, and when you bake together. In fact, I love it when you do anything together that doesn't involve a fight. Walking into your bedrooms and seeing you lying together on the bed, laughing unselfconsciously as sisters do, makes me smile.

I love it when we walk the dogs. It isn't often that you can, because you're in bed, in school, at work. But this makes when you can, a real joy. We talk with uncluttered abandon. We put the world to rights. We discover things about each other we didn't know.

I love it when another package arrives from far flung China. You are usually at school and as I place it on your bed in your full view when you walk in, I can feel your excitement. I text you to tell you it's arrived, because you've been asking when it will for days and I want to be a part of your pleasure. I love that you have worked hard to pay for it yourself and that you are really good at your work and people appreciate you. This is your well-earned reward.

I love it when, during a busy day I can text you and ask if you want to cook. I admire your confidence in creating meals for a big family and your willingness to do it. I value your independence, so I am not constantly at your beck and call. You respect, sometimes, that I too have a life and you appreciate it when I sacrifice a part of it for you.

I love it when I am going out and I can ask you, with all the uncertainty of middle age, if I look ok and you reply with all the certainty of someone who knows that I have made an effort to dress up, that I do. I listen to your arguments between each other over clothes with a mixture of irritation and fondness. I find it endearing the way you share and annoying, but understandable, the way you fight.

You are four individuals who are changing and growing. I admire your strength and your resilience to the world that you find yourselves in. It's your world for the taking. Just know that you are loved.

Mum xxxxxxxx

Dear Girls,

Thank you for coming on the dog walk today. It was fun. That is, until it ended in you getting cross with me. I refused to come into Waitrose because supermarket shopping with you is stressful enough, let alone when you're already cross with me and I felt it best to bail out. I did still trust you with my contactless credit card. You see dear daughters, I do trust you. I trust you, even though on the walk you told me that when I gave you train money in cash that you hadn't spent, you pocketed the change each week. I choose to just see that as me helping you to save your pennies and put it towards a good cause – like more clothes for your summer holidays. We laughed when you told me that you are working on your turkey body. I wondered why you wanted to look like a turkey, until I realised you meant the country. I reminded you to walk into your buttocks – a favourite phrase of mine when we're walking the dogs. It's normally partner who hears it, but today, dear daughters, it was you who got the benefit of my wisdom. All that work you are doing at the gym and a dog walk can also give you the buttocks you desire. Both of you complained that your wellies itched the whole way. I told you it was the leggings reacting with the plastic, so you pulled your leggings down and hoped no one was watching – only me, laughing. You commented very sweetly how kind the river looked. I was struck by how lovely that phrase was. I laughed when you asked me if we were getting closer to the rec and I thought you said Iraq, as we crossed the airstrip.

Dear girls, I love spending time outside with you walking. It's when things get talked about that normally get passed over, unsaid, thought of as unimportant so not bothered about. But the things we talked about on our dog walk today are the things that make you, you. The details, the throw away comments, the heartfelt words. The things that touch my heart, but you would not understand why. Like you chatting about the new skirts you are buying from American Apparel, from China. What size to get? You are both getting the same skirt and your cousin too. It makes me smile because you fight over clothes all the time, especially when one of you buys the same item as the other, so I loved hearing you chat about the same skirt together.

So thank you girls, for being so refreshingly you and for sharing yourselves with me on the dog walk this morning and for not taking the piss with my credit card (although Greek yoghurt with honey and fresh pasta were not on the list).

Much love,

Mum xxxxxx

25309030R00094

Printed in Great Britain
by Amazon

Printed in Great Britain
by Amazon

Connect with NineStar Press

www.ninestarpress.com

www.facebook.com/ninestarpress

www.facebook.com/groups/NineStarNiche

www.twitter.com/ninestarpress

www.instagram.com/ninestarpress

About Amy Marsden

As a child Amy loved reading and writing, so naturally she graduated with a degree in biomedical science and has worked in a microbiology laboratory ever since. Her passion is writing however, and she started her first novel while still at university. When she is not writing about surviving apocalypses, exploring space, and conquering magic—all featuring LGBTQ characters—she can be found reading or playing games about those very things. She lives by the sea with her wife and fifteen-year-old cat who still runs around like a kitten.

Other NineStar books by this author

Survivors

I started writing this because I was sick of daydreaming about it. Now it's all out there in the world, and it still doesn't seem real. Thank you.

Acknowledgements

When I started writing this duology a decade ago, thoughts of publishing it didn't cross my mind. It was simply a story I'd been thinking about that I decided to write. Turns out it was the first of many stories, and I'll always look back fondly on it. It's been a long process from there to here, and I'd like to thank several people who've helped make it all a reality.

First, to my wife. I was still writing this when we met, and I can distinctly remember feeling so nervous when you read it for the first time. You've read it many times since, and I'll always value your input. Your support means everything to me.

Secondly, to the beta readers who first read this years ago, when it was all still one book. I'm not in touch with you anymore, but your insights helped shape it into what it is now, and I'll always be grateful.

Another person who has massively helped me with this book is my editor, Elizabeth. You're super busy, and I can only thank you for taking the time to help hammer this into what it is today. Thank you to you and to NineStar Press.

And lastly, to you, reader. I count this book and *Survivors* as my debut, and I cannot fully express in words (funny, considering I'm a writer) what it means to have you decide this duology is worth your time and money. A decade ago,

When Jennifer and her gro  castle, she thought they w walls and strong soldiers su infected became negligible, and she could finally relax for the first time in what felt like forever. But the need for a cure outweighed Jennifer's personal comfort, and the castle didn't have the facilities needed to synthesize a vaccine from her blood.

She should have known safety wouldn't last.

Back out in the world plagued by infected, Jennifer and her group head to Paris, where they could begin to find a cure for the virus that decimated humanity. But things don't go according to plan, and they are left scrambling to get away with their lives.

Determined to find a safe place to hunker down and ride out the worst of the apocalypse, Jennifer and her broken but hopeful group return to the UK. Once there, they soon find that the infected aren't the only threat.

A story about found family and overcoming the odds, *The Safe Zone* is the thrilling conclusion to the *Survivors* duology.

THE SAFE ZONE

Survivors, Book Two

Amy Marsden

A NineStar Press Publication

www.ninestarpress.com

The Safe Zone

ISBN:

First Edition, March 2024

Also available in eBook, ISBN:

CONTENT WARNING:
This book contains depictions of death, graphic violence/gore, homophobia, death of a prominent character, and death of a secondary character.

To my wife. Now and always.

Chapter One

12TH JANUARY

When the world ended, Heather was fishing.

She didn't know anything was amiss for hours as she sat by the tranquil water, her mind blissfully empty of thoughts. Fishing allowed her to destress; she liked to imagine the river carrying her worries away as she stretched her legs out. Her serene morning came to an abrupt end as the first bodies drifted by, and she jumped to her feet, adrenaline pooling in her stomach.

Her phone, which had been switched off in her bag, showed six missed calls from her wife and three each from her brother and nephew. Ringing back proved fruitless. She packed her equipment away as quickly as she could, her shaking hands belying her efficient movements. Panic stuck her tongue to the roof of her mouth, and dread made breathing difficult. She raced back to her car—

To find it wasn't where she'd left it.

Heather couldn't hold back the terror any longer. Shouts and screams crowded the air all around her. *What's going on?* Her town was usually a quiet place. She

made her way onto the street, resolving to run home if needed, and stopped dead in her tracks.

Madness greeted her wide eyes.

Everywhere she looked, chaos reigned. People fought each other in the middle of the street, running in all directions, damaging cars and buildings. Even as she watched, a man lunged for another, punched him in the stomach, and bit into his arm as he doubled over in pain.

The paramedic in Heather froze, and she'd seen *a lot* in her twenty-year career. A tyre blew out on a car, causing it to flip, and all three occupants had walked away without a scratch. A five-car pile-up where no one had walked away. She'd held a thirteen-year-old boy in her arms as he bled out from a knife wound. She had lost count of the number of babies she'd delivered. She'd seen the best humanity had to offer and the worst, and the scene unfolding in front of her was up there with the worst.

The panic flooding her veins was thankfully tempered by her training, and her body got to work before her mind had a chance to catch up. The man who had attacked the other had left him slumped on the ground, so Heather dashed over to him. She dumped her fishing equipment at her side.

"Hi, there," she said as she checked around him for danger. "I'm Heather, and I'm a paramedic. Can you tell me where you're hurting?"

The man's glassy eyes blinked as he struggled to focus on her. "My arm," he croaked.

Heather identified the bite wound immediately. It looked nasty already. She reached into her bags for her first aid kit—she never went anywhere without one—and

pulled out some gloves and alcohol wipes as well as gauze for bandaging it. She cleaned the wound as quickly as she could, but she never got the chance to wrap it.

A heavyset woman tackled her from behind, and the two of them went sprawling over the injured man. Heather banged her head against the concrete, her vision flashing white as she struggled to right herself. Nausea hit her stomach, but she didn't vomit, thankfully. *Damnit!*

The woman wasn't there when Heather pushed herself into a seated position. She didn't know where she'd gone, and frankly, she didn't care. Pushing aside her head injury—she could feel blood seeping from a cut, but it wasn't bad—she looked around for the injured man. He was nowhere to be seen either.

Cursing again, she regained her footing only to have to jump out of the way of two men grappling with each other. *What on Earth is happening?* She ran back to her bags, pulled her phone out, and rang her wife again. Still nothing. With a frustrated growl, Heather shoved the phone into her pocket and straightened, determined to run home.

She didn't get far.

This time a man came yelling at her across the road, shouting obscenities and clearly mistaking her for someone else. Heather barely had time to drop her equipment and get out of the way. He stumbled over her bags and lost his footing, which Heather was glad for. She had no doubt he would have tried to beat her to death if he'd managed to get his hands on her. Her heart jumped into her throat at the thought.

"You, lady! Come with me!"

The voice belonged to a mountain of a man, bald, with a thick beard. He waved at her from an American-style pickup truck. Heather didn't think of the implications of hopping in—she grabbed her first aid kit and ran for it, leaving the fishing equipment behind. She had a feeling it would only slow her down. The man could have been anyone taking her anywhere but staying alone and vulnerable on the street was not an option.

The truck sped around a roundabout, jumping up onto the curb and rattling Heather's brain. "Do you know what's going on?" she asked as she fastened her seatbelt.

The man didn't spare her a glance as he shot down the road like a race car driver, swerving in between the traffic. Heather clutched on to her seat for dear life. "Probably the same thing that's happening in London. I bet it's across the country too."

She was at a disadvantage—she'd gotten up early that morning and hadn't checked the news before she left for the river. "What happened?"

The man grunted as they almost hit a bus. "The virus. Not what the news said it was. Deadly. Turns people into mindless beasts that attack everyone."

Heather turned that over in her mind, kicking herself for not putting it together sooner. *Thick fuck.* She'd seen it first-hand. Only a few days ago she'd picked up a homeless man who'd been ranting and raving. He'd bitten a police officer before they'd been able to subdue him. She'd assumed he'd been high on drugs, but the bite mark on his leg had been festering, and she'd heard the doctors whispering.

"Where are we—"

Heather didn't finish the sentence. The man—who had been driving surprisingly well, despite the reckless pace—crashed into another car that had also been speeding. The airbags exploded as metal screeched against metal, and glass sprinkled down like cutting rain. Heather would have been thrown from her precarious perch if not for the seatbelt digging into her chest.

She blinked her eyes open. Smoke rose from the engine and clogged her nose. The man next to her was unmoving, his face covered in blood as it rested against the steering wheel. She reached over with a shaking hand and checked his pulse.

Nothing.

With a groan, Heather heaved herself out of the wreck. She fell to the ground, her legs unable to support her.

Coughing through the burn of smoke and pushing aside the looming shock, she stumbled over to the other car. There was a man and woman in the front seats, both unconscious. Heather noted the careful rise and fall of their chests. She hurried back to her bags for her phone, but when she tried to ring the emergency services all she got was a busy tone.

With another curse she made her way back over to the couple. She managed to pry open the passenger side door and reach in to check on the woman. A weak pulse, but steady. She reached over for the man—

—Hands like steel grabbed her arm and yanked her backward.

"*Fucking bitch.*"

Heather fell to the ground. *What the—*

All thought wheezed out of her at the first contact of the man's foot with her stomach. Pain squeezed her chest, and it was all Heather could do to force her body to breathe. She looked up at her attacker as he lifted his leg back for another kick, saw his crazed eyes and twisted face, saw saliva dripping down his chin.

Am I going to die? The thought was distant, like it wasn't quite tethered to reality. *Oh, Kallie, I love you.* She closed her eyes in anticipation of more violence, but his foot never landed. Instead, a deafening bang left her ears ringing. She opened her eyes to see the man drop against the car, a small hole torn into his chest. She scrambled to her feet as he slumped on the ground.

She turned to her saviour—a woman in military gear—in time to see another person jump on her, sharp teeth tearing into her neck like she was a three-course meal. Heather fell back as the duo dropped to their knees. Her blood roared in her ears. The soldier managed to shove the crazy person off her, and she shot him before he could regain his feet. Heather took one look at her blood-drenched uniform, at the gaping wound on her neck, and rushed forward to help.

An abundance of caring. That's why she'd become a paramedic in the first place. She couldn't stand by when people needed her help. To do so would go against every fibre of her being.

She quickly grabbed some bandages from her kit and applied pressure to the wound. It wasn't that bad, but the soldier's face screwed up like she was the one who had been shot. "I'm a paramedic," Heather told the soldier. She had learned early on in her career that simply stating her job brought comfort to people. "Just keep pressure on

it, it's okay, it's not bleeding that much."

The soldier grabbed Heather's arms and pushed her away. She stumbled back with a gasp. How many times had she been shoved around today? "It's too late," the woman grunted as she sat up. "Get somewhere safe. Defendable. Board up the windows and doors." She gestured wildly. "Go on now, before you die too." With that, the soldier stood up, picked up her weapon, and ran screaming into the press of people fighting one another a little way down the road.

Heather stared after her. She stood up slowly, feeling somehow disconnected from her body. The roaring returned to her head, and she pressed the heels of her hands into her eyes, desperate to shut out the dread, the blood, the insanity.

"*Hey.*"

Heather let her hands drop at the hissed voice. It took her a second to locate the owner. He was a broad man with a flat face, wearing a white T-shirt stained red, his mousey hair slick with sweat. He gestured her over to him from an alleyway between two shops.

Heather didn't need telling twice. With one more glance at the fighting that was headed her way fast, she grabbed her bags and darted over to him.

"The name's Frankie. Did I hear you say you're a paramedic?"

Heather nodded and followed him away from the madness, her skin crawling with horror. How bad was this outbreak?

Chapter Two

25TH JANUARY

"Good afternoon, Sunshine."

James was a respected Sergeant of the Black Watch. He'd done three tours of duty. He'd survived ambushes, IEDs, gunfire, *actual* fire. Fuck, he'd survived Andy's practical jokes. Only his training and experience stopped him from jumping ten feet into the air at Teona's booming voice. *How is it humanly possible to move that silently?*

He grunted back, trying to act as though she hadn't scared the shite out of him. It was a good job he'd finished his drink, otherwise he would have hurled the cup halfway across the mess hall.

"Is that all I get? It wasn't even a pleased grunt." Teona pouted, sliding into the seat opposite him. She wore a dark-green tank top that showed off her toned arms. She must have recently cut her hair as well—the black fuzz was close to her scalp again.

"Your hair looks good," James said. "Did you get it done last night? Mine needs cutting badly."

"Damn right it looks good." Teona nodded like there

was no way her hair could be anything other than perfect. "There's a woman called Sara; she worked as a hairdresser before signing up." She eyed his hair critically. "Yours does look like a bird's nest, not gonna lie. You should see her soon. At least you shaved."

James rolled his eyes at her. "You say the sweetest things."

She winked at him. "I know. I'll treat you right."

James snorted. She was right though—his hair was a disgrace. It was the longest he'd had it in years. He made a mental note to find Sara after Teona left.

"Listen," Teona said seriously. James sat up straighter. "Sorry I've been so busy lately. I've been inspecting the helicopter and screening potential co-pilots and whatnot, but I just want to say that I appreciate you telling me about the flashbacks. I know it must've been hard."

James found it difficult to swallow. When she'd sat him down and looked at him with those big eyes of hers, he'd initially balked at the thought of telling her. But once the words started tumbling out of his mouth, he'd been powerless to stop them. It had been cathartic. Liberating. It was nice not carrying it alone, nice knowing she knew everything and didn't judge him.

James didn't like the thought of managing PTSD. His flashbacks, the recklessness he'd displayed at the hospital that had led to Dubois' death, his brief retreat into himself. James hadn't personally known anyone with PTSD, at least as far as he was aware. It had always been both present and not, always momentarily mentioned but never properly talked about. It was something that happened to someone else.

"You know I'll be with you every step of the way," Teona said.

He cleared his throat. "Thank you."

Teona smiled at him, and his heart danced in his chest as warmth coursed through his body.

"Now, I don't claim to be a therapist or quack or whatever, but when I put my mind to something, I'm pretty perfect at it. You're in good hands." She winked at him again, and the tension that had gripped him since she'd mentioned their talk left him as suddenly as it had arrived.

"Only *pretty* perfect? I don't think I'll accept anything less than absolute perfection."

"Well, fuck me, Mr. High Standards, you'll get what you're damn well given."

James chuckled. "I know I'm in good hands, Teona. I trust you to do your best to help."

She smiled. Not smirked, smiled. "You trust me. That means more than I can say. Trust is a big thing. I want you to know that I trust you too, James, with my life. I know you'll be there when push comes to shove."

He cleared his throat again and grunted out an "*aye*". He would train every day to get back to the way he was, to be reliable again.

To be a soldier again.

"Okay, now that all the mushy shit is out of the way, let's discuss this castle and what we can do to make everyone here fight back," Teona said cheerfully, like reclaiming the world wasn't going to be an almost impossible task.

James frowned at her. They had only been at the castle for a week. "Keep your voice down." He didn't want people thinking they thought they needed kicking into gear. *Although that's exactly what they need.*

Teona waved away his very legitimate concern. "I've talked to a few people, and everyone wants something to do, instead of sitting here on their arses and listening to information trickle in."

For the next two hours James found himself in a conversation filled with strategy and tactics, and he really did feel like a soldier again.

*

7TH FEBRUARY

"Hey, Danny!"

The soldier stopped and turned at Jennifer's shout. He was in his uniform—everyone wore military uniform regardless, even Jennifer had one on—and he had a tablet in his hand. He smiled as she jogged up to him, and they fell into an easy walk down the rest of the corridor and onto the next. They all looked the same to Jennifer. Same stone, same lights, same soldiers. Not that she was complaining. Monotony was an easy price to pay for security.

"Hey, Jennifer. You getting good use out of that charger I found?"

Jennifer beamed. "Yeah. Thanks again for that, you're a lifesaver." She had several good pictures of the castle and the people taking shelter inside its walls. She took her camera out with her most days, always ready to snap the perfect shot.

"Good. That picture you took of me and little Dan was *amazing*."

"Thanks," Jennifer mumbled, never sure how to take compliments. She changed the subject. "So, I was wondering if you had any more news of the world? I'm dying here without internet or anything."

Danny laughed. "Yeah, that is a bummer, isn't it? How will you update Instagram?"

"Yeah, yeah." Jennifer rolled her eyes.

Danny sobered. "Well, all the major cities around the world were evacuated. Or at least an evacuation was attempted. The emergency broadcasts helped with that, but it still doesn't seem to have been enough. Only a small percentage of the safe zones around the world were able to get up and running. We're getting more info now—this is *definitely* a global outbreak, and it's devastating. The world is going to look completely different when this is all over."

"It will end," Jennifer said with more conviction than she felt. She gave the scientists blood when they asked, but other than that she wasn't privy to what they did. Not that she thought she'd be able to understand anyway. Still, people assumed she knew what was happening, so she gave them simple words to assuage their fears.

Danny nodded and gave her a half-smile. "I know. Thank you again, Jennifer."

And there was that *look*, the one that made her uncomfortable. Danny switched between gazing at her with reverence and talking to her like a normal friend as easily as flicking on a light. It was unnerving.

"The military has control over some countries," he

continued, "like China and parts of the US, but we don't know how much is bravado and how much is genuine control. South America is still totally out of control, and we haven't heard anything from Eastern Europe or Russia either. We get broadcasts from the UK, but it's not cohesive—it's mainly frightened people begging for rescue from wherever they're holed up. That kind of thing is flooding a lot of channels, from a lot of countries."

These were all things Jennifer already knew from Alexia, but she wanted to have more than one source, so she didn't interrupt.

"Our most recent information is from South Africa. We've learned the reason that country fell is because people sabotaged two quarantine zones, which lead to the release of infected and kick-started the collapse. We don't know their motives, maybe fanatics? Maybe people who didn't believe it was real? Who knows. The military there is trying to claw back some control."

That was new. Why would people do that? *God, how awful.*

"In some places where the military has failed, people have risen up and taken control for themselves. We've had reports of a particularly brutal regime started in Portugal. Apparently, anyone who hasn't been initiated into this group is being murdered, infected or not. This needs to be corroborated, mind you. There's so much we don't know. I feel like we're stumbling around in the dark."

Jennifer tried to reassure him again that there would be an end to all the madness, but he continued speaking.

"Here, let me show you this." Danny tapped on his tablet for a moment before he turned it to her. "It's a news

station in Australia. They were still reporting on the out-break when infected broke in."

He pressed play, and Jennifer watched the horror un-fold.

"Breaking news," the anchor said. She was a pretty, dark-skinned woman in a red dress. "Riots have broken out across the city. Fires have had to be put out from sev-eral different buildings, and people are breaking into shops and making off with all sorts of things from food to TVs. Some people are even attacking others. Be aware, some of the images are graphic."

The scene changed from the anchor to a broad road lined by tall buildings. Jennifer saw fire spluttering out from one of the shops on street level as people ran around, seemingly at random. She noticed the attacks the anchor mentioned straight away, and she saw it for the infection it was.

The screen cut back to the news anchor. "Reports have been coming in from all over the country saying eve-ryone has gone mad, that zombies are killing people. These are unconfirm—"

The woman was cut off by a loud crash, quickly fol-lowed by screams. Jennifer knew what was coming, but that still didn't prepare her for the violence on the small screen.

The camera wobbled, then stabilised, and the news anchor jumped up with her hand clasped over her mouth. There were several more bangs off screen, almost drowned out by the screams, then the anchor ran out of the shot as two infected men ran to the desk. One was looking at the camera in confusion as the other pushed the news anchor's chair over. The resulting crash startled the

first man, and he launched himself at the second one with a wordless yell. They stumbled out of shot, grappling and biting each other as another man fell into the frame clutching his neck. Jennifer saw dark blood gushing from between his fingers as he collapsed against the desk. The camera feed cut out as he fell to the floor.

"Horrible, right?" Danny asked rhetorically. "It shows how successful the cover-up and misinformation was. People didn't have a clue how deadly the virus is. And we're all paying the price for that decision now. Society is falling apart around us at an alarming rate. Most governments have disappeared, and organisations like the WHO and the UN and NATO as well."

"Looking back, though," Jennifer said, "are you surprised? This virus has been taking people for over half a year now. Society was already struggling as more and more people were moved to those *secure facilities*. It's no wonder everything fell apart so quickly when they were breached." The more Jennifer talked, the more she realised that was what had happened. "We were stretched to breaking point, and we broke, simple as that."

Danny nodded, a far-off look on his face. "Listen, I've got to go, I was on my way to a meeting when you called."

"Oh, sorry for holding you up."

"Nah, it's okay." Danny waved off her concern. "I have a few minutes to get there. We'll catch up again soon, though, yeah? I want to hear what the doctors are doing."

"Uh, sure," Jennifer said with a smile, and she gave him a little wave as he moved off down another corridor. She was going to have to grill the scientists more when they next called on her.

She had a lot to think about. It seemed one of the many zombie apocalypse films had kind of come true, except the infected weren't really zombies and Jennifer thought humanity could be saved. She resolved to go to the lab and talk to the scientists—preferably Owain—and see what she could do to help. Despite the global devastation, motivation curled around her like humidity on a hot day. She would help get the world back on its feet. Even if it took the rest of her life. Everyone had lost too much not to try.

Chapter Three

10TH FEBRUARY

A week passed before Jennifer was able to get any time with Alexia. The soldier had been assigned several tasks since they had arrived at the castle and Jennifer had only seen her twice, and both times had been in the presence of other people. So *finally*, on a night so cold it was like winter itself stalked the corridors, she was happy to get Alexia to herself.

She half-sat, half-lay on her bed while Alexia lounged in a chair at the desk. Why she needed a desk, she didn't know. Jennifer had been given a room all to herself. She knew from Victoria that most others had to share, except for the scientists and officers. *Probably due to the bites. No one wants to share a room with me. They're scared.*

Not that she was complaining, really. Her room was nice. The low ceiling and dim lighting made it seem cramped, but Jennifer knew she had it better than most. She'd thought about giving the room to Riya and Aarav, but she didn't think Aarav would accept. It contained a single bed, the desk, and a chair, and they'd all been given a bag with spare clothing in it when they arrived, which

she'd dumped in the corner by the door.

Jennifer had been nervous about chatting with Alexia, but the conversation flowed naturally. She knew she didn't have the best track record with talking to her crushes. *I think I'm being pretty smooth, though. At least I hope so.* She gave coherent responses, and she had only gotten lost in Alexia's eyes once. She was doing well.

"Everyone knows carrot cake is the best dessert, I don't know why you would say anything else."

Jennifer laughed. "Cheesecake all the way. I *love* cheesecake."

"Cheesecake is the worst, Jennifer." Alexia pulled a face. "Think of your poor taste buds."

Jennifer felt a rush whenever Alexia said her name. She wanted her to say it more often. "I'm afraid we're going to have to agree to disagree here. I'm right and you're wrong."

Alexia fake pouted, and Jennifer had to suppress the urge to kiss it away. *Hold your horses, you don't even know if she likes women.* She would have to bring up past relationships, and that was something she did *not* want to do. *I can't just outright ask her, though. Who does that?*

"Do you at least like carrot cake?"

"Nope, it's disgusting."

Alexia shook her head. "I feel sorry for you."

Jennifer laughed again. She did that a lot in Alexia's presence. God, too much? What if Alexia thought she laughed too much? What if it grated on her nerves? What if—

"You have a nice laugh," Alexia said, and Jennifer's

brain stopped working. "It sounds...free." Alexia chuckled. "That doesn't make sense."

"No, no, I get it," Jennifer said. "You have a nice laugh too. Musical."

Alexia grinned at her, and heat diffused through Jennifer's face. God, why did she blush at every little thing? "Merci. That is kind of you to say."

"It's the truth," Jennifer said simply. They smiled at each other, holding eye contact. Jennifer was about to turn away—her face was in danger of burning off—when she saw Alexia's eyes dip to her lips. *Holy shit.* Butterflies rose up, and Jennifer had to look away lest she do something stupid like *giggle.* Ugh.

"I like horror films," Alexia said, changing the subject. "What about you?"

Jennifer fake shuddered. "I'm a wimp. I found *Jurassic Park* scary."

Alexia laughed. "*Jurassic Park*? Really?"

"Hey." Jennifer tried to look angry, but her smile refused to leave. "It was super tense when the T-rex had those kids pinned in the car."

"You are absolutely right," Alexia said seriously. "It is a horror film. How has it taken me so long to see?"

"Shut up," Jennifer laughed. "Okay, so yes to horror films. Is there any other genre you like?"

"I like thrillers, but I think that goes with the horrors," Alexia said. "I also like action movies. You know the, erm, how do you say, oh, cheesy!" Jennifer laughed at the triumphant expression on Alexia's face. "Yes, cheesy action movies."

"I love cheesy action movies too, they're a guilty pleasure," Jennifer confessed. Evelyn had hated it whenever she'd dragged her out to see the latest action blockbuster. "Anything with explosions in it and I am there."

"Never feel guilty about anything that gives you pleasure, Jennifer. Enjoy it fully." Alexia's voice was filled with sincerity, but Jennifer's mind short circuited and went to places it shouldn't. Places with Alexia and pleasure. She coughed awkwardly and hoped Alexia couldn't see her how flushed her skin was.

"I do not like romance movies," Alexia continued like she hadn't just caused Jennifer's brain to crash and reboot. "They are too straight."

Jennifer's mind stumbled to a halt. Too straight? She had to quickly school her features so she didn't blind Alexia with her smile. *Act cool, Jen, don't be a massive idiot.* "Too straight?" she repeated with nonchalance. At least she hoped with nonchalance. Too much nonchalance? Why was she so bad at talking to someone she liked? She felt like she was navigating a minefield.

"Oui." Alexia nodded. "They are all the same. Directors and actors always say they want to try new projects, so why do they always make the same movies?"

"Oh." Jennifer tried not to let her disappointment show. She hoped it was because Alexia was a lesbian or queer and didn't want to keep seeing straight shit—Jennifer was bisexual, and *she* was sick of seeing straight shit—but it was because they were all similar to each other.

"And I would like to see more, erm, representation."

Jennifer's mind started whirring again. More repre-

sentation? Did that mean she *was* a lesbian? Reading so much into everything Alexia said was going to give Jennifer a headache. "Representation?" Did her voice sound too squeaky?

"Oui, you know." Alexia gestured vaguely. "I am sure you would like it as well, yes? Seeing as you are not straight either—"

Either! "You're not straight," Jennifer all but shouted at Alexia. *So much for not acting like a fucking idiot.*

Alexia gave her a confused smile. "Yes, I thought you knew?"

"Oh no, I have a terrible gaydar," Jennifer laughed, warmth pouring through her veins. "I did hope though—" She cut herself off, her eyes widening as she realised what she'd let slip out of her stupid mouth. Alexia's smile deepened, and a light dusting of pink painted her cheeks. Jennifer stared at the colour with wonder. *Could she like me too?*

"Pretend this disease did not happen," Alexia said, breaking Jennifer out of the spell she was under. She coughed into her fist, trying to be casual. She didn't think it was working. "Where in the world would you like to photograph?"

The question surprised her. Was Alexia changing the subject because she was flustered too? Jennifer tried to rein her hopes in. She opened her mouth to give a silly answer in the hope Alexia would laugh again, but she closed it to seriously consider how to respond. It was something she often asked herself, and new places were constantly being added to her list.

"Several places. On a personal level I'd love to

photograph the Niagara Falls and the Grand Canyon and mountains like the Alps or the Himalayas. I know they're photographed all the time, but they haven't been photographed by *me*. I'd *love* to photograph an erupting volcano. There's something about forces of nature that really inspire wonder and respect. I had a lot of photos of the sea, calm and rough. Those pictures always invoke a sense of both peace and awe. Water is the most powerful thing on this planet, and to capture it on film always brings a sense of, well, power. Almost like I've tamed a tiny bit of the ocean with my camera.

"On a professional level—I wanted to be a photojournalist—I love to photograph people. Everyone has their own unique stories, and you know the saying—a picture paints a thousand words. I used to want to travel all over and capture people's stories, show their lives. Warzones, weddings, just walking down the street. I could freeze a person's smile, or glare, or tears, and it would really add an emotional depth to everything. I used to love doing that."

She lapsed into silence, lost to reminiscence. She'd known what she wanted to do with her life ever since she'd taken her first photograph, and now none of it mattered. The world she'd known was no more. The loss of a dream was too deep to put into words, and Jennifer had never been very skilled with those.

"That is beautiful," Alexia said softly, her eyes bright in the dim light. They drew Jennifer in, little liquid pools of chocolate. She almost pressed her hand into the mattress to push herself up and walk over, but Alexia blinked and turned away, and the moment was gone.

"Can I photograph you?"

Alexia blinked at her. Jennifer had already taken her picture back at the hospital—a beautiful shot of her clad in full military gear, weapon held confidently as she patrolled the perimeter—but she wanted another one. A more intimate one.

"Yes."

Jennifer grabbed her camera from the desk and perched on the side of the bed, directly in front of Alexia. How did she want the picture to look? *Natural. Not staged in any way. I need to make her laugh again.*

Alexia's short brown hair tumbled to her shoulders as she leaned back on the chair stiffly. "How should I pose?"

"You don't have to pose." Alexia raised an eyebrow. "You want to hear a terrible joke?"

A ghost of a smiled flitted over Alexia's face. "Oui."

All jokes promptly fled Jennifer's brain. *Shit.* "Erm, okay so, let me think of one..."

Alexia grinned at her. "You don't know any jokes?"

"*Pfft*, of course I do." Now was her shot. Alexia had relaxed, an easy smile lighting up her face. The shutter closed and froze Alexia's shining eyes, which were looking at her and not the camera, and grinned at the image.

"Beautiful," she whispered. Alexia blushed and looked down, grin still firmly on her face, and Jennifer took the opportunity to steal another picture. She flicked between the two—the first of Alexia grinning at her, her strong features taking centre stage, the second looking down, smile turned shy but no less striking. Jennifer couldn't decide which she liked more.

She showed them both to Alexia. "Thank you," Alexia

said, her voice thick with something Jennifer couldn't define. Alexia coughed and stood up. Disappointment surged through Jennifer like the rough sea she'd tamed so many times. "I have to be up early tomorrow, so I should go. Thank you for talking tonight."

"Yeah, it's nice talking to you." Jennifer put the camera on the bed, stood, and smiled, trying not to let any of her sadness show. "We'll do this again?"

Alexia smiled back. "Absolutely."

Fuck it. Jennifer went in for a hug. Alexia readily responded, her warm arms encircling Jennifer. She sighed into the hug, which was over way before she wanted.

"Bon nuit, Jennifer Clarke."

"Bon nuit, Alexia Lecuyer."

With one last lingering smile, Alexia left, and Jennifer suddenly felt like her room was too large. She collapsed back onto the bed and settled in for a night of second-guessing their conversation and looking at the photographs, because who needed sleep anyway?

Chapter Four

18TH FEBRUARY

Victoria was hungry, tired, and in desperate need of a shower. So *of course,* James sought her out for a bloody chat. Couldn't he see how sweaty she was? But then, he only had eyes for Wright, didn't he? Victoria kept her smirk to herself.

"How's your training going?" James asked in that gruff Scottish accent of his. Victoria wondered why he was showing a sudden interest—she had barely seen him over the past few weeks.

"Good," she answered curtly. She didn't mean to be rude, but bloody hell she looked a mess. *Shower or food first? Oh, who am I kidding?* Shower.

He nodded while he kept pace with her down the corridor, clearly not taking the hint. Victoria sighed internally. *Food it is, then. I can't believe I'm going around in public looking like this.* "Do you want to get some food? I'm famished."

"Aye, I'll never say no to food."

Victoria found herself sitting in the mess hall, sweaty

and smelly, eating with one of the soldiers who'd saved them then all but vanished from their lives. She supposed he'd been busy with his physio and forced rest. She couldn't talk anyway—she only saw Jennifer or Anthony with any regularity. She spent most of her time training with Anthony, or if he was out on duty, Louis sometimes did a workout with her.

"I've heard you're becoming a good fighter," James said around a mouthful of food. Victoria didn't look too closely. "Kickboxing, right? Trueman said you're one of the best he's ever trained with. A natural."

Pride swelled in her chest. Anthony hadn't said anything to her. All he did was constantly push her. She had always praised her students when they'd done something well, but that didn't seem to be Anthony's way. His tough love approach worked, though. She constantly tried to one up herself, pushing harder with every session.

"You've got good discipline from what I've seen and heard," James continued. "That's a good quality for a soldier to have."

Of course, she had good discipline, she used to be a bloody teacher. No discipline meant anarchy, and Victoria did not tolerate a tumultuous classroom.

What was the second thing he'd said? A good quality for a soldier? *Did he mean...?*

"You're brave as well. I saw you kill those infected easily before we arrived here."

Victoria almost flinched. She brought out the monster whenever she trained, but it always went back to sleep at the end. She tried not to think of it.

"James. What are you trying to say?"

He looked confused. She knew what he was getting at, but she needed him to say it out loud. "You'll make a good soldier, Victoria," he said, cutting straight to the point.

Some of her conflict must have bled onto her face. James frowned. "Isn't that what you want?" he asked, pausing his eating. He'd almost cleaned his plate while Victoria still had half a bowl to go.

"I..."

What *did* she want? It was her own fault, really; she was the one who cultivated this image, she was the one who distanced herself from her past self. She was the one who liked it. Enjoyed the feeling of being in control, of the wild power of her weapon, of the rush when she cut infected down.

She was the monster. She might as well embrace it. Why was it so hard?

"Being a soldier—" James stopped and sighed. "I'm probably going to sound like a mushy twat, so please don't tell Sergeant Wright."

He didn't continue until she gave her word, much to her amusement.

"Being a soldier is more than a job. It's a calling. It's about facing horrors and not breaking, not backing down from them. It's about finding family in your squad. It can also be about watching your brothers and sisters fall. It's about carrying on in the face of all that pain, all that hurt. It's about honour and respect and loyalty. We fight to protect people, to protect freedom and society and—" He shook his head, his mouth twisting into a grimace. Victoria thought she heard him mutter something about being

soppy. "It's about fighting for the love you hold for your brothers and sisters. For your family, and country. For your faith in humanity. Soldiers don't fight with hatred, to destroy and devastate. We have to be brave and compassionate, strong, yet willing to bend to a better way. Being a soldier is about fighting to protect when no one else can.

"And I think you can."

He fell silent then, sitting up straighter and going back to his food. He didn't look at her. Victoria thought he was embarrassed by his little speech. It was the most she'd ever heard him say in one sitting.

His words touched her. She turned them over in her head, mulling over everything. Before the outbreak, she wouldn't have agreed with him—soldiers could be honourable, perhaps, but she'd heard too many stories of atrocities to truly believe that. War brought out the worst in people. After the outbreak? She couldn't deny that soldiers had saved her life. They were fighting to bring some semblance of control back to the world. To help the remnants of a scattered humanity. There was honour in that, she supposed.

Could she help? Sure, she was good at fighting, but did she do it for the right reasons? She was a murderer who liked the rush and the monster, was that compatible with what James said?

In the end, if she helped people get back on their feet, did it matter?

She touched his hand to get him to look at her. When his green eyes met hers, she smiled. No words were said, but an understanding passed between them.

He cleared his throat. "If you tell Wright what I said

I'll deny it to my dying breath."

Victoria laughed and dug into her soup with renewed gusto.

*

James's heart raced, and damn it felt good. He hadn't been this free in a long time. Teona kept pace to his left, and he saw her glancing at him every few seconds out of the corner of his eye. He appreciated her concern, but it was completely unfounded. This wee jog around the castle grounds would do him the world of good. In fact, he almost started running faster. But no. Teona would call an end to it and James wasn't ready for that. After so long cooped up inside he wasn't in a hurry to get caged again.

He managed two more laps before his injury made him stop. Sweat beaded his forehead, his lungs burned, and his heart was doing its best impression of a double bass pedal, but *fuck* he felt alive.

Teona grinned that big, beautiful smile of hers, her eyes sparkling in the afternoon sun. Sweat ran down her face and onto her neck, her chest heaved with every indrawn breath—

I've got it bad.

"Good run, Sunshine." She beamed at him. "Of course, I could have continued for a *lot* longer, but I don't want to hurt your fragile male ego." James rolled his eyes at her as she snickered. "How's the shoulder?"

"It feels good," he said, declining to mention the dull throbbing that pulsed in time with his heart. That was to be expected anyway. "Have you given any more thought to taking me on a scouting mission?"

She sighed, and it sounded long-suffering. "You're not healed enough, James."

"Aye—"

"No," she cut him off. "Look, I get it. I really do. But I'm not taking you out yet. Heal more, and I'll consider a scouting mission. That's it."

James clenched his jaw. She was right, but it was still a bitter pill to swallow. He grew stronger every day, and he hated, *hated,* being stuck in this castle while others were out fighting. He resolved to keep pushing hard with his therapy, and to keep nagging Teona.

"I'm sorry, James. You'll be back out there in no time. Just keep training."

"Aye," he grunted.

She beamed at him again, and his anger started to dissipate. "Glad we're in agreement. Now"—her smile morphed into a smirk—"I'm going to have a shower before my guard shift. I suggest you do the same."

James didn't blush. Was her voice full of suggestion, or was he imagining it? He cleared his throat to say something witty in response, but the words wouldn't form. What was wrong? His injury? He had read that PTSD caused difficulties with intimacy. That didn't feel right. Could it be he'd never felt so strongly about a woman before? It both scared and exhilarated him.

He must've looked a right idiot staring at her like a fish out of water. She took pity on him, her eyebrow twitching upward in amusement. "See you soon, Sunshine." She winked as she sauntered off.

James tried not to be obvious as he watched her walk away. The last thing he needed was for her to catch him

staring. He'd never hear the end of it.

He need not have worried. She didn't turn around. James huffed as she disappeared from sight. *Life will never be boring with her.*

He turned to stretch and cool down when he caught sight of Jennifer by some trees with her camera. He wondered how the cure was coming along, and after his stretches—he ignored the flare from his shoulder—he strolled over to her.

He leaned against smooth bark and watched as she raised the camera to her eye, the castle looming over them. She took several shots before she lowered the camera and started fiddling with it.

"Do you take a few pictures and pick the best?"

James held back an amused grin as Jennifer nearly fell over.

"*James.*" Jennifer clutched her chest, and he would have been concerned he'd caused a heart attack if she'd been older. "Don't creep up on me."

He didn't bother to hold back a small smirk. "Sorry," he said, not sorry at all. She needed to improve her spatial awareness.

She took a deep breath and mock glared at him. "To answer your question—yes, that's basically it."

James frowned. "But it looked like you took the same picture."

She waved her hand. "I edit them all differently and see which one looks best."

He nodded, accepting what she said. He'd never had a talent for photography. "How are you?" Jennifer

squinted at him. "What?" James added defensively.

"Nothing," Jennifer replied. "I just didn't take you for the 'how are you' type." She held up her hands as James scowled. "Sorry," she laughed. "I'm fine, you? How's your recovery coming?"

"It's fine," James said. "Hurts like fuck, but it's getting better," he paused. "Don't tell Wright I said it hurts."

She laughed again. "I won't tell, don't worry. I'm glad you're on the mend."

"Thanks," James grunted. The conversation danced too close to coldness and agony as the bullet tore into him. James shook his head as if it would rattle the memories loose. "So, how's the cure coming? You were with the doctors again this morning, aye?" A safer topic. And what he had wanted to ask her about in the first place.

Jennifer nodded slowly. "You're not the first person to ask. I tell the others that it's getting there, to be patient, that sort of thing. But to be honest, I'm not really sure." James noticed she clenched her hands. "They only started telling me what they're actually doing because I insisted, and I don't know what they're talking about half the time. The general mood is still positive, though, so I take that as a good sign. Well, Louise and Owain are positive, Dickface is never happy."

"Dickface?"

"Dr. Evans." Jennifer grimaced. "It wouldn't kill the man to be nice for once."

James snorted. He hadn't interacted with the doctor since their first day at the castle, but by all accounts he was an arsehole. "It's good that they're pleased so far. Do you think they're close?"

"Honestly, I have no idea. Sorry I can't give you more."

James nodded, not letting his disappointment show. "No, that's good. It's something."

Jennifer looked at him as if she saw through his façade. "What do you think the world is going to be like now? Like, I know the latest about South Africa and the new stuff coming out of Egypt—" *What is she talking about? Has something happened?* "So even if we develop a cure, how will we mass manufacture it? How will we mass distribute it? Governments are falling left, right, and centre leaving a power vacuum, and anything that rises in its place either gets toppled quickly, like in Egypt, or is just plain horrible. How do we get the cure to everyone when people are greedy bastards and will hoard it for power?"

James realised he was at a disadvantage. He was going to have words with Teona for not giving him the latest updates. "Tell me everything you know, starting at the top."

He knew his tone was wrong the moment she tensed up. "I'm not revealing my sources—"

"No, no, I don't care about that," he sighed. "You know more than I do. Tell me, please?"

She did. James knew the world was fucked up, but it had been remote, like watching events on TV and them not directly affecting him. Hearing all the shite going on made it all seem more immediate, more real. The chaos in South Africa and Portugal and Egypt, the martial law of America and China, the contradicting reports of Spain and Australia and just about everywhere else. He really needed to heal and get back out there. *I'm going to go*

straight to Roux after this. Maybe we can increase my training.

"So, what do you think?" Jennifer asked. It was a vague question. What did he think about the state of the world in general? A specific country? The cure?

"I think it's one hell of a shit show out there, and that it's going to be one hell of a clean-up operation. We're probably going to have to remove the threat of infected before we can start rolling out the cure."

"But then that brings up its own problems," Jennifer countered. "People are becoming newly infected every day. If we wait there will be no one left to give it to."

"Wait. When we talk about a 'cure', it's a vaccine, right?"

"Yeah, I think so."

"Okay, so we vaccinate everyone here, then start sending out teams to find people, bring them back and check for infection, obviously, then vaccinate them. We then escalate operations and go further afield with the helicopter." Even as he said it, James saw the issues that would plague such a plan.

"We send out teams now to scout the area." Jennifer sighed. "There's no one around here for miles."

"Aye, we'd need a lot more manpower too." James estimated there were no more than a hundred and fifty personnel at the castle, including the civilians and scientists. "We could broadcast the vaccine?" He shook his head. "No, even if people heard and believed, we'd bring potential hostiles down to our doorstep."

"Exactly," Jennifer agreed. "There's no easy way to go about it. The more I think about it the more obstacles it

throws up. We could try to approach the governments still standing. But then there's still the problem of mass production."

"Aye." The more James thought about it the more his head hurt. "Listen, try not to worry about it for now. Wait till they've actually got a vaccine, and then we'll cross that bridge when we get to it."

Jennifer nodded, but she didn't look reassured. He could tell from the crease between her brows that she was going to continue thinking in circles about it. James mentally shrugged. Maybe she would think of a solution.

"I'm going to go see Roux about my shoulder," James said as he started to walk away. "Keep me updated, aye? On everything."

Jennifer smiled. "I will." Her smile transformed into a smirk, not unlike Teona's had. "Say hi to Wright for me."

James frowned at her as she laughed. He wasn't going to let her have the last word like that. "Say hi to Alexia for me."

It was James's turn to smirk as a blush swept across Jennifer's face. He turned and walked back to the castle, chuckling under his breath.

Chapter Five

1ST MARCH (PRESENT DAY)

The wind whipping at Victoria's coat didn't seem as cold as yesterday. Was spring arriving after what seemed like an eternity of winter or was it a fluke in the weather? Whatever the reason, Victoria walked up to the castle wall with extra vigour lent to her by the warming sun.

Once at the top, she leaned on the ramparts and stared out over the town and fields. She had gotten into the habit of going up on the wall in the month and a half they'd been at the castle, away from the frenetic bustle so she could be alone with her thoughts. *I still can't believe I'm here.* The breeze pulled at her hair in its ponytail. *I've gone from staring at the same four walls to looking out over all this.* Could she be thankful for a virus while also hating it?

Jennifer had acquired "sources"—she tried to be mysterious, but Victoria guessed they were certain soldiers, Alexia and Danny in particular—and had kept them up to date on the military activity and state of the world. All their information came from Jennifer. If one wanted to find out anything, one went to her. Victoria

wasn't bothered. She'd rather train with Anthony than shoulder the responsibility of people's expectations. Jennifer could handle that.

She sighed, and rested her head on her arms, leaning further out on the ramparts. Everyone she used to know would have laughed at the thought of her learning kickboxing. When James had told her Anthony thought she was one of the best he had trained, Victoria had tried not to let her ego grow too much.

She'd seen Anthony the most out of the soldiers who'd rescued them. The soldiers ate meals with them when they could, but Wright was out flying often—Victoria didn't know where they got the fuel from—and James kept himself busy with his shoulder.

Victoria didn't know much about the command here, only that Commandant Phillipe was in charge. There'd been a shift in the power dynamic that, according to Jennifer's sources, happened when they'd arrived. Louis didn't talk about it, and her time with Anthony was spent training. Jennifer said the French lieutenant had all but begged Commandant Phillipe to take over.

A fluffy cloud drifted into her line of sight, and it reminded Victoria of the castle's latest arrival. A little girl had arrived alone, covered in blood and dirt, her curly black hair frizzing with grease. She must have been though some awful things, and it had obviously left her traumatised. Victoria hadn't heard her talk the entire time she'd been there.

Jennifer had tried to get her story, but she wasn't getting far. The girl couldn't have been older than five, and she was most likely French, so she probably didn't understand a word of what Jennifer said. She'd managed to

bring Dan more out of his shell a little, so maybe she'd succeed with the girl as well. Victoria sighed. They were too young to be going through so much horror.

Victoria turned at the sound of boots scraping across the ground. *Speak of the devil.* Dan walked over and leaned his skinny arms on the ramparts in imitation of her. He didn't talk, and the silence settled around them like a familiar blanket, warm and easy. Victoria let her thoughts trickle from her mind as she gazed out over the landscape.

According to what she saw of Dan's expensive watch, they stood together for about half an hour. More clouds drifted across the bright sky, but nothing else changed. It was the first time the boy had joined her. Others had come for a while, idly chatting until they got the hint she wanted to be left alone.

Dan was different. Silence with him felt...comfortable. The only other person she experienced that with was Jennifer, and Victoria knew that was partly because of her resemblance to her sister, Katherine, but also partly because she didn't try to talk or pry. Victoria frowned. That wasn't like her. Jennifer loved snooping into people's pasts. Was she waiting for Victoria to open up? Victoria didn't think that would ever happen, so Jennifer would have to keep on waiting.

Dan sighed next to her and leaned his head on his hand. His watch flashed as it caught the light, and Victoria blinked the brightness away. Was he taller now than when they'd first met? He had a few more spots, but his skin was quite clear as far as teenage faces went. His voice seemed deeper too, on the rare occasions he spoke. *He's well into the throes of puberty, poor kid.*

"Where did you get your watch from?" Victoria asked, surprising herself. She mentally rolled her eyes. She disliked idle conversation, yet there she was, starting up small talk.

"Oh, erm, my uh, mum gave it to me." Dan also seemed surprised she'd said anything. "For my birthday last year."

"It's nice." She smiled at him. Was he stuttering less? It was hard to tell.

He ducked his head. "Thanks. She said, erm, that I was becoming a man now so, uh, she got me a nice watch. I don't take it off," he continued in a much quieter voice. Victoria had to lean in to hear him. "It's the uh, only thing I have left. From her, y'know. I don't have anything from my sister."

Victoria's stomach twisted. "You've got your memories of them," she said as she put her hand on his shoulder. She felt him tense, but she kept the pressure there until he slowly relaxed. "I lost everyone too." Truth was, she'd lost everyone before the virus outbreak, but he didn't need to know that.

A sudden desire to talk about something else jolted her, and she clasped her hands together. "So, as you know, I used to be an English teacher," she blurted out, louder than expected. Dan looked at her with wide eyes. "How good are you at English? Maybe I'll start teaching you." Even as she said it, she knew she'd never go back to teaching. It had a wrongness about it—it wasn't for her any more.

Dan's eyes widened even further. "Erm, I was pretty good at English, I think. History was my favourite subject, but I liked English as well."

"History? I know about the Elizabethan and Shakespearian era, but not much more than that I'm afraid."

The next thing Victoria knew, she was embroiled in a deep conversation about sixteenth century England with a teenage boy. There was no trace of his shyness as he got more into the discussion, and he even started to gesticulate, which was something she had never seen him do before.

They must have talked for a good forty-five minutes, at least. Victoria started to feel pangs of hunger when she heard running footsteps behind her. She spun around and in front of Dan as energy flooded her muscles and she fell into a defensive stance without thinking about it.

It was Jennifer.

She tutted as she relaxed. At least it wasn't infected. She took one look at Jennifer's stricken face and her body tensed again.

"What's happened?"

Jennifer's breaths came in harsh gasps as she stopped in front of her. She'd been practising her running, so Victoria thought the breathlessness was more due to the news than the exercise.

"It's the doctors," she gasped. "Evans in particular. He says there's nothing more they can do here without better equipment. He said we have to go to a proper research facility to do more." She wiped some loose hair from her forehead. "Fucking hell, but it feels like they've bled me dry already."

Dan's voice trembled as he spoke. "We have to leave? Go back outside?"

"Evans said we're leaving as soon as they have

everything ready. I left them arguing about the best place to go. I didn't want to leave without saying goodbye." Jennifer seemed close to tears. "There's no way I'm making you come with me, Dan. You don't have to worry about going back out there."

The thought of splitting up tasted bitter in Victoria's mouth. They'd been through so much together. Could she leave Jennifer to go alone? She'd be with the doctors and soldiers, but she'd no doubt *feel* alone. Victoria looked deep inside herself, felt the connection she had to Jennifer, to the others, and knew she couldn't. James's words echoed back at her, and she knew she needed to protect her as they searched for a cure. The bond of those who'd survived something traumatic together vibrated in her chest. She wouldn't leave Jennifer. She *couldn't*.

"I'll go with you."

The resolve in her voice didn't surprise her. She'd been going through the motions here, training with both her hands and weapons but growing restless all the while. If she admitted it to herself, she felt the most alive amongst the infected. It was like she was living in black and white, and colour bloomed vivid in the midst of madness.

Making sure Jennifer stayed alive for a cure to be found, that she could do. Going back out into the chaos, that she could do. Maybe it was her atonement for killing her sister. Her reparation.

Her purpose.

"No, Victoria." Jennifer sounded scandalised. "I can't ask you to do that. You're safe here."

"I want to," she said with steel in her voice. Jennifer

wasn't going to talk her out of this. No one was. Her mind was made up. "I want to, and I'm going to. You can't stop me."

Jennifer's mouth hung open as she struggled to find something to say. She looked equal parts pleased Victoria was accompanying her and distraught that she was leaving the safety of the castle.

"We should find the soldiers, ask them to come with us," Victoria suggested. "Get the old team back together again."

"James and Wright and Anthony are out on a mission right now," Jennifer said sadly. "Danny said they left early this morning and he doesn't know when they'll be back."

"Oh, okay." Victoria tried not to let disappointment seep into her voice too much. "What about the others?"

Jennifer perked up a bit. "Alexia is coming. She didn't hesitate." Victoria thought of how transparent Jennifer was when it came to Alexia and smirked. *She's got it bad.* "And she said Elise will come too."

"Elise?" Victoria frowned. They'd barely seen the woman since they arrived. Victoria thought she didn't like them.

"Yeah, that was my reaction too, but Alexia said that Elise is chafing to get back out there."

"What about Louis and the Commandant?"

"I couldn't find them. But honestly, I think the Commandant will stay here, I mean, he is in charge. And Louis will go wherever he goes."

"I'm coming too," a small voice piped up.

Both Victoria and Jennifer whirled on a red-faced

Dan, who took a step back. They started talking at the same time.

"Absolutely not—"

"No way, Dan—"

"—Just a child—"

"—It's safe here—"

"I'm coming," he repeated in his quiet voice. "I'm in this with you, till the end. We've been through so much together; you can't leave me here. This castle may be safe, yeah, but I feel safest around you guys."

He looked them both dead in the eye, and Victoria had a glimpse of the man he would hopefully grow to be.

His mature speech was ruined by the childish exclamation of, "And if you don't let me, I'll sneak out after you anyway."

Jennifer burst out laughing. Dan looked startled before he joined in. Victoria didn't think she'd ever heard him laugh. Looking at the two of them, with twin grins decorating their faces, Victoria was struck with an emotion she hadn't felt in a long while.

Happiness.

Somehow, out there with the infected and the crazy, desperate people, she knew they would be all right as long as they had each other.

Chapter Six

James stirred before dawn, but that was nothing new. His shoulder had improved, and was continuing to do so, but it still woke him through the night occasionally. He couldn't lift his arm above his head, but that still left a small range of movement he was happy about.

He could hold and aim a rifle, which was one of his goals, so he couldn't complain. Hand-to-hand combat was another beast altogether. It was a massive struggle, and he knew if he was in a position where he had to fight with his fists, he'd do more damage to his shoulder and would be next to useless.

That morning, however, pain didn't wake him. It was anticipation. He had finally convinced Teona to let him join one of her recon missions. He could tell she wasn't happy, but he had been nagging her for a while and even she couldn't deny the progress he'd made. He would prove to her that he could do it. He would show them all. *Please be a soldier again.* He was finally starting to feel like one.

Their destination was London. *Assess the capital and report back.* Simple enough. Up until now, Teona and her crew had been flying around the nearby area, with the occasional jaunt further afield, but this was the first time

they were going back to the UK. It was probably part of the reason Teona and the Commandant had agreed to let him be part of her crew.

Eagerness at being back in the UK, even if it was England and not Scotland, flushed the sleep from his veins. James didn't think he'd ever forgive himself for taking leave when he did, but that was neither here nor there. Scotland would have to wait.

He was the first one to arrive at the helicopter. The grounds were quiet, and the moon was a bright-silver orb hanging in a clear sky, scanty stars dotted around it like white paint splattered on black canvas. It was chilly, but the air barely penetrated his armour. That had been a chore getting into, but he had managed it. As he waited for everyone else, he went through his pre-mission checks, making sure everything was on properly and his weapon was fully operational.

The helicopter was a Puma, and all James knew about it came from Teona. She'd drafted in an eighteen-year-old ex-air cadet named Charlie to help her fly it, because, in her words, "I've never actually flown one of these fuckers and even I need help sometimes". Despite that, James wasn't feeling nervous. The two of them worked well after a rough start, and they hadn't crashed, which was always a good sign.

James waited for about five minutes before Teona showed up. She materialised out of the predawn shadows, yawning and rubbing her eyes. Even tired, she moved gracefully.

"Morning, Sunshine," she said as another yawn took over.

James smirked. "Missing out on your beauty sleep?"

She scowled at him. "Sometimes, I make poor decisions. Nobody's perfect, you know."

"Really? I seem to recall you claiming to be perfect. Several times in fact." He couldn't keep the laughter out of his voice, and Teona rolled her eyes.

"I am mostly perfect, of course. Just the occasional slip up." She pretended to flip imaginary hair. "My imperfections are what make me perfect."

James snorted and Teona gave a tired smile. "Where are the rest of them?"

"They're on their way, you're early. I hope you're not always this premature." She waggled her eyebrows. James frowned. "I want to be in the air in the next fifteen minutes, so you better get on board, Sunshine."

James nodded and pulled open the sliding door. Inside there was enough space for sixteen fully equipped soldiers, though only seven were going on this mission, including James and Teona. Trueman, Millar, Davison, Ota, and Woods were the others. James only knew Trueman. The rest were all from the same regiment; Teona had been out with them before and reported that they were good, and James trusted her assessment.

He sat himself down and waited for the others. Trueman arrived next, closely followed by the rest of the soldiers all at once. Charlie arrived last, yawning and sleepy-eyed. He was under strict instruction to stay in the helicopter if they had to land.

They were up and flying on schedule. Excitement and nervousness thrummed through James like out of tune music, and he discreetly rolled his shoulders as the others chatted around him.

*

They had to land.

While flying low over Westminster, Teona said she spotted a group of people waving up at them. They had promptly disappeared, however. She brought the Puma down on the grass outside the Abbey, and James and the rest jumped out and formed a defensive ring around the helicopter. His shoulder twinged as his boots hit the ground, but he ignored it. He already knew this mission was going to test his physical limits. *No point worrying about it,* he reassured himself.

There was no movement. Even the air was still, and James had an unobstructed view of the devastation around him. Rubbish littered the streets—paper, cans, bullets, bodies. Fire had caused a lot of damage as well, with the front of several buildings blackened by smoke, and one double-decker bus was a gutted ruin at some traffic lights. The heavy smell of smoke and fire still clung to the calm air, like it refused to leave, a dark reminder of the destruction that had ripped through the area.

The Palace of Westminster hadn't fared any better. Big Ben still stood, but the main building had a section completely blown away and the other tower simply wasn't there any longer. Rubble from the blast had made it to the grass where they all stood, and James kicked a little block of stone away. *That had stood for centuries.* He had never been particularly interested in history, but he felt saddened at the thought of something so old just gone.

The Abbey still stood, dark stone against an overcast sky. It looked like it was going to rain, which, James thought, was fucking brilliant. They couldn't even catch a

break with the weather.

According to Charlie, the people they'd seen had run into the Underground, so that was where they'd start. Teona ordered everyone forward, with Trueman and Woods taking point and Ota and Millar at the rear. James knew he was the weakest one there, so he'd stay in the middle the whole mission. He was annoyed by it, but there was nothing he could do, and the last thing he wanted was to endanger the rest of them.

The sky started spitting as they entered Westminster station. James remembered it as a massive maze of escalators, but they didn't have to go that far in. The people who had waved them down were just inside the doors.

Teona's group fanned out into a straight line in front of them. James angled his body at the other group, but he let his eyes wander. The station bore little resemblance to the one he'd walked through at the start of the year. Like the scene outside, rubbish of all kinds littered the ground, with broken bodies scattered around the large space. There was a faint hint of smoke in the air, but the smell of blood was stronger, and James saw pools of it on the floor and splashes of it up the walls. His skin tingled against the uncleanliness of the place.

He turned his attention back to the new people. There were six in total, all men. They all looked filthy and exhausted, which was nothing less than James expected. *Poor bastards, out here all this time.*

One of them stepped forward, a man with a narrow face and a nose that looked like it had been broken and not set properly. His wide, red-rimmed eyes didn't blink. "My name is Corporal Simon Johnson." His voice had a hysterical edge to it James didn't like, and he started to

pay more attention to the people and less to the surroundings. *Should we bring them on board if they're unstable?*

"Sergeant Wright," Teona said. James noticed her wary expression. "What is the situation here?"

Johnson shook his head, but James thought it was more like a twitch. "Shit, Sergeant. We've been scavenging from place to place, hunting infected, them hunting us in turn. It's been one big shit show. There used to be more of us. Our sergeant sacrificed himself not a week ago so we could get out of a shitty situation. That's what we've been doing really. Running from one shitty situation right into another."

He barely paused for breath as he spoke, his sentences short and sharp. James was *definitely* concerned about his mental state. He'd have to pull Teona to one side and discuss it with her.

"What about civilians? Government? Military?" Teona eyed the soldiers cautiously, and James knew she was having the same doubts he was.

"The first few days we were evacuating people. But then it got too chaotic. Then the order came down to start bombing the city. The power cut out shortly afterward. Then we didn't receive any orders. They left us to live or die down here like rats!" Johnson's face grew more flushed with each word. "We've been trying the radio, but it's flooded with too much traffic. There are some civilians alive in the city, but they run away from us. Haven't seen any other soldiers except you now. Infected are everywhere."

The civilians run from them? Something didn't sit right with James. He looked over the soldiers again, took in their ragged appearances and jumpy eyes, and shuffled

his feet as adrenaline pooled in his muscles.

"Why do the civilians run away?" James asked slowly. None of Teona's soldiers had lowered their weapons.

Johnson gave a shaky laugh. "Because they're scared? Too stupid to accept our help? Who the fuck knows?" He shook his head. "It doesn't matter anyway. You've got a helicopter, let's get on it and leave this fucked-up place."

Teona tightened her grip on her weapon. "Why do the civilians run away, Corporal?" Her voice was steel.

The soldiers started to fidget. Johnson clenched and unclenched his jaw several times before he answered. "So, we may have used them as bait sometimes to lure out infected. Or left them to infected so we could get away. Live and fight another day. They don't appreciate that we're helping them! Without us there would be a lot more infected running around!"

Disgust rose like bile in James's throat. Looking at the men standing across from him, he couldn't see any humanity left in their frantic eyes.

Johnson shook his head again. "Look, we don't have time. We've stayed in one place too long, especially with the noise that helicopter made. We need to go."

Teona stood her ground. "Let me get this straight. You fucking pigs use civilians as bait instead of helping them, and you expect us to lift you out of here instead of them?"

That struck a nerve. The other soldiers with Johnson lifted their weapons, nervously moving from one foot to the other. One of them even groaned, a high-pitched sound like an animal in pain.

A young, blond man took a step forward, his eyes

pleading. He looked on the verge of tears. "You can't leave us here, it's *hell*. We're going to die here!"

That statement set the others off, who all started talking at once. James's heart rate spiked as the situation started to decay. Who knew what they were going to do? Their behaviour was erratic, and they clearly didn't want to stay there. James could see them attacking if things didn't go their way.

Teona remained unmoved by how critical everything had become. "Everybody shut the fuck up!" she shouted over the cacophony. James winced—her voice carried, and if things here were as dire as they were told...

"Lower your fucking weapons—"

Johnson cut her off. "You lower yours first!"

Before things could devolve even further, a shriek came from outside and everything went crazy.

Chapter Seven

Jennifer had woken up that morning feeling pretty good, all things considered. Sure, she had to work with Dr Dickface, and had to endure more needles stabbing into her, but she was still riding the high of Alexia's company the night before, where they'd stayed up late talking about anything and everything, and Alexia had left with a lingering hug and secret smile.

She wasn't happy anymore. When she arrived at the lab, she'd accepted another day of getting poked and prodded—why they needed so much of her blood she didn't know. She knew they stored some, couldn't they use that?—but when the doctors dropped the leaving bombshell on her she felt her entire world tilt off its axis, and she'd struggled to breathe as Dickface rambled on about needing better equipment.

The only silver lining to leaving the castle was that she'd be doing so in familiar company. She wasn't so hot on Dan coming with them—she wanted him safe, not running for his life with them, but she accepted he wasn't going to take no for an answer.

Victoria was a welcome addition. The ex-teacher's fighting skills improved every day, and Anthony had

started training her in different weapons. The fact that Anthony and Wright and James were gone was extremely disappointing, and Jennifer felt less safe without them around even inside the castle. She clenched her fists and pushed her fear to one side. *You didn't expect them to always be there, did you?* They had other soldiers accompanying them. Not a lot—they didn't want to draw the attention of anyone who roamed the outside, but enough to be safe. She hoped.

The biggest surprise was Elise, but Jennifer understood. The soldier didn't like them, and Jennifer had long since given up trying with her, but she was like a caged lion in the castle. Jennifer hoped she didn't get anyone killed because of a reckless disregard for her own life.

Alexia coming warmed Jennifer in a way she couldn't quite describe. She hadn't really felt this way since Robin, and that scared her. Robin had broken her heart. She did *not* want to go through that again. But Alexia was warm and soft and whenever her dark eyes landed on Jennifer, she felt like Alexia was devoting her whole attention to her. Jennifer couldn't imagine her being as cruel as Robin, who'd thrown five years away with a single, devastating sentence.

Jennifer turned her mind away from her ex. She wasn't worth thinking about. Instead, she frowned as she helped load food supplies onto a truck similar to the one they'd arrived in. They were taking "enough" according to one of the soldiers who was going with them—a dark-haired French man called Pierre with a face like an arrow—and that was the end of that conversation.

Jennifer huffed as she picked up a heavy bag, and nearly dropped it as Dickface shouted at her to be careful.

His Welsh accent had long since begun to grate, and today was no exception. She'd asked him why they were leaving halfway through the day—hoping to stall him in case James and Wright and Anthony returned—but he'd snapped at her as usual and said the sooner they left the sooner they'd get to wherever the fuck they were going.

"Hello," Alexia said, smiling as she hefted a large backpack higher on her back. "I was rushing around because this was very short notice, but I think I have got everything I need. Have you packed everything?"

"Hey." Jennifer grinned back. Seeing Alexia always brought her mood up. "Yeah, I have everything—clothes, toothbrush, my camera and charger." She hardly went anywhere without both. She needed to capture the collapsing world, and she never again wanted to experience the crushing stillness that was her camera dying. She'd triple checked she had them with her.

"Good." Alexia nodded. "And please do not worry too much. I'll protect you. It will be okay." Her big brown eyes looked so earnest all Jennifer could do was nod in return. She wouldn't allow her fear to get the better of her.

"Right," Dickface shouted. "That's everything packed. Let's go. No more dawdling." Pierre shot him a dark look as he climbed into the cab. Jennifer rolled her eyes. *I guess no one likes Evans.* She couldn't decide if she should pity him or keep being annoyed at his abrasive nature.

Jennifer had been holding out hope the helicopter would suddenly appear in the sky and the others would come with them, but that bubble burst at Evans's words. With a sigh, Jennifer followed Alexia up onto the truck and settled on the bench as Dan hopped up next to her.

She had said goodbye to Riya that morning, interrupting one of her advanced first aid sessions with Louis. Riya had hugged her and told her to be safe. Jennifer was glad she had opted to stay—Riya was a friend, and she didn't want any harm to come to her. She was going to miss her and her stories.

Pierre was driving, and in the passenger seat was another French soldier called Léa. Her curly hair reminded Jennifer of Rachel, and she was easy to talk to and laugh with. With the cure and the pressure and the darkness weighing down on her, it was nice to forget about it for a while and laugh at Léa's silly jokes.

Danny was another one of the soldiers going with them, which Jennifer was in two minds about. He was a nice guy, but he could get intense about the whole cure thing. She was sure he would do anything she asked, which freaked her out a little. He nodded at her as he sat down.

Dickface, Owain, and Louise were all up next to the cab. Elise sat next to Owain, with Danny next to her and another British soldier next to him. Jennifer had never spoken to her before, but she knew her name was Naomi, and she made Jennifer uncomfortable the same way Danny occasionally did. Naomi was more full-on, though. Jennifer had caught her staring a few times like she was some kind of saviour. The back of her neck prickled. She had never been the focus of awe before, and she didn't know how to deal with it.

Victoria dropped down next to Naomi, talking to Dan all the while. They both leaned forward with their elbows on their knees and looked deeply engrossed in their con-

versation. Something about a play, but Jennifer wasn't interested enough to get involved.

Instead, she leaned back and shut her eyes. She couldn't look at the receding castle, couldn't bear to watch safety dwindle from sight. The relief she'd felt upon arriving vanished along with the high stone walls, and Jennifer struggled not to become too upset. She would find somewhere else safe. And if she didn't, she'd damn well make her own safe place. She pursed her lips as an idea took root. *We'll find somewhere and settle. Properly settle. People can come to us for a cure and a safe place.* It was a rough idea, and she didn't know how likely it was to ever see the light of day, but she held it close and let it warm her.

As the truck picked up speed, Jennifer did her best to relax.

Chapter Eight

James whirled in time to see infected stream through the entrance, and the air ignited with the shouts of men and the screams of guns. He discharged his own weapon, cutting down an overweight man and an old lady. Teona's soldiers started backing away, holding the line formation.

As they edged further into the station, the horde of infected showed no sign of letting up. James didn't know where the other soldiers had gone—they clearly had experience in running away. *Maybe that's the best option here.* Their bullets did little to slow the mass of bodies that were throwing themselves at them. Screaming nonsense, clawing forward, spraying spittle. James couldn't hear his own thoughts over the horrific noise. His heart went wild in his chest, and the strain in his shoulder eased as adrenaline kicked in.

"This isn't working," someone growled. James thought it was Davison, but he didn't know for sure.

"*Retreat.*"

Teona's sharp voice sliced through the cacophony. James didn't turn away from the infected, but he could sense her solid presence on his left, his weak side, and he took comfort in that. The sound of bullets threatened to

dump him right back on the cold ground in France, but Teona was right beside him, so he'd be all right. He'd be all right. Maybe if he told himself often enough, he'd believe it.

She yanked him back and he stumbled into the barriers, righting himself in time to follow her over them. He fired indiscriminately into the surging crowd as the rest of their squad jumped over, silently hurrying them on. They needed to get out of there.

With the infected temporarily slowed at the barrier, James and the others ran further into the station. Even as he looked back, some had already climbed over and were running after them. He fired as he ran, getting the wall on his first attempt and a girl in the leg on his second. *Fuck, there are children in that chaos.* He hadn't expected to see children. *Don't be a naïve idiot, James.*

Deciding to save his ammunition and strength, he focused on running. Sweat rolled down his face, soaking into his helmet strap, but he pushed through the pain. His heart beat so hard it shook his bones, but he kept running, *running*, his neck straining as he tried to keep track of everything at once. Trying to keep one eye on the scene behind him, and spying out his next move in front of him was impossible.

"*Down*," Teona shouted, and James scrambled not to fall down a steep escalator. Catching his footing in time to not make a complete arse of himself, he rushed after her with the others hot on his heels.

"They're gaining!" Ota yelled. He discharged his weapon, momentarily deafening James as it echoed around the underground.

He saw an infected man fall, blood and broken bones

clearly visible as he was trampled by those behind him. *One down, what feels like a hundred more to go.*

The other soldiers who'd run shouted to them, and they hurried down more banks of escalators until James was sure he was as far underground as he had ever been. Darkness crept up on them like a thief, stealing the light inch by inch until they had to switch their torches on. The only good thing about the situation was the fading sounds of pursuit once the darkness became absolute. James's eyes tried to drink in as much light as they could, but the torches were dim compared to the pressing dark, and the beams jumped around too much as they ran.

Teona called a stop down some tracks leading to who knew where. James realised he hadn't heard the infected for some time. He strained to hear anything beyond the loud panting of people trying to catch their breath, but he didn't pick up any of the pursuing madness.

"We tried to tell you," Johnson wheezed as he leaned against the wall. "This city is lost. Overrun. We *need* to get out of here!" His shout echoed down the tunnel, and everyone twitched as they tried to look everywhere at once.

"Keep your fucking voice down," Teona hissed. "The first thing we need to do is take stock. When I call your name say '*here*'. Mollino?"

"Here," James said, standing right next to her.

"Trueman?"

"Here."

"Woods?"

"Here."

All the soldiers from the castle were present, and

Johnson took stock of his soldiers too. No one was missing.

"Right, now we work to get out of here," Teona said.

"Yes," Johnson agreed. "And once we're out we get on that helicopter and leave this fucked-up place."

"Corporal, I'm not promising you shit," Teona said, her anger spilling over like a rough sea over rocks. "You think you deserve to be saved more than those poor people you fucking terrorised?"

"This isn't about what people deserve," Johnson shot back. "We've done our time in hell. Now we want out. Besides, we're more useful to you than some fucking civilian!"

"I can think of several civilians who are more useful to me than you, and they don't have the same moral depravity you do."

James couldn't see Johnson letting up any time soon and standing around arguing would achieve nothing. They needed to get out of here. "Enough," James growled. He turned to the others and ignored the corporal altogether. "Did anyone see any signs? Which way are we headed?"

Johnson's eyes burned a hole in the back of his head, but James continued to ignore him as he looked at Davison, who shuffled on his feet. "I think I saw a sign?" he said hesitantly.

James frowned. "Is that a question? Did you, or didn't you?"

The stocky man nodded. "Yeah, we're on the Jubilee line to Waterloo."

"Are you sure?"

"Yes, sir." He sounded more confident than he had a second ago. James decided to believe him. They didn't have much else to go on.

"Okay, people," Teona said. "Let's continue. The sooner we get out of here the better."

They started forward, the thin beams of light drifting around, trying to push back the unrelenting darkness. It almost had a weight to it. James could *feel* it all around him, heavy and demanding, and his small light seemed feeble in the face of it.

After a few minutes' walking, a ripe smell wafted down the line. James grimaced but kept both hands on his weapon despite wanting to cover his nose. They came upon a train a short while later. Splashes of dried blood stained several of the windows. He tightened his grip on his weapon and ignored the pain building in his shoulder as his heart once again picked up speed. He drew in a deep breath as he signalled Woods forward. The small man pried open the door and squeezed on board. He signalled them to follow after a tense moment.

James breathed through his mouth, but it didn't help much. He heard gagging behind him. Blood and bodily fluids covered almost every surface, and the dead's eyes followed them, almost as if the torches disturbed their rest. It was eerie, plain and simple. He couldn't wait to be off the other side.

They edged forward more quickly, an unspoken urgency pushing everyone on. James kept his breathing even. It wouldn't do to show the others he was scared, especially Johnson's soldiers. He stayed close to Teona as thoughts of getting shot kept trying to rip through him,

and he focused on the here and now.

Focused on the dry, stale air. Focused on the different smells of death and decay. Focused on the way he could almost taste the tangy blood, on the dim lights of the torches surrounding him, on the faint sounds of dripping water, of heavy breathing, of shuffling feet, of muted screams and running.

Muted screams and running.

Getting louder.

Getting closer.

"We need to hurry," James said, unable to keep the unease from his voice. "You hear that? Move. *Now*."

They raced through the train and James was surprised no one tripped in the confined space. Carriages passed by in a blur of chaotic light and dark, half seen faces and shadows, and someone behind him letting out a steady stream of curses. They got stuck at one of the doors for a few precious seconds before Trueman shoved his way through.

They burst out of the end of the train, James stumbling as pain shot through his shoulder, then they were running again.

A station coalesced out of the darkness ahead and the sight gave everyone an extra burst of speed, with Johnson being the first one up onto the platform, closely followed by his soldiers. James turned to watch their six, but Teona grabbed his good shoulder and shoved him forward, telling Davison to help pull him up while she pushed. She shot him a wink as she heaved herself up after him, and they ran to the stairs.

"Fuck—"

The shout was cut off as a bald man jumped on one of Johnson's soldiers, the young, blond one who'd pleaded with them earlier. They tumbled down the stairs in a mass of flailing limbs and bitten-off shouts, the light from his torch spinning wildly. Instinct kicked in and James jumped back, then his training reasserted itself and he raised his weapon and started firing at the infected spilling down the stairs like floodwater.

The others were firing as well. For a few seconds, all their light was beamed at the stairs and the gunfire lit up desperate faces. Then, nothing. It was clear as suddenly as the infected had appeared. James looked down at the mangled body of the blond soldier and didn't feel any stirrings of pity.

He took the stairs two at a time, dodging bodies and blood, thankful for the adrenaline pumping through his system that blocked out the pain in his shoulder. It felt better than it had in a long while. His heart still beat out a rough rhythm, but he was almost at peace with it. *Please be a soldier again.* He felt like he had years ago, on deployment. The rush of the fight, the thrill of survival, the buzz of battle.

The cold, cold ground, the bullet tearing its way into him, his warm blood draining out. James fell to the hard ground, his shoulder screaming as it was ripped apart, his body screaming, the world screaming. He was trapped in ice, all heat fleeing from him as he clawed for it, begged it not to leave him.

Someone was yelling at him. A man? Yes, a man. James focused on him, saw his blue eyes, his pale skin, his dark stubble. Who was he? James shoved him away—he

didn't like people getting in his face like that, and this bastard was no different. He was so cold, was this the bastard who'd shot him? White-hot anger ignited in his stomach and flooded his bones. Clenching his jaw, James went to lift his weapon—

"*James.*" That voice he recognised. Teona. She filled his vision, an avenging angel releasing him from the past's icy clutches. He snapped back to the present and heard the howls of infected and shouts asking what was wrong with him. Millar stood next to them with his weapon aimed down the stairs. Teona pulled him up. When had he fallen to the floor? "We have to keep moving. Stay with me, James, please." He nodded, making a mental note to apologise to Millar later. If they made it out.

The others waited a little way up the corridor, and everyone started running when they caught up. James didn't see anyone give him any *looks,* but he could feel them questioning him. *What's wrong with him? Can we rely on him? Is he going to get us killed?*

James didn't have the answers. *Please be a soldier again.* He hadn't had an *incident* the whole time they'd been at the castle, bar the nightmares, but this *was* the first time he'd been out in the field again. He'd thought he was ready. Clearly not.

They made it out of the Underground and into the station proper. It was deserted. The scene mirrored that of Westminster—bodies littering the floor, pools of black spreading out of them like poison. James took care not to step near any of it.

They advanced out of the station onto the street, where a similar sight greeted their eyes. It all screamed of a city abandoned, left to the wilderness to reclaim what

man in his arrogance once took. The rain fell harder than before, but it was still little more than a drizzle. The deceptive type that didn't look like much but got you drenched in a matter of minutes. James welcomed it. He lifted his face up to the sky and let the raindrops mingle with the sweat on his face. He felt cleaner as it washed over his skin, and he scrubbed a hand over his eyes and blinked away the water.

"We have to keep moving," Johnson said, his wide eyes and not-healed-right-broken nose giving him a feral look. "This is life now. Never stop. Never stop. If you do, you die."

"Thanks for the life lesson I didn't ask for, dipshit," Teona returned curtly. "Of course we keep moving."

Contrary to her words, she paused, and James knew she was mulling their options over. The quickest way out was the helicopter, but she didn't want to bring the civilian-terrorising pieces of shite.

"Let's get away from this station, get somewhere secure and plan our next move," James suggested, hoping to buy them some time to decide. Aye, these soldiers were off the deep end, and they couldn't be relied upon to fight, not after all they'd been through, but could they in good conscience leave them?

"We need to get to the helicopter," Johnson hissed angrily. "You don't get a say anyway, not after what happened back there. You got scared and shut down. Never seen infected up close?"

James knew he was trying to get a rise out of him, and it was fucking working. He threw his best glare the arsehole's way, but Johnson just sneered back. If Ota hadn't stepped in, James would have punched the bastard right

in his mocking mouth.

"He's a sergeant, corporal, so watch your mouth. We don't have time to talk about what happened right now. They're coming up through the station."

"There's a place we can go that's not far from here," said one of Johnson's men. His eyes held a sadness that suggested he knew they didn't want to take them and had accepted it. "Follow me."

Johnson looked about to contest but a howl rang up from the city. James shook his head, muttering to himself.

That man needs careful watching. James tightened his grip on his weapon, willing himself to be ready for whatever came next.

Chapter Nine

They jogged down the steps, the rain giving everything a dreary, washed-out look. James shoved down his fear of having another *incident* at a crucial moment. *Keep going, focus on getting out of here. Focus on Teona, she'll keep me grounded.* He glanced at her jogging next to him, always next to him. On his weak side. He'd only known her for a short time, but he knew she would never let him down.

There was a sudden clattering to their left, and twelve guns were pointing there in a split second. Everyone was jumpy. It was a young lad, no more than Dan's age James guessed, and clearly infected. He blinked up at them all, confused and agitated as he crouched beside a blue car that had crashed into the wall. He looked like he was about to dart in any direction.

Before he had the chance to so much as twitch, a weapon discharged and a red hole bloomed in the boy's chest, like some disgusting parody of flowers in spring. James jerked at the gunshot, but Teona was there, and he wasn't in France. He was all right. He was all right. He was all right.

The noise would attract others, so they moved on

quickly. James tried not to think about the kid, but a sadness rose within him at the pointlessness of it all. Last year that boy was in school, having fun with friends, thinking about his future. Maybe he'd had a girlfriend or boyfriend. Now it was all gone. *Children without childhoods. That's what the world has fallen to.*

Two more infected stumbled out of a bombed building a little further down the road. Both had visible bite marks, but one was clearly deeper into the psychosis than the other—the brown-skinned man was drinking a bottle of water while the ginger woman was practically foaming at the mouth.

The man spotted them first. He threw his bottle at them and tried to run away, but the woman shrieked and ran at them. They both died in a storm of bullets before they could take two steps.

Again, they moved on. And again, they didn't get far. Anger gripped James. *We haven't even made it to the end of this street.* It wasn't infected this time, however—Johnson grabbed the man who was leading them and hauled him around, stepping right into his space.

"Hey!" Teona admonished, but Johnson ignored her.

"What the fuck do you think you're doing, you spineless twat!" Johnson shouted. "We need to go to the helicopter. Why can no one see that but me?"

The man tried to push him away, but Johnson was clearly the stronger of the two. They grappled until they were pulled apart by Davison and Trueman. James noticed none of Johnson's soldiers got involved. They studiously ignored the whole thing, which made James suspect Johnson had done this before. Had he killed some of his own? James wouldn't put it past him. It would explain

why the others feared him.

"Infected at six o'clock," Millar announced calmly.

James looked behind, and sure enough four people were cautiously making their way out of a relatively intact building. Only two bore visible bite marks on their arms, but the other two were just as agitated. James sensed the madness coming from them in waves, like heat haze from a hot engine. They spotted the soldiers and froze, but before James could so much as think about firing his weapon there were loud discharges from his right as Johnson's soldiers gunned them down. *Fuck me, they're trigger happy.* Or maybe he was slow. A burst of worry flashed through him. What if he was losing his edge? The only reason he hadn't been dumped right back to that night at the sound of the gunfire was Teona standing next to him.

He needed to get his fucking act together. He wasn't there any more. Aye, his shoulder was damaged, but he was still alive, and he was on the road to recovery. James knew it wasn't as simple as that, but he was still annoyed at himself.

Before they could start walking again a middle-aged man stumbled around the remnants of a building in front of them. Fat tears dripped down his round face and got lost in his impressive tangle of a beard. James felt itchy at the sight of it.

"Please," he begged them. "Help me. One snuck up behind me. Please help." The rest of his sentence was lost to incoherent rambling, but James got the gist. Freshly bitten and panicking. Sorrow once again welled up in James—they'd come here to assess the city and to try to rescue any survivors. So far all they had done was meet up

with some cowards and barely survive an hour or so on the ground.

"You have to help me, take me to a doctor, please, please, get me out of here, help—"

His pleas were cut short by the roar of a weapon, silencing his voice forever. James jumped at the unexpected sound, but he was all right. He was all right.

"What the fuck, Johnson?" Teona snarled. "What the fuck is wrong with you?"

"He was infected," Johnson said. "We put infected down." His voice took on a mocking tone, like he was talking to a five-year-old instead of a grown woman.

"Yes, I am aware of that," Teona sounded like she was grinding stones with her teeth. "But we don't just put people down like animals. We could have at least explained the situation and heard his last words. Show some humanity."

"You really don't get it, do you?" Johnson laughed. "We've been here for what feels like forever. This is the way it is now. Pause for breath and you're fucking dead!"

Teona shook her head. "Yeah, this is a shitty mess we're all in. But the moment you abandon your humanity is the moment you're lost. You've let this world beat you. We all need to rise above it and keep showing some damn *compassion*."

Johnson shook his head in a manner that said, *you're clearly an idiot and I'm done trying to explain shit to you.* James wanted to knock the bastard out.

"We need to keep moving," Trueman said. He and the rest of the soldiers with James and Teona had formed a rough circle and were watching the area, which was more

than what Johnson's lot were doing. Oh, they were looking around, but it had the appearance of scared little boys instead of trained soldiers. There was no order to them. They were acting like people who had been randomly placed together instead of a coordinated unit. James wondered how they'd lived so long.

"Yes, we do," Teona agreed, frowning at Johnson. The sudden sound of running feet cut off the rest of what she'd been about to say, and two women burst out of the torn-up rubble the bearded man had stumbled from. One with short blonde hair was chasing one with black tangles, and the blonde was shot by Millar as the black-haired woman ran past him.

She dived on one of Johnson's men, a beanpole of a man, and they fell to the floor as bullets ripped through their flesh.

Quiet settled around them once again. The smell of blood lay heavy on the air, the drizzle doing little to dampen the metallic odour. Blood ran in a rivulet toward James, who stepped out of the way and watched it continue unimpeded down the street, a dark stain forever tainting the ground.

"We meet you and now two of us are *dead*," Johnson growled.

"Your men killed one of your own," Teona shot back.

"Fuck you!" Johnson yelled. "We're better off on our own. C'mon, boys, we'll take that helicopter for ourselves."

Teona's men got fidgety at that. James saw Ota frown, and Davison half-turned from his watch to glare at Johnson. "Sure, and I suppose you know how to fly it?"

Teona asked sweetly, with a grin that was more teeth than mirth.

"I don't need to," Johnson spat. "We'll take it and force you."

They had their weapons trained on James and the others as they backed away. Davison completely turned from watching behind them and pointed his weapon on the retreating cowards. "Sergeant, we can't let them take the helicopter. It's our only way out."

Teona didn't respond. Johnson grinned at them as he withdrew back the way they'd come, and James felt the anger boiling off Teona. She was calm the way a bomb was calm.

She opened her mouth and a shriek came out. It wasn't her voice. James whipped around just in time to see a woman dive on Davison. He let out a yell and all hell broke loose.

Several people fired at once, and the multiple bangs from different directions briefly disoriented James. He followed Ota behind a collapsed bit of wall as pops continued to go off, from them or the cowards, James didn't know. He needed to take stock. His mind fell into its ritual of checking his armour and weapons, then into assessing the situation. That was good. It was almost as if there was nothing wrong with him.

He peeked over the top of the rubble and saw the cowards running down the street away from them, five infected hot on their heels. One half turned and discharged his weapon, but it went wide and embedded itself in a wall that was nowhere near those chasing them. An infected man with his hair greased to his head stood underneath where the bullet landed, and he jerked and let out a roar,

stumbling around and clawing at his face as little bits of debris rained down. When he looked up his crazed eyes met James's, and with another roar he charged.

James raised his weapon. It was like someone else was in control of his body. With a gentle squeeze of his finger, he ended the man's life. Just like that. Thoughts of Martin flitted through the bubble his mind floated in, but he pushed them away as they threatened to burst the tentative tranquillity that had stolen over him.

With the immediate threat dealt with, James looked around for Teona and the rest of their soldiers. They were crouched on the other side of the street, weapons trained all around them as they hunted for more threats. James nodded to himself. They were all right. *What about Davison?*

The soldier lay face down in the middle of the road with both hands clutching the back of his neck. Red squeezed its way out between his fingers. The woman who had jumped on him lay dead down the street. Acid churned in James's stomach as he watched the soldier bleed. Seeing cowards die was one thing, but one of your own was something else entirely. Shame engulfed him like fire ripping through a forest. They weren't going to bring them all back.

"Fuck," Ota cursed next to him. "Fuck."

James knew the pain of losing a brother, so he didn't bother with words. He grasped Ota's shoulder and poured his understanding into that. Ota nodded back at him.

They slowly rose from behind the rubble, the other four across the street mimicking them. They made their way to Davison as a rumble built, coming from the direction of the station. Ice ran down James's back. It was the

horde of infected. It had to be. Nothing else would make that noise in London. That screeching. That blood-curdling screaming. The pain of insanity.

They all froze.

"We have to move," Teona said with an urgency James had never heard from her before.

Millar moved to pick Davison up, but the fallen soldier pushed him away and sat up himself. He grabbed his weapon and winced as his pushed himself to his feet. "Go," he said, putting on a brave face. "I'll give you as much time as I can."

Woods almost spoke, but one look from Davison shut him up. He had the look of someone who'd made up his mind and nothing was going to make him change it. James respected that.

"Thank you," Trueman said quietly. Millar and Woods echoed the sentiment.

Ota said something James didn't catch, and Davison nodded, his red-rimmed eyes gazing past them. With a shake of his head, he walked a little way down the street and readied his weapon.

James and the others started the other way. He looked back once and saw the silhouette of a person standing tall, ready to face what was coming.

He was growing tired of people dying so he could live.

Chapter Ten

26TH JANUARY

The day dawned bright and cold, and hope flourished in Heather for the first time in days. She'd almost forgotten the feeling.

"Stay low," Frankie whispered as he peered over an abandoned car. He didn't seem to be experiencing any of the relief lighting up Heather's heart. Walking down the street were five men and three women, all heavily armed. She could have jumped for joy at the sight of them. The army had fallen or abandoned them after the outbreak, so seeing these capable people was like a balm to Heather's incessant fear. Why Frankie insisted on hiding she didn't know.

The group checked every nook and cranny as they passed. They would find them soon. She might as well stand up. They'd get to her quicker. But what if they mistook her for a diseased person and shot her?

She took her cues from Frankie and stayed down. Maybe he thought they would shoot as well. It didn't matter. Frankie had kept her alive this long—she trusted his judgment and did what he said in times like these.

The group walked closer. They would have to move if they didn't want to be spotted. Heather looked at Frankie again. He watched them with an intensity she'd begun to associate with him, all unblinking stare and thin mouth. What was he going to do? They were almost on them.

"Okay," Frankie said, shuffling low again. "I'm going to shout over to them—they're going to find us anyway. Maybe this is what we've been waiting for. Rescue."

Heather nodded. She couldn't think of anything better. The past fortnight had been ripped straight from her darkest nightmares. Death stalked these streets, pounced like a hunter in the night. They'd been a group of five for a while, but now it was only the two of them again. Heather caught the food and bandaged the cuts, but she hadn't been able to do much for Mitchell without his insulin, and none of them had been able to do anything when a group of seven diseased people had attacked. Heather and Frankie had been lucky to escape with their lives.

"Here goes," Frankie took a deep breath. "If they shoot me, don't run. Announce yourself to them. You'll have more of a chance that way." He didn't wait for a response. He thrust his hands into the air and eased himself to his feet. "Don't shoot! There's only me and one other, we haven't been bitten!"

Heather's heart leaped into her throat as the guns were all pointed at Frankie. Luckily, no one seemed trigger happy. "Come out," the man closest to them called. Heather pushed herself to her feet, her knees protesting after so long crouched. She settled her bags on her shoulders and shoved her hands in the air, copying Frankie. *Please don't shoot, please don't shoot.* They

hadn't survived this long for it to end here. Sweat beaded on her forehead as none of the soldiers made any effort to lower their guns.

"Who are you?" the same man asked. He had about a week's growth on his face and eyes that never stilled. Heather's stomach twisted itself into knots.

"My name's Frankie, and this is Heather. She's a paramedic." They had agreed to mention her job whenever they met new people. They were always quick to change their tune when they heard her skills. It had saved their lives three times now. Heather still found it hard to believe how far society had fallen in such a short time.

This group was no different. Immediately, all but the bearded man in charge lowered their guns, and Heather saw smiles break out on some faces. "A paramedic?" Bearded Man looked to be mulling something over. It didn't take him long before he also lowered his gun. "Come with us. We have a safe zone nearby."

Heather's knees almost gave way. She released a deep breath as tears stung the back of her eyes. With a big smile to Frankie, which he didn't return, she hitched her bags higher on her shoulder and followed this group to their safe zone. After not being able to find Kallie or her family—she held on to hope they were alive somewhere, they *had* to be—this win gave her the boost she needed to keep going. She *would* find them. She had to. Her wife was her life, and the outbreak wouldn't keep them separated.

*

The safe zone turned out to be a pub called the Red Lion. A bus had been parked across the bridge next to it, blocking that road entirely. Cars and vans were parked over the

other road and roundabout, forming a blockade that would slow diseased people down. More people were guarding them with weapons, and Heather was struck by how capable it all looked. The only thing that gave her pause was how jumpy everyone seemed, but she supposed that was to be expected.

The pub itself had all its windows boarded up, blocking her view of the inside. She and Frankie were halted outside and given a cursory once-over that Heather didn't think was good enough at all, but before she could voice her concerns, a man walked into the sunlight.

Tall and handsome, he was dressed, inexplicably, like he was going to an interview. His light-brown hair was impeccably styled, and he wore blue trousers and matching blazer over a white shirt. It wasn't his smart attire that told Heather he was in charge, however; it was the way everyone around him stood up straighter and seemed more vigilant.

His smile was bright and easy. "Hello, my name is Brendon." He held out a hand for them to shake. His grip was firm, and in contrast to his appearance, his hands were rough, like he used to work a labour-intensive job. "You're both safe here." His smile never dimmed. "I hear one of you is a paramedic?" A spike of annoyance stabbed through Heather as he directed the question to Frankie, but she pushed it aside.

"I am," she said, holding her head high. Kallie would be so proud of her standing up for herself, helping these people through this shit storm. Brendon was the one dressed for an interview, but Heather felt like she was the one on the other side of the table. *Better sell myself.* She gestured to her bags. "I can also fish and hunt small

animals. My dad taught me when I was young." She didn't like the way Brendon's eyes lit up like she was a great prize he'd won, but again, she pushed the feeling aside. Her skills would help everyone. This was a good place. Safe. Secure. That it had been created in such a short time spoke volumes to the competence of the people involved.

"That is marvellous." Brendon clapped his hands together. His smile hadn't changed. "Welcome to our little safe zone. It's not much, but it's certainly better than anything out there. I run a tight ship here, as is necessary for our continued survival, so don't be alarmed at how militaristic it may seem at first. Eli, our soldier, may he rest in peace, was the one who taught us how to use the weapons and fight and survive. I've kept running the place as close to his model as possible.

"Come on in, make yourselves at home. I'll give you a tour and explain how things work around here."

They followed Brendon through the door, and Heather let herself relax as she entered the gloomy interior.

Safe at last.

Chapter Eleven

PRESENT DAY

"Do you have any tattoos?" Alexia asked out of the blue. They had been driving for what felt like ages, but Jennifer knew they hadn't made it far from the castle. Why Dick-face had insisted on leaving so late in the day was beyond her. It didn't help that he and Pierre kept arguing about which way was best—Pierre wanted to take a long route to avoid infected, while Evans wanted to drive straight to Paris. Fucking Paris. If it was even remotely similar to what London had been like, Jennifer didn't have high hopes for their trip. "I have one—"

"What? Really?" Jennifer exclaimed. "How come I haven't seen it yet?"

"It's on my thigh." Alexia laughed at Jennifer's amazement. "Maybe you will see it one day."

"Yeah?" Jennifer tried to look cool and casual. "I'd like that."

Alexia smiled. "So, do you have any?"

"No, I've thought about it but never got one." Jennifer had held Amanda's hand when she had gotten a rose on

her shoulder and seeing her pain had put her off. "What's yours?"

"It is a lioness's head."

"Nice," Jennifer smiled. "Did it hurt?"

Alexia shrugged. "It was painful, oui, but it was not as bad as people make it out to be. It was like a scratch over and over again."

The truck slowed to a stop. Never a good sign. Jennifer hoped the road was merely blocked and they would soon be on their way.

The soldiers and Victoria jumped out, weapons ready to blow anyone away. Jennifer moved to the end of the truck, placing herself in between the others and whatever was outside.

Loud, incessant voices. None she recognised. *At least it's not infected.* Pierre's voice. Just as loud. An argument? Jennifer held her breath. What if it went badly? What if they had weapons and opened fire? She could feel herself getting worked up and released her breath in an effort to calm down. Nothing would happen. They were all right. Everything was fine.

She leaned around the side of the truck to get a better view of what was going on. From her vantage point, she could see three men, all armed. They had messy hair and beards and torn clothing. The gleaming weapons did *not* fit with their image. *Probably stolen.*

"What's going on?" Louise asked in a hushed voice. It was the quietest Jennifer had ever heard her. "It's not infected people. Obviously. You can't reason with them. So, who? Soldiers? We'll be able to reason with *them.*"

If you stop talking for a second, I can tell you.

Exasperation curled around the thought as Jennifer fought not to roll her eyes. Talking seemed to be Louise's default setting, but she detected a slight nervous lilt to her strong Manchester accent.

"It's some men," Jennifer replied. "I can't really see how many, but they have guns."

"Not infected, then." Louise nodded. "That's something at least." She still seemed on edge, but a tad less so now.

"It'll be all right," Jennifer reassured her. "The soldiers are talking to them, which is always better than bullets, and if it comes to that they'll protect us. They're good at their jobs."

Jennifer saw Louise and Owain take deep, calming breaths and give twin nods. *Huh, that comforted them.* She turned back to see what was happening outside. More talking, or arguing really, and a lot of posturing from what Jennifer could make out.

"I can't see a lot," Jennifer said, "but they're still just talking—"

"Move aside, girl," Evans snapped, cutting her off. "I'll give a more accurate description of what is occurring."

Jennifer's eyebrows slammed down as she turned to snap right back at him. How *dare* he speak to her like that. She'd put up with his disrespect and arrogance at the castle, but now they were out of his territory, and she was damn well putting a stop to it. *She* was immune, *she* was the one who could end this. Out here, Jennifer realised, she was one of the safest people to be around. He was going to show her respect even if he choked on it.

Deafening bangs silenced her reply. She ducked automatically, whipping back into the truck as five more shots were fired. The air was still ringing when Pierre's angry voice carried over to them.

He shouted in French, so Jennifer didn't know what he said, but as the soldiers rounded the truck—Alexia and Victoria included, both fine—she saw the look on Elise's face and knew the woman was the one to open fire. Her face was slack, like she couldn't care less she was getting shouted at.

"Give it a rest," Victoria cut in. The Frenchman stopped talking with a surprised snap of his teeth. "They were unhinged, Elise could see it, I could see it, you *all* could see it. They were seconds away from shooting. Elise did the right thing getting there first."

An angry growl sounded deep in Pierre's throat. "You are not a soldier, so I don't expect you to understand." He turned away from Victoria and scowled at Elise again. "Do *not* disobey a direct order again. Do *not* open fire on potential hostiles while we are all exposed. If you don't follow my orders, I will take your weapon and leave you in the truck."

Elise shrugged, not looking the slightest bit repentant. Pierre was so red in the face Jennifer worried he was going to have an aneurysm. "Back up," he barked before storming around to the driver's seat.

Everyone filed back onto the truck, and once they were underway again, Jennifer leaned over to Elise. "What happened?"

Elise glanced at her, then turned away. She closed her eyes and rested her head back, clearly content to leave Jennifer in the dark. Jennifer sighed. Their relationship

with Elise had most definitely *not* improved. She turned to Victoria instead, raising her eyebrows in question.

"There were seven people altogether," Victoria said, her weapon held loosely, like it was an extension of her body "They looked rough, like they'd been struggling to survive ever since everything went to hell. They all had weapons, ranging from machine guns to pistols, and one only had a knife. They were clearly desperate, attempting to rob fully armoured and armed soldiers. Elise did the right thing—they *were* going to attack. We would have driven straight into an ambush if Léa hadn't seen them. When they saw that we saw them, they stepped out and came up to us. I don't know what they were hoping to achieve, to be honest." Victoria shrugged and settled back.

Jennifer found it increasingly difficult to think of Victoria as a schoolteacher who loved fashion and hated doing physical activity or going outdoors. She'd told Jennifer she'd only ever been bowling once because she'd broken her manicured nails and had grown to harbour a resentful hatred of the activity. Now she bit her nails to keep them short and talked about ambushes and pre-emptive killing. Jennifer couldn't merge the two versions of Victoria in her brain.

Although I know she still shaves, like me. She had seen the razor Victoria had packed. *Part of the woman she was is still in there, she's just adapted quickly. I wish I could do the same.*

As Jennifer settled back into the drive, she noticed how shaken the scientists looked, even Evans. Had they not experienced *any* of the world falling apart? Louise had talked about being transported from one army base to the next until they ended up at the castle, but Jennifer had

assumed they'd seen at least some of the shit that had happened. *Never assume. Get the facts and let them speak for themselves.*

She estimated about fifteen minutes passed before they slowed again. The soldiers and Victoria all jumped out, but they didn't move around the truck. Instead, Pierre walked into view, looking grim.

"There's infected up ahead," he said. "They are fighting amongst themselves. I was going to drive around them and not get involved, but Léa suggested we kill them so they don't go on to infect or kill others. She's covering them now. We should save ammunition, so I only want Lécuyer and Fuller with me, the rest of you guard the truck."

Alexia and Danny left with Pierre. Elise shook her head and jumped back up into the truck. She threw herself onto the bench, sulking like a child. Naomi frowned at her but didn't say anything as she moved to cover the left. Victoria shrugged and turned to cover the right.

"Will we be all right?" Louise nudged Jennifer. Back when they were at the castle, the scientist hadn't struck Jennifer as a worrier, but you never really knew how someone was going to react in a situation until it was happening.

"Everything will be fine," Jennifer said soothingly. The scientists looked to her for reassurance and she didn't know why. The soldiers were right there to ask. *You do know why. You're immune. It's as if they think that grants you some special kind of composure.* In reality, Jennifer battled her own fears. She tried to project a calm air, tried to seem relaxed and at ease with the infected so close by. Everything was fine. The soldiers would quickly

deal with them, and they would be driving again in no time.

Everything wasn't fine. There was a screech from the opposite direction Alexia and the others had gone. Victoria and Naomi spun to the sound and opened fire as infected ran to them, weaving in and out of the handful of cars strewn around the road. There were only four—they were clearly at the scene of an old accident—but there may as well have been four hundred. Bullets ricocheted off the abandoned metal, missing their targets as they ducked and darted about.

Similar to what happened at the hospital, seeing the infected brought a startling clarity to Jennifer's mind. She grabbed Dan and shoved him further into the truck, yelling at the scientists to stay in it as well. Elise jumped down and started shooting in a matter of seconds, catching one infected in the stomach and another in the leg. Jennifer couldn't count them all as they dived around.

Victoria shouted at her to get into the truck, but Jennifer ignored her. *I'm the safest person,* she reminded herself. *They can't infect me. I'm safe.* She knew she wasn't, not really. Safe from the virus yes, but they could still quite easily kill her. Her mind repressed that thought as a pale woman snarled and ran at her. She had the look of someone who had lost a lot of weight in a short amount of time.

Jennifer was nowhere near as good as Victoria when it came to unarmed combat, but she thought she could throw a decent punch. She squared up to the infected woman and directed a fist at her cheek. It landed on her jaw and sent a shockwave of pain up Jennifer's hand, but it had the desired result. The woman fell to the ground

and a bullet caught in her chest. That was the end of that.

Jennifer looked up in time to see a large man barrel down on her, and she threw up her arms in defence. The impact sent them both smacking into the side of the truck, and pain lanced across Jennifer's back. *Shit, I'm not very good at this whole fighting thing.* The thought flashed through her mind in the spilt second it took for the man to right himself, then there was no more time for thinking.

Instinct took control.

Jennifer kicked him in the knee, hoping to knock his leg out from under him. He stumbled but didn't fall. With a furious growl he moved to punch her, and with an insane amount of luck Jennifer ducked out of the way. He yelled in pain as his fist connected with the truck, and his dark eyes seemed to get even more enraged, if that were possible. Jennifer sent a punch of her own back at him in the ribs, but it had little effect. She was too close to him. She needed some space to get power behind her attacks, and maybe get in a kick to the balls. She was able to easily avoid another punch that was wildly thrown, and duck out around him. Rage made him sloppy.

She was so focused on him that she bumped straight into another infected man. This one was shorter than the first, and less solidly built. Without thinking, Jennifer brought her elbow up and slammed it into the second man's face, and he fell to the ground with a surprised yell.

With a burst of dread, Jennifer moved to face the first man again. Too slow. *Too slow.* She was lifted into the air before she had finished turning back to him, and she slammed down onto the bonnet of a car. Her head whacked off the windshield, and Jennifer's vision went white for a few precious seconds. She still had the

presence of mind to throw her arms up in front of her. That was probably what saved her life. The man moved to tear into her throat with his stained teeth, but her right arm got in the way. He didn't bite down on it—*thank fuck*—as she caught him on the chin and heaved with all her strength.

All her strength wasn't anywhere near enough. He grabbed her arms and threw them to the side, leaving her in an awkward position with the top half of her body twisted to the right and her legs trapped straight under him. She had no way to push back. *Fuck. Fuck.* She was going to die. He couldn't infect her, but he could kill her. Why the fuck hadn't she listened to Victoria and gone up into the truck? She'd left the others exposed up there. *Dan, oh shit, Dan.* She was going to die, and she wouldn't be able to protect him anymore. *Fuck!*

The bite down never came. He abruptly arched, letting out a godawful scream and falling away from her. Jennifer wasted no time in scrambling to her feet. Her head was *pounding*. She spared him a glance as she stood up and noticed the messy bullet hole in his upper leg, bright-red blood spurting out like streamers. She let him crawl away. He would be dead soon.

She got her bearings. The air was filled with the shouts and screams of infected and non-infected alike, as guns blasted in every direction. Jennifer's ears rang with the sounds of desperation and fear, and she felt them echo through her bones, the screams going on forever. She saw Victoria and Naomi standing close to each other, guarding the truck and killing any infected who got too close. Elise was a little way apart from them, facing Jennifer and shooting behind her. She must have been the one who'd

shot the man. Gratitude for Elise ignited in her chest, but she knew Elise would hear nothing of it.

She saw a small woman sidle up behind Elise. The soldier didn't see, focused as she was beyond Jennifer. Victoria and Naomi were too occupied as well. A surge jolted through her, and she was sprinting as fast as her legs would carry her. She had been practicing over the past month. Hopefully the training had paid off.

Elise saw her mad dash toward her and frowned. Jennifer waved behind her. Elise's steel eyes widened, and she spun around. *Too slow.* Jennifer watched her turn, her gun not coming up fast enough. *No, no, no!*

Jennifer barrelled into the infected woman—who looked more like a teenager up close—and together they tumbled to the ground. Jennifer became disorientated as the sky and the road danced around each other. When they stilled, she didn't have time to move before sharp teeth sank into her left hand beneath the thumb and pain bloomed fresh. She screamed, and with a burst of energy she shoved the girl off. Jennifer shuffled away as Elise stepped in front of her and shot the infected girl.

That gun shot was the last, and its cry vibrated in Jennifer's ears. It took her a moment to catch her breath. *In and out.* She closed her eyes and focused on her hand. The pain was incessant, and it made her whole hand throb. *In and out.* She opened her eyes and looked down. Blood trickled out, tickling her as it made its slow way down to her fingers, where it leaped off her hand to crash into the road below.

More running footsteps. Jennifer scrambled to her feet as Elise spun, but it was only Alexia and the others. The wild worry in Alexia's eyes warmed Jennifer, and she

smiled tiredly.

"We heard the gunfire," Léa panted. "We came as soon as we could."

"What happened?" Pierre grunted.

Victoria stepped forward and shouldered her gun. "Infected. No one was hurt except Jennifer." Victoria eyed her hand, sympathy forming a grimace on her face. "You okay?"

Jennifer nodded, still cradling her hand. Her breath caught as she realised Evelyn had been bitten in a similar place. She was now experiencing what her friend had gone through, but she wouldn't be executed for it. White-hot anger burned through her gut at the thought of Johnson. She hoped he was dead. She hoped he'd died in a very, *very* painful way.

Evans emerged from the truck like frightened prey leaving its den when a predator lurked nearby. Again, the feeling that he was in her territory came to her, and she felt bolstered. She hoped it wasn't an after-effect of the adrenaline.

"It's safe now," she called. "The infected have been dealt with." She liked the way condescension swirled around her words. *He can have a taste of his own medicine.*

Evans frowned at her. He hopped down and walked over to them with a firm step, no doubt terrified of appearing weak.

"Give me your hand," he snapped.

"Give me some bandages and I'll wrap it myself," Jennifer snapped right back. The adrenaline began to wear off and the gravity of what she'd done sank in. Exhaustion

squeezed her body. Had she really fought four people? She scarcely believed it.

Evan's frown looked to be turning into a permanent fixture. "I don't know where this attitude is coming from, girl, but give me your hand so I can examine it and bandage it. I'm the doctor here."

Jennifer opened her mouth to give him *attitude*, but slowly shut it instead. He was right. The adrenaline had worn off, and her forceful demeanour had bled away with it like the life from the infected people around them. Suddenly unsteady on her feet, she held up her hand so he could look at it.

As with all the times working with him, his delicate touch never failed to surprise her. He lifted her hand up to his eyes, turning it this way and that before grunting and gesturing for Owain to pass his first aid kit.

While he wrapped her hand, Danny jogged over. She hadn't noticed he'd been guarding the perimeter.

"More infected on the way, sir," he said with a wide-eyed look at Jennifer's bloodied hand. "They'll be here soon, unless they tear themselves apart first."

Evans finished with her hand. "Let's keep going, then. The sooner we get to Paris, the less we'll have to deal with madness like this."

Pierre scowled. He sucked in a deep breath to no doubt rehash the same arguments again, but Evans cut him off. "No, soldier. We tried it your way, and this was the result. We drove *directly* into the criminals and infected you were hoping to avoid. No more dallying, no more detours. *Straight* to Paris."

The two men glared at each other, neither looking to

back down anytime soon. Jennifer sighed. She was getting so tired of all this stupid infighting. Civilisation collapsed and people still found things to argue about.

"Get back in the truck," she snapped, pushing her exhaustion down and standing up straighter. "Straight to Paris, please, Pierre." Without waiting for a reply, Jennifer walked past everyone and climbed back into the vehicle. She wanted nothing more than to slump down on the uncomfortable bench, but she resisted the urge, instead sitting straight-backed with her head held high. Everyone's eyes were on her. She let her irritation bleed into her voice. "Well? What are you waiting for?"

They moved. Jennifer would have felt more exuberance if not for the weariness beating down on her. *Four* people. She was amazed at herself.

Only when they were underway again did Jennifer relax her stiff posture. Victoria gave her a look she didn't quite understand, then stared out at the scenery. The soldiers and scientists were quiet, each in their own world, but Dan was nattering away. Shy, awkward Dan?

"That was *so cool,* Jennifer. The way you elbowed that guy and ducked out from that other guy and dived on that girl. You saved Elise's life. And then you ordered everyone back on the truck, even the soldiers. So cool!" He barely paused for breath. Was he getting the same look Danny and Naomi had? Jennifer tensed. That would be horrible. *Not Dan. The little brother I never had.* She watched as he continued in his retelling of the fight, including what Victoria, Elise, and Naomi had done. No, he wasn't looking at her with reverence. It was just his boyish enthusiasm coming through. She relaxed again. *At least he's talking more, and not stuttering.*

Dan's voice eventually faded away as he sat back with a satisfied look on his face. She didn't think he had realised he'd been talking for so long. Was this the true Dan? The boy who didn't have to carry the loss of his mother and sister around with him? Jennifer hoped he was starting to heal. It was nice to see him so talkative.

As they continued driving, her exhaustion didn't fade. Feeling emboldened by her tiredness, Jennifer tentatively leaned her head on Alexia's shoulder. When Alexia didn't move away, she closed her eyes with a small smile.

Chapter Twelve

James and the others ran down the street as the rumble got louder. They reached an intersection next to a little shop when the gunfire started. It seemed so loud, almost like he was standing right next to Davison.

James didn't know London well at all, so he hung back as Teona took the lead and directed them left under a bridge. They passed people lying dead in the middle of the road, their thoughts and dreams snuffed out forever. They passed abandoned cars and bikes, some of them still sheltering their owners' gutted bodies. The sight of all the blood was managing to turn even James's stomach, and he'd seen some horrific things in his time.

The gunfire stopped. James knew they didn't have long before the infected reached them.

"In here!" Teona shouted. She darted right through a fence and ran up to the building beyond. It looked untouched by the violence that had blighted the city—all the pillars were still standing, and the clock tower was defiantly upright, gleaming in the rain.

James wasted no time diving after her. Woods slammed the door behind him, and their heavy breathing filled the air as they waited for the infected to pass. If they

even came this way at all.

It was dark and silent inside the building. The pattering of the rain could barely be heard through the thick doors, and it gave James a feeling of false security. Trueman, Ota, and Millar were watching the interior in case they were surprised again, and Woods was still pressed against the door like he expected infected to try to push through at any second. James and Teona stood in the middle of them all, weapons trained at the door.

Seconds dragged into minutes, and still there was no sound from outside. Sweat or rain or both ran down James's face. He clenched his left hand on his weapon. His shoulder was screaming, but there was nothing he could do about it.

Teona's whisper almost made him jump. "We need to try to get to Westminster Bridge, that's the quickest way back to the helicopter. On my count, open the door, just a crack, and see what's outside."

Woods nodded and did as she ordered. As he eased the door open, James tried to relax his shoulder—the last thing he needed was for it to fail him and to become even more of a liability. His heart hammered out a gruelling rhythm that put the drummer in him to shame. A thin sliver of light appeared as Woods opened the door as much as he dared, and he leaned forward slightly to peer out.

James realised he was holding his breath and released it in a long exhale. *Fuck this city. Fuck this entire fucked-up situation.* He had never wanted to be somewhere else as much as he did in that moment.

Woods stood still for what felt like an eternity, and James was sure his heart was going to drill right through

his chest. Eventually, Woods opened the door a little further and brought his weapon up, gesturing for them to follow him out.

James got to the door ahead of Teona and slipped out after Woods. The streets were quiet. Empty. That was good. He hoped it stayed that way. He moved to the fence next to Woods and trained his weapon down the other side of the street as the others made their way to them. His ears picked up faint sounds of fighting, but they were distant, and James thought they were getting quieter. Maybe they were about to have some good luck.

Sudden, sharp sounds of running feet. James resisted the urge to turn around—he was covering the opposite side. "Leave me alone!" It was a deep, masculine voice, but the pitch was raised in terror. "I have to get to my wife! Go away!"

"You tried to kill me! You tried to kill me!" That voice was feminine. The shout was followed by a shrill scream. *They must not be far into the psychosis if they can still reason and speak.* James was by no means an expert, but he'd seen enough to know that the more the disease progressed, the more they screamed and grunted instead of talked.

A weapon discharged two times and their shouts came to an end. The echoing sound made worry gnaw at his stomach. That had been heard. "Move," Teona ordered, and they started forward in a tight-knit group, heads swivelling all around.

They made it back to the little shop under the bridge before they had to stop again. James was in the middle of the group, so he didn't see, but Ota halted them as he scouted around the corner. He pulled back around almost

immediately, shaking his head and forcefully gesticulating back the way they'd come. Teona didn't ask for an explanation. She nodded and they moved off at a steady jog.

James's shoulder felt like a nail with a chain attached had been driven into his flesh and was dragging his whole body down. He gritted his teeth. There was no way he would slow them down. Besides, he didn't think Teona would let him stop even if he was at death's door. Ignoring the burning agony as it set fire to his shoulder and neck, James ran on, focusing on his surroundings through the pain.

They reached a big circular building that, like the pillar building, was still mostly standing. They hurried around it. As they ran, James saw a young man, around Jennifer's age he thought, dart out at them. He had blood all down his chest and arms and lacked shoes. His bright-blue eyes were crazed, and he ran at them with the speed of a sprinter. James stopped to aim and killed him before he got too close. The gunshot seemed unusually loud again, ringing out across the street and through the buildings. James cringed.

"Keep moving," Teona shouted, and he sprinted to catch up. Her worry warmed him, but now was neither the time nor the place for fuzzy feelings. They made it to a bridge, still running. Gunshots would attract infected like flies to shite. The Thames was choppy, the rain coming down heavier. James thought the weather summed the day up well.

They made it to the other side only to be ambushed by three infected running out from behind an overturned bus. Two women and one man. He didn't have time to think. He took aim at the man and fired, catching him in

the chest. The man screamed and fell back, writhing on the ground as he died.

One of the women was dead, but the other had managed to make it up to Millar, who grappled with her. James didn't want to shoot in case he hit Millar, so he pulled out his knife and made to run forward when Teona beat him to it. Her knife sunk into the woman's back, and the scream she unleashed was ungodly. *Like a banshee.* James had to fight the urge to cover his ears.

Teona ripped her knife out as they stumbled back, and she twisted round the front of the woman and slammed it into her chest. She was dead before she hit the ground. Teona carefully wiped her knife and hands free of blood before they moved on.

"Did she bite you?" Ota asked.

"No," Millar replied. "She came pretty close, but no."

"We don't have time to properly check you," Teona said. "We'll all get checked back at the château anyway. We have to keep moving."

"Sergeant!"

James looked to where Trueman pointed and counted eleven infected running toward them from one street, and thirteen running at them down another. "As fun as standing in the rain is, it's time to go," he said, pushing Teona ahead of him. She frowned and dropped back next to him, on his left side. Always on his left side.

They were running in the right direction according to Teona, so at least something had gone right for them. The clouds grew thicker, and the rain came down harder— their boots splashed through expanding puddles and their skin was soaked through. James was no stranger to rain,

but this wee downpour pissed him off. He had to constantly wipe water from his eyes so he could see where he was going.

They ran past another burned-out husk of a double-decker bus, the shadows of people still inside. They ran past rubble, half collapsed buildings, buildings that had somehow escaped the bombardment. They ran past bloody bodies, broken bodies, bodies of children and animals. James tried not to look too closely at those, but it was all hard to miss.

The howls of the infected kept them going. Ota asked at one point if they should stop and fire, but after a quick glance over his shoulder James shouted a firm "*No*" back to him. Several of the infected were right on their tails. They wouldn't have time to turn and fire before they were on them.

And *fuck* were they on them. James chanced another quick glance behind and felt dread hit him square in the stomach as filthy hands grabbed at him, clawing at his injured shoulder. Pain raced through his body, blinding him to all else as he was pulled back.

He hit the ground hard. His helmet took the brunt of the impact—if he hadn't been wearing it, he would have split his head open. He had never felt such gratitude to an inanimate object before. They skidded on the wet road and before James could bring his arm up the man who'd caught him bit down. James yelled in horror as his stained teeth clamped shut, but the pain never came.

At first, he thought it was because his shoulder was eclipsing everything else, but then he realised the fucking bastard had bitten down onto his armour. He was shaking his head trying to tear it open like a rabid dog and having

absolutely no success. James could have danced a jig. He slipped his knife out of its sheath and rammed it into the bastard's side. Once. Twice. Three times.

He heaved the dead man off him—no easy feat with one working arm—and quickly rolled the other way lest he be trampled by two infected. They ran straight past him. James pushed himself up and ducked out of the way of a sloppy punch. A grey-haired old man growled at him, swinging punches left, right, and centre. James backed away to give himself more room and stumbled into a young woman trying and failing to keep the gaping knife wound to her stomach shut.

She was drenched in blood. James jumped away from her only to get hit in the side by the old man. The blow wasn't hard, and James returned it with one of his own, square in the man's jaw. He went down like a stack of bricks.

He managed to pull his weapon up as another woman slammed into the side of him, screaming bloody murder. He lost his grip with the impact and the FAMAS went spinning round his side again. She was a large lady, and he almost fell to the ground for a second time. His shoulder had transcended agony and was now on another level entirely, and he was *pissed off*. With a wordless yell he jumped forward and stabbed his blade straight into the woman's throat. He didn't wait to see her die. He spun around and kicked the leg out from under a man as he stabbed another and punched another and elbowed another and on and on it went.

James didn't know how long he danced among them. When it ended, it ended suddenly, without warning. Silence. Glorious silence. He stood still, gasping for breath

and about ready to keel over with exhaustion. All around him were the lifeless bodies of people who had tried to murder him. Blood. Urine. Vomit. All washing together in the rain.

It was ugly.

It was survival.

The pain in his shoulder came rushing back into focus, pulsing in time with his heart. He was surprised it hadn't given up on him. He tried to concentrate on something else, anything else, but the blood and the death and the pain were all conspiring to send him back to that air base in France, and he was growing colder even as he sweated.

Teona. He needed to find Teona. James spun in a wild circle and saw her making her way over to him from the other side of the street. The ice thawed from his bones at the sight of her. He expelled a breath, half expecting it to mist in front of him, but it wasn't that cold.

"You all right, Sunshine?" Teona asked, her eyes moving frantically over his body.

"Aye, you?" James did the same anxious search but found her skin to be unbroken. He couldn't have described the relief if his life depended on it.

"Sergeants." Trueman nodded as he jogged over to them. "Are you both okay?"

"Yeah," Teona answered. "How are the others?" She looked around, frowning. "*Where* are the others?"

James copied her, looking over the devastation. "Ota, there." He pointed. Ota climbed to his feet a short way off next to a hotel, pulling his weapon out from under a dead body. "I can't see Millar or Woods, though."

"Okay, spread out, we'll have a quick look for them." Teona's voice held a sadness that said she didn't think they'd find them alive. James secretly agreed. *I'm not going to be able to apologise to Millar.*

They fanned out, checking all the bodies. It didn't take long to find them. Trueman was the first one to shout as he pulled Woods's body out from under a small pile of three other people. Teona shouted not long after, standing over Millar's mangled corpse, regret painting a morose scene on her face.

Ota fell into a squat, his head held in his hands. James thought it was what Jennifer would call a poignant moment, and she'd immortalise it on her camera. But she wasn't here, and James didn't need her camera. The image seared itself into his brain. A man losing his brothers all on the same day, crouching amongst bodies as rain washed over him and their final resting places.

"John Davison, Mark Millar, Adrian Woods," Ota said as he slowly rose. His eyes were wet. He closed them, his chest heaving with silent sobs, pain twisting his face into something James couldn't look at.

After a few moments, he sensed Teona take a deep breath. James knew what she was going through—he felt that stinging shame as well. He'd lost people under his command before. James would be there to support her.

"Right," Teona said. "Fuck. Okay. Let's continue." She exhaled forcefully. "No one else is dying today."

James admired her fierceness and hoped beyond hope she was right. He didn't want to lose anyone else either.

Chapter Thirteen

They continued down the street, jogging as the clouds dumped water on them in a torrent. James scrubbed himself as they ran. It wasn't his most thorough clean, but it would have to do. He didn't think he would ever feel truly fresh again.

The familiar sights of destruction greeted him as they moved on. They ran past three buses in a row, but only the middle one was blackened by fire. James saw the aftermath of a four-car crash on the other side of the road, the driver of a white Mercedes half hanging out of the window, his expensive suit splatted with blood. *Money doesn't help you when you're dead.*

They ran past a big building with the glass in the middle still standing but most of the concrete on either side in ruins. James wondered how that had happened. It slipped from his mind as they continued on. He didn't look too closely at the bodies, but he was sure they passed a group of children still holding hands. Bile burned the back of his throat. How had it come this far? How had they let this happen? He shouldn't have blindly followed orders—he should have leaked it to the press. Maybe then people would have been more prepared. But there were already

riots and protests, already people shouting that not all was what it seemed. Would his leak have gotten lost in all the noise? *I guess I'll never know.*

They passed an old-looking spire thing and Teona said Trafalgar Square was up ahead. They slowed to a walk and moved closer to the buildings for cover. James had been to Trafalgar Square a few years ago. A big open space. He didn't like it.

They edged forward, cautiously, methodically. A car had crashed into the end building before the square and they all crept up and took cover behind that. James peeked over the banged-up bonnet.

Not that there was much to look at. The pillar and statue of Nelson were miraculously still standing, but the surrounding space looked like a war zone. Which James supposed it was. The museum was half destroyed, and a tree lay broken across a road. There were craters where bombs had exploded, the white ground and stonework blackened and burned, and pockmarks aplenty where bullets had ripped through indiscriminately. It looked like something out of a film—not quite real, even though James was staring right at it all.

The bodies went without saying, and the thick stench of blood and death hung like a rancid perfume, heavy and clogging, refusing to be washed away. James had been breathing through his mouth for a while now.

"Look there," Trueman said, pointing across the Square. A man dashed through the open space, his legs pumping like his life depended on it. Judging from the two people chasing him, it did. The bulky bag strapped across his back clearly weighed him down.

"Do we intervene?" Ota asked.

"Yes," Teona answered without hesitation. "This is what we came here for, to save people."

"I can't see anyone else, civilian, soldier, or infected," James said. "We should move fast, pick the two off, and continue to the helicopter with the civilian without stopping."

"I agree," Teona replied. "Okay, when I say, Trueman and Ota move first and take an infected each. Mollino and I will pick up the civilian and we'll all be on our merry way. Three, two, one, go."

James forced aside his fatigue and pain and pushed his legs on again. After an initial protest, they fell back into the rhythm of running, and James was halfway across the Square before he knew it.

The man angled toward them. Trueman and Ota stopped, aimed, and fired, and the infected fell with two loud yells. Teona gestured at the civilian, telling him to keep running in the direction he originally was. He adjusted his course back, and Teona and James caught up, just ahead of Trueman and Ota.

They continued running in silence, for which James was grateful. He started to flag. The adrenaline that had rushed through him during the fight was fading, leaving him drained and hurting. He could see Big Ben in the distance, though, the street acting like a tunnel toward it. He couldn't stop. Not yet. Almost there. Not far now. Not far now.

The man dived into a bus next to a statue of a man on a horse, furiously gesturing for them to do the same. Without thinking, James jumped up after him, ushering Teona and the others in before following. They ran up the stairs and copied the man in lying down. James held his

body rigid as he lay on the dirty bus floor, his face inches from chewing gum and blood and who knew what else.

Silence, then he heard it. Feet pounding on pavement, along with panting breath and the odd snarl as they ran right past the bus. James held his breath. The man gestured for them to stay still while he checked out of the window. A few seconds went by as James watched him, his heart rate climbing and climbing until the man finally relaxed and slumped down into a seat.

The others were up before James. Trueman gave him a hand, and he slouched into a seat as Teona and Ota looked outside for movement.

James turned to the man. He was younger than he'd originally thought, with messy brown hair and a tangled beard. His eyes were also brown, and they were deep set in his face. His clothes were ripped and stained, but his hands were surprisingly clean.

"Have you been bitten?" James asked, diving straight in.

The man shook his head. "No, sir." He spoke like a soldier. "I've had a few close calls over the weeks but I'm all right."

"Are you a soldier?"

"Yes, sir. I never made it back to my regiment, and I've been scavenging ever since, trying to help people where I could, trying to kill as many infected as I could. Mostly just trying to stay alive, sir."

Teona sat down across the aisle from the man. "What can you tell us of what happened here after the evacuations?"

"Not a lot, I'm afraid," he answered, looking down.

"It's all one big blur now. I tried to get my friends to safety, but some died, and others were separated. Then, it was just me. I tried to join a squad, but it was too crazy, and everyone was too busy. When the bombing began, I tried to get as many people as I could underground. I was able to obtain several weapons from fallen soldiers, but I always ran out of ammo, and the sound is too loud anyway. For the past few weeks, I've just been keeping my head down. I still try to help people, but more are infected every day, and people don't trust as easily as they once did."

"Sounds like you've done the best you could," James said. He thought the lad was telling the truth—he certainly looked sincere enough. This was what a soldier was supposed to do, not what Johnson and his cowards had done.

"Yeah," the lad sighed. "Was it good enough though? I couldn't even save my friends." His shoulders drooped, and pity stirred in James's chest.

"Would you agree this city is a lost cause?" Teona pressed.

He looked up at her, opened his mouth to reply, and shut it again. He thought for a couple of seconds before answering. "Yes," he said slowly. "It pains me to say it, but yeah. Like I said, more people are getting infected every day. Better to leave while still you have the chance."

That last sentence was phrased like a question. Hope blazed in the lad's dark eyes. James was glad they'd been able to save someone. The day wasn't a total failure.

"Yeah," Teona smiled. "We have our very own helicopter. There's one complication, however."

A flurry of emotions flew across the man's face, the last being confusion bordering on apprehension.

"Some shitty soldiers, who do not deserve to be called soldiers, may have reached it first and may be holding it hostage," Teona explained. "We need to get it back from them before we can fly off into the sunset."

"I'll help," the man said quickly. "Anything to leave this place." He paused. "Am I the only person you've found besides those soldiers?"

"Aye," James said sadly. "We lost a few of our own in the process." He looked at Ota, but his back seemed a fortress.

"I'll help," the man reiterated. "Lance Corporal Rhys Coyne." He extended his hand.

The lad had a strong grip. "Sergeant James Mollino. This is Sergeant Wright, Corporal Anthony Trueman, and Private Ota." James realised he didn't know Ota's first name. He'd have to rectify that soon.

"The name's Edward," Ota said, as if he'd sensed James's thoughts. "We should move again. We've been here too long."

"He's right," Coyne said. "Never stay in one place too long. It'll get you killed."

"Okay, people." Teona stood up. "Let's get a move on."

James was the first off the bus and back into the rain. They made their way cautiously at first and broke into a jog when they didn't see anyone.

It didn't take long to reach Big Ben and Westminster. The helicopter was right where they'd left it, except there were several infected between them and it. About forty or fifty James guessed. On the plus side, he didn't see the cowards.

"Shit," Teona muttered loud enough for him only to hear. The infected were right up to the helicopter, banging on it, shouting, and screaming. More were arriving even as they watched, no doubt drawn by all the commotion. James hoped Charlie was all right and had kept his head down inside.

"What's the plan?" Coyne asked, staring at the helicopter like a man dying of thirst would water.

"We have enough ammo to carve our way through to the helicopter, but not enough for all of them," Teona mused. "Not much of a plan, but we have to move soon. More of the fuckers keep arriving."

"Let's go, then," James said, his heart in his mouth. He gave his handgun to Coyne, who nodded.

"Okay," Ota said. "If we don't make it, sergeant, I want you to know I'm glad you chose us for this mission, that you thought we were good enough. I'm also not glad at all, because it's been a fucking disaster."

Teona smiled. "That it has been. I'm truly sorry, Ota." He bowed his head. "Right, enough of all this touchy-feely shit. Try to keep close together, I don't want anyone separated in all that. Let's go!"

James pushed his tired body forward, his shoulder screaming in protest. Again, he ignored it. They opened fire and the sounds of nightmares filled the sky. Weapons roaring, people shouting, yelling, dying. It was as if the very air was screaming. James witnessed it all in a haze of red, cutting infected down until his clip ran out, then cutting through them with his knife. His mind retreated as he went into survival mode, only thinking as far into the future as the next kill.

He slashed his knife across a man's face, causing him to rear back and out of the way. He brought his left arm up to block a blow from a skinny man with long hair, and the reverberations from the impact rattled his core. James twisted and was able to slice the man's gut. He didn't know if it was a thin cut or not before he was carried away in the wake of the other soldiers.

He stabbed another man, another woman, another man, and it went on and on. His world boiled down to his knife—it became an extension of his hand, cutting his way through all the insanity to the salvation that lay ahead. He kept one eye on the helicopter as he slashed and cut and stabbed, but the infected seemed never ending in their rush, pressing in on every side so all James could see was madness personified in the warped faces around him.

He almost ran into the helicopter. Not his finest moment. Ota and Coyne were already on board, and he couldn't see Teona anywhere. Panic flared. The blades were starting to move, however, so she must be in the pilot seat. James let out a long exhale filled with relief.

He punched a man who got too close, causing him to fall back as Trueman jumped over him. "Get on," James shouted. Trueman wasted no time diving on board. James was about to follow when someone grabbed his armour and yanked him back. He stumbled and almost lost his balance, but someone else grabbed him before he could fall over.

He didn't get a chance to see his rescuer as he dived onto the helicopter. Ota pulled him further in. The door slammed shut and James lay where he was, gathering his breath and trying to calm his frantic heart.

He didn't open his eyes until he felt the helicopter

take off. He took stock—Teona *was* in the pilot seat, working her magic and taking them into the air. Charlie was there as well. Trueman, Ota, Coyne, Johnson. Everyone was accounted for.

Wait.

Johnson?

James was on him before the thought had fully formed in his mind.

"Hey—" The shout was cut off as James punched him in the face, busting his lip.

"What the fuck are you doing here?" James growled.

Johnson spat out blood and glared. "A thank-you would be nice. I did just save your life."

James opened his mouth to shout some more but Trueman's calm voice interjected. "He followed us through the path we carved, and he's right, he did pull you back." He sounded like he didn't want what he was saying to be true.

Johnson smirked. "I don't give a shit what you think of me, *sergeant*. I did what I needed to do to survive. And now I'm out of that shithole."

"What happened to the rest of your men?" Ota asked. James could tell he was furious and barely refraining from attacking Johnson.

"Dead, no thanks to you bastards," Johnson spat back. "We were chased through the city after Waterloo."

James tuned the arsehole out. He'd probably sacrificed them to save his own skin. They'd deal with him when they reached the castle. He leaned back and closed his eyes again.

They'd succeeded in one of their missions—accessing the situation in London. *FUBAR*. They'd managed to save two people, but at the cost of three. It was as Ota had said, a fucking disaster. James looked forward to getting back to France. He listened to the hum of the helicopter as they flew away from the madness below and allowed himself to relax.

Chapter Fourteen

James kept his eyes closed as they descended. Maybe if his shoulder was better the others would have survived. Maybe they could have found more people and saved them too. He struggled not to drown as guilt flooded his stomach, more painful than his shoulder.

The helicopter touched down, and Johnson was on his feet and chomping at the bit to get out. No doubt he wanted to escape the choking atmosphere inside and the barely veiled contempt everyone fired his way.

Well, James would make sure he was the last one off the helicopter. It was petty but fuck it. James wasn't feeling magnanimous.

He stood up slowly, his shoulder having long since seized up. Trueman pulled open the door and Johnson rushed to jump down but James blocked him, standing in his way like a pissed-off wall. Johnson frowned, and James bared his teeth back. No fucking way was this rat getting off until he said.

The others all jumped down, and only when Teona had finished her checks did James move. Johnson glared at him as he passed, and James glared right back. He'd tell it like it was in the debrief. The Commandant wasn't going

to suffer this one for long.

He waited for Teona and together they caught up with the others, jogging past some men going to check and refuel the helicopter. The fuel stocks were running low, but that wasn't something James could do anything about. He hoped Teona would be all right on a mission for more.

They were a solemn group as they trudged up to the castle, dropped their weapons off at the makeshift armoury, and marched on to the debrief room. James kept Johnson in front of him—he wasn't going to let the bastard out of his sight until they reached Phillipe and Roux.

The debrief room was an average size, but with eight people crowding inside it seemed smaller than it was. A large dark wooden table took up most of the space, and even the bright lighting did little to chase away the cramped feeling. The Commandant sat at the top of the table furthest from the doors with Roux at his right hand.

Teona fell into a chair halfway down the table without her usual grace, and James felt a flash of worry for her.

He took a seat next to her more slowly. The pain in his shoulder flared every time he moved, and it dulled to a sharp ache as he stilled. It wasn't until after he'd sat down that he realised he'd put himself on her right, his injured side next to her.

The others all filed around and sat down, tiredness etched into their faces. Ota shut the door, and the debrief started.

"I see two new faces amongst us, and three missing ones," the Commandant said, in that smooth voice of his. "Let me start by offering my condolences. They were good men, and they will be missed. I'm sorry. We'll hold a

remembrance service for them." Ota bowed his head. "And let me extend a welcome to you two." He nodded to Johnson and Coyne. "I can't imagine what you've been through. This castle is protected, as much as anywhere can be these days, and you can rest and recuperate here.

"Now, sergeants, your statements, please."

Teona went first. She recounted, in minute detail, everything that happened on the mission. It took a long time. Johnson tried to interrupt but the Commandant silenced him with nothing more than a look. When she fell silent, James started talking, adding his perspective. Not that he had much to contribute. Round the table they went, Trueman and Ota adding their comments, until they reached the two new men. Johnson opened his mouth to speak but the Commandant held up a hand, once again silencing the bastard without saying a word. James could have grinned at that, were they in a different place and time.

"Let me reiterate my sorrow at losing Woods, Millar, and Davison. By all accounts they died bravely," the Commandant said. He turned cold eyes to Johnson. "We'll get to you soon enough. Now, I want to hear from you, Lance Corporal Rhys Coyne."

The lad sat up straighter. "Yes, sir." He took a deep breath and launched into his story. "I want to start by saying I abandoned my post, sir. Loads of people did. Officers I admired, friends I'd worked with for years, all left. So, I did too. I apologise for that. I went to my friends. They were my family. Literally. My parents were both only children and they died in a car accident when I was sixteen."

James grunted quietly. He didn't have any family left either as he was also the only child of two only children.

"They're gone now as well," Coyne continued, sadness settling on his square face. "I saw two of them die, but I don't know what happened to Damien or Evelyn or Jen." James saw Teona flinch at the names, but she didn't say anything. The lad went on without seeing anything.

"I couldn't help Rachel or Amanda. Rachel was beyond my control, but Amanda...she was taken right next to me. I had a tight grip on her hand, but she was still... I should have saved her. I should have *done* something." Anger replaced the sadness.

The Commandant interrupted. "I'm sure you did what you could. Don't beat yourself up over things you couldn't have foreseen and, as you say, had no control over."

"That's kind of you to say, sir, but I know I'm going to live with it for the rest of my life." James felt sorry for the lad—the anger in his eyes was directed at himself. "After I lost contact with the others, I tried to get to Knightsbridge—that's where I was originally taking everyone, so I hoped they'd continue there."

James frowned as something clicked in his mind. Jen—Jennifer? She'd mentioned friends called Evelyn and Damien, hadn't she? She'd certainly been at Knightsbridge.

"—But I was pushed in the other direction by people, infected, the military. By the end of the night, I'd stopped trying and had joined a squad. It was all right at first, we seemed to be making progress. But the sheer number of infected was just too much."

James remembered that night like it was yesterday. Coyne was right, James had thought the exact same thing until a wave of infected had overrun the barricade they'd

been setting up in a street. He had been lucky to get out alive.

"The squad I joined, they're all dead or infected now. And when the order came down to bomb the city, well, that was it, wasn't it? After that I scrambled from place to place, scavenging for food and water. I helped people where I could. I helped this kid, Ethan, he stayed with me the longest." The sadness entered his eyes again. "I couldn't save him either." He sighed. "Every day was a fight to survive. I'd just escaped a little cluster of newly infected people when you found me."

Coyne stopped, looking down at his clenched hands. James was about to ask after Jennifer, but the Commandant spoke first. "Thank you for sharing. Like I said, you can rest here. We'll draft you in when you're up for it again." Coyne nodded. The Commandant turned to Johnson. "Now, tell me your story."

Johnson started speaking immediately, like he was afraid they'd try to stop him. "I was moved to Knightsbridge that night—" James frowned again, had everyone been to Knightsbridge? He couldn't recall seeing Johnson "—and it was like he said. Fucking chaos. Everywhere. It was clear no one knew what they were doing. After the bombing me and some other forgotten soldiers banded together. I'm not proud of what we did, but we did it to survive. You understand, huh? Self-preservation is a powerful thing."

"Powerful enough to turn you into a disgusting piece of shit who uses people as bait," Teona snarled, leaning forward to glare at Johnson.

"Quiet," the Commandant said. Teona sat back, but James could see she wasn't happy. He gave her a look that

said, *I'm with you*, and she nodded back at him.

"Wait," Coyne said, speaking rapidly. "You were at Knightsbridge? Did any civilians make their way there? Damien, he had brown hair, blue eyes, he was six foot. Evelyn had long black hair—"

"And brown eyes?" Johnson cut in. "And Jennifer also had brown hair and blue eyes? Both pretty?" Coyne was nodding so hard his head looked to be in danger of falling off. "Never saw the guy, but the women made it."

Coyne sat back, clearly floored. A massive smile spread across his face, twisting his beard even more than it already was. James was reminded of his own beard, which he'd shaved off almost as soon as they'd arrived at the castle. He rubbed a hand over his cheek. He'd need to shave again soon. The rough stubble prickled his skin. "Where are they? What happened?"

"Dead." Johnson shrugged, devoid of empathy. Coyne deflated, his smile fleeing like it was never there. "Killed one of them myself—she'd been bitten," Johnson continued, uncaring. Coyne's face darkened with each new word that came out of the bastard's mouth. "Don't know what happened to the other one. Probably dead as well." He rubbed his nose.

Before James could shut him up, before Coyne started throwing punches, Ota stood. "Shut the fuck up," he said forcefully. "Show some fucking decency. People are dead because of you. Good people. If I had my way, I'd throw you to the infected and be done with it." He turned to the Commandant. "That's my recommendation."

The Commandant nodded. "Noted. Please sit down." Ota did as he was told, throwing a nasty look at Johnson, who sneered back.

"Jennifer isn't dead," Teona said. "Trueman, Mollino, and I were also at Knightsbridge, it was clearly the place to be. We evacuated the civilians who were there, and Jennifer was one of them."

"Are you serious?" Coyne asked apprehensively.

"As a heart attack." Teona smiled, the first one in hours. "Wanted to be a journalist, surgically attached to her camera, immune. She's alive."

Coyne's grin returned. Were there actually tears in his eyes? "Yeah, she took her camera everywhere she went. Where is she? Can I see her?" He paused. "Wait. Immune? What do you mean? She can't get the virus?"

Johnson shook his head like he was a fucking virus expert. "Don't be ridiculous, nobody's immune."

"She is," James said, annoyed at the bastard's assumptions. "She's been bitten twice now. The doctors here are working with her to find a cure."

Johnson was still shaking his head, but the movement was slower.

Coyne looked floored again. "Jen? Immune?" He stood up. "Please take me to her."

Roux spoke for the first time. "I'm afraid I can't let any of you leave until I've checked you all for bite wounds."

James frowned. "I thought Evans always does that."

Roux looked uncomfortable. "That's another thing. The specialists need better equipment. They couldn't do much more here. They have left for Paris. Several soldiers went with them. Jennifer, Victoria, and Dan also went."

James saw Coyne's shoulders slump. *Shite*. He felt...

strange. They'd always been together, ever since everything went to shit. He'd always thought they'd get split up eventually, but when that didn't happen, he took it for granted they'd always be close. A certain type of bond formed amongst people who went through hell together, and to find out they'd gone, well, it left him feeling... strange.

"We need to go after them," Teona said, like she also felt their absence wasn't right. "When did they leave?"

The Commandant and the pilot seemed to be holding a staring competition. James held his breath.

The Commandant abruptly smiled. It was a rare sight—the man was as stoic as they came. "Why do I get the impression you are going to go regardless of whether I give you permission?"

Teona shrugged, not the least bit sheepish. James admired her nerve. "We've been together since the beginning."

James glanced at Coyne, who was red in the face, no doubt from the tension. The Commandant sighed. "Take the helicopter in the morning. You can get an up-to-date report on the status of Paris while you're there, and we can kill two birds with one stone."

"Thank you, sir." Teona nodded. "Where did they go?"

It was Roux who answered. "They went to the Institute national de la santé et de la médicale. It's a medical research facility. The doctors said they needed to take the chance that it was not destroyed and is still functioning. They've run out of ideas here. Dr Evans thinks the facility will have all the equipment they need."

The Commandant stood up. "Thank you, soldiers. It is clear to me that London is lost. I'm sorry, the price was high for that information. I suggest you all rest after Capitaine Roux has looked you over, you'll no doubt have a busy day tomorrow. You, Johnson, stay behind after the others have gone."

It didn't take long for Roux to check everyone, and he was nicer about it than Evans. As James walked through the stone corridors, passing tired face after tired face, fatigue came crashing down on him like an obsessive lover who never intended to let him go.

Teona strode next to him, a silent shadow on his left. He'd never known her to be so quiet. She would grieve in her own way, and he'd be there for her. One look at her face told him she wanted to be left alone. He respected that.

He tuned into the conversation behind them, where Trueman and Ota were walking a couple of paces back.

"I'll write a poem for them when I next have time," Ota was saying.

"You write poetry?" Trueman sounded surprised.

Ota got defensive. "Yes, what of it? Poetry is beautiful, more people should write and read it."

Trueman sounded taken aback at how vehemently Ota had spoken. "No, I agree. I'm sorry, I didn't mean to sound condescending in any way. I just wasn't expecting it. Poetry *is* beautiful."

Ota relaxed. "Sorry I lashed out. It's been a—" he searched for the right word "—*difficult* day."

James snorted softly. *That's a wee bit of an understatement.*

Ota continued. "I was often ridiculed for my interest in poetry. It's never really left me, so I get overly defensive about it."

Trueman nodded. "I understand. I was bullied at school too. But I think it's a lovely gesture. Maybe I could read it?"

James sensed Ota's smile. "Of course. And I'm sorry you were bullied. It's shit. It took me years to get over my insecurity and start writing again."

James looked over his shoulder. "I'm sorry too, for both of you."

Trueman waved them off. "It's fine. It was years ago."

"Fuck those pricks." Teona spoke for the first time since the meeting. "They're probably dead now anyway."

They lapsed into silence once more as they neared their sleeping quarters. James wondered what Trueman had been bullied about, but once he bid the others farewell and fell onto his bed without washing or getting undressed, sleep swept all thoughts from his mind.

Chapter Fifteen

The morning after leaving the castle dawned overcast and chilly. Pierre pulled over to the side of the road as the surrounding area became more built up. Victoria jumped down, animal drawn and eyes scanning the area. It was deserted. The monster in her was disappointed at the lack of confrontation, but Victoria was all too happy for it to remain quiet. *Oh, get over yourself, woman,* she chided herself. *Part of you wanted a fight. The monster isn't real, it's all you.*

It was still difficult to accept that part of herself. Half of her hoped she'd be at peace with it sometime soon, while the rest shied away from the implications. She was a murderer. How did one come to terms with that?

Jennifer had suggested they go the rest of the way on foot as the truck would have attracted too much unwanted attention, and the others agreed. Victoria was glad she'd stepped in and stopped the arguing. It had been beyond irritating.

Victoria had never been to Paris. As they walked, she had to admit it did seem like it had been a beautiful city. If one looked beyond all the rubbish and debris and death that accompanied a city abandoned to infection. Victoria

admired the buildings as they passed, always keeping one eye open for any movement.

They'd entered the north-west portion of the city. Pierre had said they'd take the wide streets as much as they could, which was how they ended up on the Champs-Élysées walking around the Arc de Triomphe. Victoria recognised it from TV, and she supposed it had once been very grand. Now, however, cars were piled up where they'd crashed, bodies were scattered everywhere, there was evidence of fire damage, and a young, infected girl saw them and ran off before any of them could put the poor kid out of her misery. The destruction drained the splendour from the monument.

Victoria walked in the middle next to Jennifer, whose head never stopped swivelling as they edged forward. Victoria understood—they were in the middle of the road, and the feeling of being exposed was insidious, curling around them like the smoke in the air.

Victoria followed said smoke with her eyes, up into the grey sky where a cool breeze blew it away. New scents hitched a ride on that wind. She wrinkled her nose as the smell of ash and bodies assaulted her senses. The whole city stank something terrible.

The group carefully picked their way around the blown-out rubble from a building that had been destroyed. When Jennifer had told them the military had been bombing major cities, Victoria hadn't known what to think. Seeing the evidence right in front of her, she still didn't know. Did she feel sadness at the destruction of humanity's accomplishments? Anger at how flagrant said devastation was? Pierre said they'd walk to the Louvre and turn south over the river there. When they reached

the famous museum what would they find? More rubble? Priceless art simply blown out of existence?

Yes, Victoria felt sadness. Anger. Maybe even a little disgust at her own species over how quickly they laid waste to their homes. But then, humans had always had a destructive nature. One only needed to open a history book to know that.

A surreal feeling hung above all her emotions. The collapse of civilisation still hadn't really sunk in.

Shaking off her wistfulness, Victoria straightened and turned her attention back to their surroundings, where it belonged.

*

Jennifer stared at the mess that was Paris. She'd heard the reports of a world gone mad, but *seeing* it? She couldn't stop staring.

There were blown-up buildings, burnt wood and cars, rubbish and clothes and bodies strewn everywhere. She tried to not look too closely at those. There was even a mattress out in the middle of the street. Graffiti graced walls and roads. *Who has the time to do that?* Jennifer wondered, perplexed. She couldn't read it, so she quickly moved on.

About halfway down the Champs-Élysées they walked past a little bike. There was nothing particularly special about it, but it stood out to Jennifer's eyes like it was illuminated by bright light. She switched her camera on and walked over to it, ignoring the flash of pain from her hand. The rest of the group stopped, and Victoria saved her from a tirade of scathing remarks from Pierre

and Dickface. Not that she would have listened to them anyway. They'd lost the right to lead when they couldn't stop bickering.

She put them out of her mind and focused on the bike. It was built for a child. Pastel pink, with tassels hanging from the handles. The chain was broken. There'd been a basket attached, which Jennifer found ripped off not too far away.

Next to the back wheel was a little shoe. One of the ones that lit up while walking. The white colouring was marred by splatters of red, and Jennifer swallowed a sudden rush of emotion. Next to the shoe and bike was a little splash of green—a tiny leaf shoot, growing up between a crack in the pavement, growing among all the death and destruction. The bright green shouted *life*, and Jennifer almost felt like crying.

It was a perfect picture.

She took several, fiddling with the settings to get it right. The shoot in the foreground and the shoe and bike behind, just out of focus. Or the blood on the shoe taking centre stage, or the broken bike. When she was satisfied, she turned back to the group, not caring about their disapproval. The shot was too good to pass up.

She quickly raised her camera again and took a picture of the group, standing in the middle of the street surrounded by ruin. She captured them all: the fear, the determination, the impatience. *Another good shot for my collection.*

It showed the horror of this virus and the loss of children. It showed the ruins of once beautiful cities. It showed the cycle of death and life. The broken bike and

forgotten shoe, left to be reclaimed by nature. Nature, already pushing through, taking back what humans had borrowed for a brief time. *Nature always wins. At least the planet will survive this.*

Shaking herself partly out of her melancholy, Jennifer frowned at herself. *Humanity* would survive as well. *They* would survive. She had to believe that. Find a cure and rebuild civilisation. Easy.

A few streets over, a dog howled. Everyone jumped. They shook it off with nervous smiles and laughter, but the fear clung to them like a bad smell. Jennifer switched her camera off and was unable to hide from her own anxiety, which ate her from the inside out. The last big city she'd been in was London, and all her friends had died. It was difficult to shake the nagging fear people were going to die here as well.

She tried to keep a tight rein on her dread as they continued down the wide street. She plastered a frown on her face to mask how frightened she was. She remembered James at the little airport as they'd refuelled the helicopter. God, it seemed like an age ago. He'd been so calm and collected, so ready to face whatever came flying their way.

Jennifer tried her best to channel how he'd been on that day.

*

They entered the grounds of the Louvre. It looked like a war zone, which, Victoria surmised, it probably had been. Bodies and blood, rubble and ruin, dust and debris. The main building seemed to have survived all right, but the big glass pyramid was gone, and only half of an archway remained standing. Sandbags and the remnants of half-

finished fortifications littered the area, and people in uniform stared sightlessly at them.

Victoria felt sorrow for the dead, and for the ruins of the history lost there. Maybe some of it could be salvaged.

She let herself feel the sadness, then moved it to one side. Now was the time for pragmatism. She eyed those unfinished fortifications, the rubble, the buildings. Any number of them could be hiding people, infected or malicious. Her skin crawled at the thought of being watched while unable to see anyone. She did *not* like how exposed they were.

Victoria relaxed her grip on her animal and let some of the monster bleed free. Nausea stole through her at the thought of unleashing it fully again, but the sick feeling was nowhere near as strong as it had been. Did that mean she was accepting this part of herself? Accepting the violence? What kind of person did that make her?

Murderer.

The whispered word sounded a lot like her mother. She'd screamed it at her, tears crowding her eyes, but Victoria had rejected it. Now, though, she truly was a murderer. Although she hadn't actively gone out of her way to try to kill people, the title still stood.

Pierre turned them to the right, and they started walking though the shadow of the Louvre to the road beyond. Cold stole over Victoria's flesh. Those unseen eyes dug into her like needles under her skin, and the hair on her arms stood on end.

She scanned around quickly, and Jennifer seemed to pick up on her agitation. Jennifer frowned at her, and her step became lighter. She moved closer to Dan.

Victoria made sure her safety was off. She scanned around more slowly. *Still nothing.* She couldn't shake the feeling of being watched, and it started to creep her out. Others picked up on her mood as well—Elise glared about them so hard Victoria thought she was going to start shooting at anything and everything, and Danny kept clenching and unclenching his jaw. Alexia and Naomi moved closer to Jennifer, and the three scientists bunched so close to one another Victoria was afraid they'd trip themselves up.

Still no movement. They emerged from the shadow of the building back out into the chilly sunlight and continued on over one of the many bridges spanning the river. They turned left and walked up the street a little bit before Pierre hesitated next to a narrow side road. Some chairs from a café were scattered about, which added to the cramped feeling of the side street.

"We shouldn't stand around for long," Victoria said, still unable to shake the uncomfortable feeling of being watched. "We have to keep moving."

Pierre nodded, although he didn't look happy. But then, when did he ever? They turned into the claustrophobic street, a sense of urgency pushing them forward. On either side of the road were shops of all kinds, from chocolate to jewellery to small art galleries. Some had the windows smashed in, the glass crunching under Victoria's boots, the sound too loud in her ears.

Victoria glanced behind them as Léa was slammed against an intact shop window, an infected woman screaming as she clawed at her. It was all so sudden—the explosion of noise, of movement, of panic. Victoria raised her animal, but Dan was in front of her, and she couldn't

get a clear shot.

Luckily, Léa was able to hold the woman off long enough for Pierre to shoot, and the street once again fell into tense silence.

The stillness only lasted a beat as Pierre pushed them on at a faster rate. "Too much noise," he said. "Quickly now."

A yell echoed down to them, startling a cat out from under a car. Victoria watched the little streak of ginger disappear down another side street. She shivered. Their position had been compromised with that gunshot.

The city—which had been abnormally quiet—erupted with ubiquitous noise.

Chapter Sixteen

Jennifer clutched her camera close as she ran, terrified of losing it. Blood-splattered buildings flashed by as they weaved their way through the winding streets. She darted past a silver car with one of its doors ripped off and jumped over a box of spilled figurines before almost tripping over a body. Her breathing came in increasingly short gasps, and she had to consciously take deeper lungfuls of air lest panic suffocate her.

Dan was ahead of her. She made sure to keep him in her sight. He kept glancing over his shoulder at her and the infected chasing them, but she kept her eyes forward. Alexia and Naomi kept pace near her, and Victoria and Danny were behind. While Jennifer's stamina had improved, lugging her backpack around was starting to wear her down. She didn't know how the soldiers did it.

Even weighed down and tiring, though, she knew she could go faster. They were running at the pace of the scientists, who weren't the fittest. Jennifer felt like a horse biting at the bit, the adrenaline surging through her and urging her to *move,* to *run.*

The abrupt, loud discharge of a weapon sent a ringing through Jennifer's ears and down into her bones. She

glanced behind her even though she didn't want to, and saw insanity reaching for them, stretching and clawing. Danny twisted and fired, opening a ragged hole in an infected man's stomach. Jennifer gagged as he fell, tripping three more in the tight street. Still more came. *Will it ever end?*

"In!"

The shout came right as Dan swerved in front of her, and Jennifer stumbled into a sharp turn. They barrelled into a shop that looked to have escaped the rioting and chaos. Victoria was the last person through the door and Pierre and Danny slammed it shut seconds before bodies crashed into it on the other side. Léa pushed a bookshelf in front, jamming it, and Jennifer finally saw they were in a small bookshop. The smell of old books washed over her, almost drowning out the stench of death that throttled the air outside.

"Keep moving," Pierre panted. "That will not hold them for long."

"It's fascinating," Louise wheezed as they moved to find another exit. "They are suspicious and paranoid, and they fight each other, but they also seem to move together in this massive group. It's almost pack-like behaviour, like dolphins in the ocean. Could they sense the infection in each other? Or it is the similar behaviours that bring them together? But they still fight each other. It's bizarre. How can they move together yet fight at the same time? I suppose it's only the ones infected for the longest time who fight, the others must stick close to each other out of commonality perhaps—"

Jennifer wanted to tell her to shut the fuck up, but she knew rambling was Louise's way. *Snapping at her*

would only show my own fear. Take a leaf out of the soldiers' book. Calm and collected.

Easier said than done when about thirty insane people were banging on the door, and they couldn't find another way out.

Jennifer pushed down the panic before it could incapacitate her. There was no other way out. The door into the back room had been barred from the other side and they couldn't get through. She clenched and unclenched her fists. Could they go back out the way they'd come in? Judging by the banging, that would be a very bad idea. What else? *Think, Jennifer, think.*

Dan pressed against the counter next to her, her constant shadow. The scientists huddled near her as well. Louise had fallen quiet. Danny and Naomi held the bookshelf in place while Pierre and Alexia kept trying the inner door. Victoria and Léa were guarding the windows.

The windows. Could they?

"Jennifer? Do you know what we can do?" Owain asked in a small voice. The skinny man had been kind to her during the weeks she'd spent with the scientists, but he'd never shown her this deference before. It was so *weird*. They were *scientists*, didn't they know immunity didn't automatically grant the ability to know what to do?

"Shoot the windows out," Jennifer said.

Victoria frowned at her. "Shoot the windows? Really?"

Jennifer nodded. "Yes." She made her voice firmer. "There's no other way out. We go through the windows. Shoot the glass, and infected while you're at it. It will disorientate them, and we can escape down the street."

Jennifer remembered running through London with her friends and how the bright flash from her camera had startled some infected. Maybe that would happen here too. "We'll get past them."

It was incredibly risky. Some would probably get caught. Looking around, Jennifer saw that the same thought was going through their minds as well.

Dickface was frowning, but he didn't say anything. He was a smart man; he no doubt saw it was either stay here till they broke through and killed them all or make a run for it and hope for the best.

"Everyone get ready to run," Jennifer said, pouring as much conviction into her voice as possible. "Don't be afraid to cut your hands on the glass when you jump out, we can't afford any hesitation." She nodded to Victoria who moved up next to the window on the right side of the door.

Jennifer pushed Dan in front of her, ready to help him through the window. Alexia gently touched her arm. "I'll protect you."

Jennifer looked into her dark eyes. She took in her sweaty face and the hair poking out from under her helmet, the sweep of her cheekbones and the determined set of her lips. She wanted to kiss her there and then, but it was certainly not the time. Jennifer nodded instead, and Pierre called out the order to shoot.

*

Victoria was the first one through the window, and she landed in a maelstrom of glass and bullets. She didn't think. If she did, she was sure she'd be screaming in

horror.

Boots thumped down next to her, but she didn't turn from her onslaught. Bodies screamed and died by the monster's hand. *No. My* hand. The animal roared and raged, and Victoria almost lost herself to the sweetness of obliteration.

The nausea she felt pulled her back from that cliff's edge. It was noticeably less than the last time she'd massacred people, but it was still there. It was still there. She wasn't completely heartless, despite what people said.

Pierre was the last out of the shop. "Cover our retreat!"

Victoria and Danny—who turned out to be the person next to her, also firing into the crowd—started edging back slowly. Victoria made sure to keep pace with him. The screams were quieter, but there were still plenty of infected people running at them, and Victoria did *not* want to get caught by madness's twisted fingers.

She reloaded and kept firing. Blood bathed the street, sliding down to coat her boots. It was ugly. Some of the infected were crying as they died. The monster relished it all. Not killing for the sake of killing, of course, but because it meant she was winning. It meant they were still living, still *surviving*. That was something to celebrate, not be sickened by. Victoria knew her thinking was distorted, but murder did that to a person.

Aim, squeeze, release. Only, she didn't need to do that here. She didn't need to aim—the crowd of infected was right in front of her and they barrelled straight into her bullets. She didn't take her finger off the trigger unless she needed to reload. She inched back, slowly sweeping her animal from side to side. The bodies fell like breaking

waves, one atop the other, smashing and roiling and screaming and dying.

The mass was suddenly no more. The remaining infected broke and scrambled back the other way, desperate to escape the ferocious teeth of the animal. Victoria let them go. It was better to save ammunition than to pick off stragglers.

Danny gave her a nod, then they jogged to catch up with the others. She ignored their bloody footprints.

Nobody said anything as they ran on. Best to get as far away as possible from all the commotion they'd created. Victoria checked her ammunition—she only had two magazines left, not including the half empty one in her weapon. Disquiet built inside, but there was nothing she could do. They'd been given five magazines each, all the castle could spare, and she'd used up two of them. She pushed aside her worry. She would make do. She'd have to.

A wail pierced the quiet a street away, but to Victoria's ears it could have been right behind her. She almost tripped over an empty bottle in her surprise. Berating herself, she pushed forward, mentally shoving the scientists on as well. *Have they never ran a day in their lives?* Still, they were some of the most valuable people left alive, and they needed protecting. *And what about your vow to protect Jennifer? Why aren't you with her?* Jennifer was up in the middle of the group with Alexia, Naomi, and Léa all surrounding her. She'd be all right. Besides, part of protecting Jennifer was protecting the scientists. If they died who knew if they'd find someone else to synthesise a vaccine?

Shouts and screams came from what seemed like

every direction. Victoria pushed her tired limbs on, relying on adrenaline to keep her going.

They blew through an open gate and ended up running on stones instead of asphalt. Trees appeared as if out of thin air, and were those tennis courts? Where were they?

Victoria stopped asking questions as a new crowd of infected almost charged into them.

Chapter Seventeen

The loud wailing of an alarm dragged James from unconsciousness. He took a moment to orientate himself, then he shoved his helmet and ran out of the door. He grabbed a man running down the corridor who was still putting his armour on.

"What's going on?" James shouted over the noise.

Confusion filled the man's eyes as he pulled away, continuing his dash down the corridor. James belatedly noticed the French flag on his uniform. He growled and followed him, fully alert now as adrenaline burned away the last remnants of sleep.

"Breach! Breach! Get a move on, you lazy shits! Plug the breach!"

James entered an atrium where a thick-shouldered man shouted from a corner, directing people down another corridor. His strong cockney accent was a welcome sound amid all the commotion.

"What's happened? Where's the breach?" James asked. He still had to shout to be heard over that awful wailing.

He was grabbed and towed away before he got an

answer. He pulled out of the grip and yanked his knife out of its sheath, but it was only Teona. "There you are, Sunshine," she yelled over the noise, looking refreshed and well-rested. James felt like his head had barely touched his pillow before he was rudely awoken, and knew he looked like shite. How did she do it?

"What's going on?"

Teona shrugged as they started running again. "From what I've been able to gather fucking infected are somehow on the grounds or in the castle itself. Don't ask me how, it shouldn't be possible."

James shook his head. The perimeter was watched, patrols were always out. Was it a drill?

But no. As they neared the doors he heard real gunfire, real shouts and screams. *Fuck, we need weapons.* He was about to pull Teona toward the armoury when he noticed the crates of weapons in the room ahead. They must have carted them here for easy access. James grabbed a pistol and an L85, the familiar weapon boosting his confidence as he and Teona burst out of the confines of the castle and into the stinging predawn air.

James saw the gate he and the others had arrived through was wide open, and infected poured through like people at a festival. Only the music here was the jarring sounds of people fighting, yelling, dying while infected screamed their madness to the black sky.

James's shoulder was surprisingly quiet as adrenaline thrummed through him. *Let's hope it stays that way.* He raised his weapon and fired at a middle-aged man. His bullet caught the infected in the gut and he went down with a thud.

James fired at five more people before the weapon essentially became useless. A young woman with blonde hair that seemed to shine even in the darkness got within his reach, and he had to drop the L85 in favour of bringing his elbow up and slamming it into her face. She fell with a scream, and James barely held in one of his own. He'd hit her with his left arm, and no amount of adrenaline could block the sudden, sharp, *intense* stab of agony. Fuck, he felt like he'd ripped his shoulder open again even after a month of healing. A cold sweat broke out over his skin, but he'd be damned if he lost himself now.

With a growl, James ignored it as best he could. He brought his weapon up and cracked it against a man's head, who fell without a sound. Spinning, James frantically searched for Teona and found her not far away, taking down infected as if fighting for her life was no big deal.

A body rammed into him from behind, and together they crashed to the ground in a heap. The air rushed out of James like he was a deflating balloon. He was almost dumped right back at the air base, bullet tearing through him, but he somehow held on to the present. His helmet took the full force of the impact as it had in London. Without it he'd have been stunned, completely at the mercy of his attacker.

But he wasn't stunned. He wasn't at anyone's mercy. He was Sergeant James Mollino of the Black Watch and *fuck it* if he didn't show these bastards that.

Ignoring the pain and cold that raced through him, James *shoved*, and the man fell to the side with a surprised grunt. That was all James let him get out. With a quick thrust, James's knife slid into the man's eye and brain, ending him where he lay. James yanked it out in a

spurt of blood and quickly stood up as two more infected rushed at him.

He stopped thinking. Teona could take care of herself, and he stamped down his worry. He hadn't seen Trueman or Ota, and he pushed aside his concern for them as well. He became pure instinct, letting himself get lost in the heat of survival. No thoughts, just actions.

Men, women, old, young, they all blurred together. James moved through them as smoothly as he was able, leaving a trail in his wake he couldn't look back at. Adrenaline coursed through him, lending him strength that convinced him he could scale mountains and swim oceans. His heart beat out a powerful rhythm, and James let himself *feel* the fight, the heat, the raw struggle to win. To *live*.

Baring his teeth, James continued to throw himself into the press of bodies. He was finally a soldier again. No more cold, no more incidents, no more weakness. Just the fight.

A young soldier was about to be overrun, and James ran to help. He let his momentum carry him into an infected who'd been about to take a chunk out of the soldier's neck, and he stayed on his feet as the infected fell. James ended him a second later with a slight pull on the trigger. The young soldier nodded their thanks and turned to engage more infected.

There were *so* many. It must have been another horde, like the one in London. James shivered as memories surfaced, and he quickly shoved them aside as more infected came at him. The thrill of survival took on a desperate hue, and James struggled to hold off four of them at once. He stuck his knife in an infected person's chest. A bad move: it jammed there, and he lost his grip as they

fell. James bit down on frustration. He pulled his L85 up and slammed a man in the cheek with it, the bone giving way under the impact. Two more women were already attacking even as he dealt with the man. James trusted his armour to blunt one woman's teeth, and instead stepped into the other woman's reach. He battered aside clawing hands and punched her in the solar plexus. The woman wheezed as she crumpled.

He needn't have worried about the other one. Trueman was there, and the infected was dead from a bullet buried in her back. There was a lull, and James came back to himself. *Shite.* All around him was a clamour of noise, and the stench of blood clogged the air, hovering over them like the heavy clouds obscuring most of the sky. His shoulder screamed, his breathing was laboured, and his heartbeat pulsed in his skin. He pushed past all the distractions, refocusing on his duty. *Please be a soldier again.*

"Status report," he shouted at Trueman.

The corporal looked worse for wear. Sweat made clean trails through the all the blood and grime on his face. "They're in the castle, sir! I don't—" He cut off as three infected charged at them.

As the last one fell, James saw something small next to the castle doors. He couldn't properly see in the night, but he knew the little figure had black ringlets that framed a face much too joyless for her age.

James moved. He ran as hard as he could, his muscles straining as he pushed faster, *faster*. An infected woman was also running for the girl, but James was faster, *faster*. The little girl looked up with wild eyes as he scooped her into his arms, his shoulder protesting the

sudden weight even though she was as light as a feather. She wrapped tiny arms around him as he struggled to bring his L85 up, but it was all right as Teona, Trueman, Ota, and Coyne formed up around him, and Ota shot the running infected.

The little girl buried her head in his neck. He could feel her tears. James's heart broke for her, for all the children lost and abandoned to this virus. The world had always been a shitty place, but children were supposed to be protected from it all. They were supposed to be free and innocent, unrestricted by the burdens of adulthood. This little girl had been deprived of all of that.

"We have to get to the helicopter!" Teona shouted. "This place is lost!"

James looked around. He saw bodies everywhere, people running, shouting, dying. Soldiers fought alone or in pairs, and those who formed groups disintegrated immediately. He saw people run past with fresh bite wounds. There was no cohesion, no discipline. Anger bubbled up, but it dissipated a second later. Facing enemies on a battlefield was one thing, but this screaming insanity was something else entirely.

A body was thrown out of a window next to them, causing them all to flinch as another fell from the walkway above and landed with a sickening crunch. *"Helicopter,"* James agreed.

They set off together, keeping close as infected ran at them. James was in the centre with the girl, and they moved as fast as they could, which wasn't as fast as James wanted. They were mobbed by infected. There didn't seem an end to them—for each one they cut down two more clambered over the bodies.

James's world boiled down to gunfire and screaming and holding the girl as tight as he could. Her tears burned him. They had to be near the helicopter. The gloom obscured his vision, but they *couldn't* be too far away.

An explosion rocked the sky across the grounds, and heat washed over him as sudden light blinded everyone. He crouched down, blinking to clear his vision. One of the cars had gone up. Burning bodies surrounded the fire in a blown-out ring. Some were still moving. James turned away, unable to help.

The extra light illuminated the helicopter, and they ran to it, free from attacks as the infected took longer to gather themselves after the explosion. Teona ducked into the pilot seat as Trueman slid open the doors and jumped up, and James passed the girl up to him.

As her weight lifted, James sighed in relief. He didn't think his shoulder could have supported her for much longer.

Coyne scrambled up next, but James stepped back. He'd cover everyone. Raising his weapon was like lifting dumbbells that were too heavy, but he strained anyway, unwilling to be beaten by his injury. A small voice in the back of his mind said he'd damage it further if he kept pushing, but he ignored it. He'd protect his friends as they got in the helicopter. *Please be a soldier again.*

It seemed to take an age for the blades to begin turning. James willed them on as he fired his last bullet and grabbed more ammunition from a pocket. His shoulder was on the verge of giving up on him, the pain so constant now he was almost beyond feeling it, but he kept firing, kept pushing. *Just one more infected, then I'll jump up. Just one more.*

One turned into five, into ten, into fifteen. The blades were faster now, blurring into one as the wind whipped at him. James was about to jump up when he saw the Commandant and Roux, with Charlie, Riya, and Aarav, and the bastard Johnson. They were running toward the helicopter, so James shot two infected and cleared a way for them.

Riya, Aarav, and Charlie jumped up immediately, as did Johnson, much to James's dismay.

"Evacuate as many as it can hold, sergeant!" The Commandant and Roux fell in next to James, fighting to clear a way for the soldiers trying to reach them.

The next few minutes—hours? Time lost all meaning—were filled with loud bursts of gunfire, scenes ripped straight out of nightmares and the strong smell of smoke blanketing everything. It was all tinged with pain and that persistent cold feeling as he struggled to hold back another *incident*. James stepped aside as a soldier ran past and was pulled up by Trueman. The only one to make it to them so far.

Teona shouted something he couldn't hear, but he could guess. *Time to leave.* James started inching back toward the helicopter, and everything went wrong.

A big, infected man slammed into the Commandant, pushing his weapon down and biting into his neck. Roux screamed as his cousin grappled with the man, and James had to spin and protect the now unguarded right side. Together, Roux and the Commandant managed to get the infected away, and Roux killed him as he regained his balance.

The Commandant clutched his neck as he winced, blood seeping out. "*Go,*" he roared at them, and threw

himself into the mass of madness, wordlessly yelling as he fought with a ferocity that shocked James.

He pulled Roux back, but the doctor yanked himself out of his grip. "I'm not leaving him! I can't! He's the only person I have left!"

James opened his mouth to shout him back as he dove after the Commandant, but a grunt came out instead as two infected rammed into him. He felt a moment of blind panic as he fell back against the helicopter, which had started to lift off the ground.

Adrenaline surged through him, and he managed to shove away one of them, and they were promptly shot by someone from the helicopter. The other one, though...

James heaved, desperate, but the man had the upper hand. Still, James pushed, throwing all his depleted strength against him, trying to get him off, trying to stop his mouth from inching closer. He could already smell his rancid breath.

Something gave, and James screamed in agony. His left arm fell uselessly to his side, and it was all he could do to keep the teeth away, to keep the cold away. His heart pumped out a panicked beat, and James almost lost himself before his assailant grunted and some of his weight lifted.

Hands on him, pulling him up and away. The infected man didn't give up easily. He grabbed James's clothing, straining to pull him back down. When James continued up into the helicopter the man yelled and tried to bite him, but his teeth were rebuffed by his armour. James still had the presence of mind to kick him, and he stumbled back. James almost cried as he was dragged further into the helicopter.

Someone slammed the door shut, and an odd weight-lessness settled over James as the helicopter lifted into the sky. He lay there, staring at up at nothing, trying to bring his erratic breathing under control.

His mind fell back into old rhythms. *Take stock.* He started with himself. He felt drained, bruised, and bat-tered, and he was pretty sure he'd damaged his shoulder beyond repair, but he hadn't been bitten. He hadn't been bitten. That was a win.

James gritted his teeth against the unrelenting pain. *Fuck, it's fucked.* He tried to focus on something, *any-thing* else, like who'd made it, how many, was anyone in-jured? But he couldn't. His thoughts moved more sluggishly, slipping away as he struggled for clarity. Obliv-ion whispered to him, sweet promises of no pain, no struggle.

In the end, James sighed and let the warm darkness embrace him.

Chapter Eighteen

Jennifer ran, looking alternatively at Alexia, Dan, and everyone else to make sure they were still with her. She couldn't believe her half-thought-out plan had worked. Victoria and Danny had blown them all away. She was still shocked at Victoria's cold, methodical way of cutting people down, but she was more than thankful for it.

Her thighs burned, her lungs burned, her wound burned, yet she kept on going. To stop now would be death. They ran through a gate in a stone wall and Jennifer almost lost her footing on loose gravel. Trees rose all around her, bare branches still in the chilly air.

She'd been able to hear a low rumbling for a while, below all the shouting and noise, and it seemed to be reaching its peak as they continued past some tennis courts. She risked a glance over her shoulder in time to see another large group of infected swing round at them. One man almost grabbed Victoria, but she twisted out of his reach.

Jennifer's heart continued its frantic beat as her lungs took in ever greater gasps of air. She was sure she shouted, "Keep going," but she had no real recollection of doing so. The pathway split into two sets of steps, and she

followed Dan down and out onto an open area that would have been a gorgeous photo opportunity if she wasn't running for her life.

A huge building stood tall and proud to their left—it had to be a palace—and a large pond spread out in front of it with a fountain in the middle. To the right, a massive wall of trees began, with two corridors of gravel cutting through them. Jennifer couldn't see where they went. She was too preoccupied with the infected chasing them and the other crowd of infected in front of them.

If they weren't practically mindless, Jennifer would have thought it a perfect execution of the hammer and anvil strategy Rhys had told her about once.

Some of the ones in front of them had been fighting among themselves, some were drinking from the dirty pond, others sat on the ground and rocked backward and forward, while still others paced around, muttering to themselves. Some were emaciated, others looked freshly infected. As their group skidded to a halt at the bottom of the steps, Jennifer felt the weight of hundreds of eyes abruptly trained on her, and the hair on the back of her neck stood on end.

She couldn't see a quick way out of this. This was going to be a slaughter worse than the one Victoria and Danny had committed.

People were going to die.

Perhaps all of them.

Fuck.

*

If Victoria cursed, she'd sound like a sailor as her eyes drank in the horror around them. Years of her mother drilling into her that swear words were horrible, terrible things, and later when she became a teacher and couldn't swear in front of the kids, she had never gotten into the habit.

If she did swear, though, she would be saying things like *shit,* and *fuck,* and maybe even *motherfucking twat.* She'd heard an eleven-year-old girl say that once.

They were surrounded.

She moved over to Jennifer. They had a snowball's chance in hell of getting out of this, but if they did, she needed to protect Jennifer. *What is she doing?* Victoria frowned as Jennifer turned her camera on and took several pictures in quick succession. Victoria almost batted the damn thing out of her hands. *Idiot. We're about to be killed and she's taking pictures?*

Everything happened quickly after that. The frenzied infected behind them whipped those in front of them up, and a deafening roar took residence inside Victoria's ears. The infected surged forward like a tsunami tide, intent on wiping everything from its path. Victoria became aware of sensations instead of thoughts—the sting of sweat in her eyes, the smell of unwashed bodies, the weight of her animal in her arms. Not a lot of bullets left. Certainly not enough for all this. She would have to rely on her hand-to-hand skills. She was good enough, wasn't she?

Looking at the running press of infected in front of them, she felt her confidence dwindle to next to nothing.

Shouts from behind. Gunfire rang loud, cutting through the roar as Pierre gestured desperately for them to follow him. He ran to the wall the steps split around

and put his back to it. *Yes, we can hold here.* Hold for what? They'd be safe from attacks from behind, but they'd be stuck. Still, Victoria ran over. *It's not like we have a multitude of options.* She dropped her backpack on the ground and squared her feet.

They would have to cut their way out eventually, but for now it would do. The scientists were against the wall with Dan and Jennifer, and Victoria and the soldiers formed a semi-circle around them.

Victoria's world deflated to right in front of her.

Blue sky. Dusty ground. Red splashed across the middle. She unleashed the animal, and with it, the monster. *No holding back.* She hadn't truly felt this in almost two months, not even killing the infected earlier. This, *this* was pure instinct. Pure survival. Victoria revelled in it.

The animal was music to her ears, spitting out bullet after bullet until there was none left. She stepped back and let the others expend their ammunition, which happened all too quickly for Victoria's liking. They didn't seem to have even made a dent in the bulk of infected.

Behind her she could hear faint crying. She didn't turn to see who it was. She couldn't turn from the boiling press of madness, screeching, clawing, unrelenting in its push ever closer.

As soon as the last bullet flew, Victoria threw herself forward. She didn't think. The monster was fully in control, and she trusted it to keep her alive for as long as possible. She didn't focus on the infected. To her, they were all one big creature with seemingly never-ending teeth and claws. She threw punch after punch, kick after kick. They landed on jaws, cheeks, stomachs, groins, legs. One man fell with a broken arm, another with a dislocated

knee. A woman got within her reach, so Victoria elbowed her in the face and felt her nose smash like an egg. Blood coated her, and none of it was hers.

She didn't think about potentially contracting the disease herself.

She didn't think about anything.

She found she had an open space around her as the others held back. Good. She didn't want them to get caught up in her whirlwind.

A young man ran at her, so Victoria kicked him in the stomach to keep out of his reach. A middle-aged woman jumped forward next, spraying spittle, and Victoria punched her in the face. She reared back and tripped another woman. The young man was back, hands balled into fists and teeth snapping. Victoria ducked a punch and slammed one of her own into his kidney, causing him to flinch to the side. She straightened up and smashed a fist across his face. He dropped with a grunt.

A muscular woman stepped up next. She looked like she knew what she was doing. The monster purred at the challenge.

Victoria blocked a punch and returned one, only to have that blocked as well. The woman shouted something at her in French, but Victoria ignored her. She smiled a feral smile that Victoria wanted to wipe off her stupid face.

Another punch, another block. The monster growled in frustration. A kick, a dodge out of the way. She was getting nowhere. A flurry of moves. She managed to land a punch, but the woman twisted in time, so it had no force behind it.

Blinding whiteness. Ears ringing. Sight returned,

blurry. Victoria spat out blood, shaking her head to try to clear the sting. Two women shook into one, smirking that annoying smirk. Victoria growled. She wanted a fight? She'd give her a fight.

Bringing her guard up again and planting her feet, Victoria smiled a bloody smile right back. Stepping forward, she feigned a jab and twisted for a hook. She failed to complete the move as something rammed into her back and knocked her off balance. The woman sensed her opportunity and leaped forward, only to be hit in the side by Léa. The soldier continued forward—Victoria thought she had *fallen* into the woman by mistake instead of purposely attacking her.

That was all Victoria had time to see as she yanked her arm out of the way of snapping teeth. Pivoting on the ball of her left foot, she smashed her fist into an infected person's face whilst simultaneously kicking the leg from under another. Unable and unwilling to quench the bloodlust rising inside, Victoria let it consume her.

Infected after infected fell to her one-woman army. She felt herself tiring, but if she fell here, she'd die. *That* was a certainty. She pushed on through the haze of fatigue, fists and feet flying almost with a mind of their own. She faintly registered pain from her knuckles but carried on. She'd deal with the bruising when she made it out. *If* she made it out.

An uppercut to a jaw. A kick to a shin. A jab to a nose. A knee to a groin. On and on and on. She wasn't killing, unfortunately, but at least she was incapacitating and knocking out.

She was so lost on the exultation of the fight that she almost missed what happened next.

Léa, having recovered from her fall earlier, flew past Victoria in a whirlwind of fists and steel. *Bloody hell, how did I forget my knife!* Victoria was still rebuking herself as she dispatched yet another infected and turned to block another. Léa's knife stuck in a body, and that split second of stillness ruined her momentum and opened her up to attack. No less than four infected crowded her, and she fell to the ground under their weight with a ferocious yell.

Victoria didn't see what happened after that, but she could guess. If the poor soldier wasn't ripped apart, she'd be trampled by the rest of them. A dull sense of grief was overwhelmed as the bloodlust surged anew. *She* wouldn't be overcome. *She* would beat them all.

Victoria spun away from where Léa fell, only to see the same thing happen to Pierre. One infected man had a tight hold of his arm as another tackled him to the ground. Three more jumped in, and the whole mess devolved into infected fighting infected. She saw Pierre briefly push himself to his knees, but that was as far as he got before a woman dived on him from behind, teeth sinking into his neck as they fell back to the ground.

Grieve later. Panic later.

Terror knocked its way to the forefront of her mind. There were simply too many infected to fight. She fought down a further two that charged at her, and her exhaustion tightened its grip, making her feel like she had weights tied around her arms and legs.

Need a new plan. This is going to get us all killed. She didn't know what to do. Both the soldiers and Victoria had been pulled out of their tight ring around the others, exposing them. Jennifer was fighting off two women, but she wasn't as good as Victoria, and she was almost

overpowered. Victoria noticed no less than three new bite marks on Jennifer's arms.

She made the split-second decision to abandon her little holding area and dash back to the wall. On her way she knocked down four people, but they'd rise again. She reached the scientists in time to stop Owain from being bitten, and she sent the infected man stumbling away with a broken nose.

Louise was crying. Owain looked like he was in shock. She left them in relative calm to help Jennifer, picking up her animal on the way. She rammed the bayonet into one woman's back as Jennifer punched the other in the face, making her lose her footing and opening her up to a bayonet in the gut. Jennifer was breathing so hard Victoria was afraid she'd start hyperventilating and pass out.

She didn't have time to ask how she was as the four infected she'd knocked down reappeared, like stupid kids with bad attitudes. Victoria whacked one woman around the head with the butt of the animal and slit another man's throat as she swung the animal back around, but the others crowded too close. She had no option but to drop the weapon. She snapped the man's leg easily enough with a sharp kick, but the woman dodged out of the way of her jab. The kick and punch left Victoria overextended, and the monster in her cried out as the woman grabbed her and pulled her in. Her mouth was a gaping maw of bad breath and yellow teeth, and madness lurked within.

Victoria thought her life was supposed to flash before her eyes at this point, but all she saw was the woman's frizzy hair and saliva-coated chin. And...Jennifer?

Jennifer barrelled into the infected woman, sending them both tumbling to the ground. Rugby tackling people

seemed to be her go-to move. It gave Victoria the precious seconds she needed to grab her animal again and ram the knife into the woman's face.

Victoria pulled Jennifer to her feet as a large, infected man slammed Naomi against the wall and ripped her helmet off. Before Victoria could even think to help, he banged her head against the wall once, twice, and dropped her lifeless body to the ground, letting out an ear-splitting yell as he did so. He seemed more like a beast than a man.

His howl turned from triumphant to pained as Danny stuck his knife in his back. Danny ducked a wild swing and lost his grip on the knife, which remained lodged in the big man's back. Victoria ran, pushing her tired limbs forward. They were slow to respond, but she got there in time to rip the knife out, prompting another violent roar. Danny kicked him in the groin and when he doubled over Victoria slammed the knife home in his throat. The man fell like a puppet whose strings had been cut.

She and Danny shared a look that said, *this is hopeless*, and the soldier jumped back into the fray. Victoria had a second to catch a breath before she too threw herself back into the fight. She dispatched an infected man and saw three dart past their failing defences. Only Victoria, Danny, Alexia, and Elise remained.

She couldn't extract herself. The infected ran to the scientists who cringed back against the wall. *Fight them! Defend yourselves!* Victoria wasn't going to lie to herself, the pitiful way they conducted themselves brought disgust, not pity. They were the smartest people here and they didn't know how to throw a punch between them.

Owain died first. He fell with a broken neck. Louise went second, swarmed by two of them as they all fell to

the ground. Victoria heard her piercing cry above all the cacophony. A small stirring of pity arose then, but it faded in the face of desperation.

David was bitten, but Victoria didn't see his death as three people crowded her. She fought them off, but at a cost. Her muscles were like jelly, and the sting of her bruised knuckles was getting harder and harder to ignore. Sweat stuck her hair to her head under her helmet and she couldn't catch her breath. She was dying for a drink. Water sounded like the best thing in the world.

She thought she heard a low humming above all the screaming and fighting and dying, but she put it down to her fatigued mind playing tricks on her. Side kick to the stomach, jab to the cheek, duck a powerful swing. She barely got out of the way. So tired. So thirsty. She took hits. Got in a few of her own again. Block. *Get out of the way of those teeth.* The monster in Victoria was quieter, although it still rumbled. How long had they been fighting? It seemed like hours and minutes all at once.

Sudden roaring. Like her animal, but more. *What is that?* Infected around her were running, scrambling over each other in their haste to get away. Victoria stared after them, her sluggish mind not comprehending. She was slow to register the wind slashing at her face, the thrum of blades slicing through the air, the sharp pop of gunfire. She turned and saw salvation hanging in the sky, spitting fire at the fleeing infected. Victoria fell to her knees, her tired legs giving out in the face of rescue.

The helicopter landed upon what seemed like hundreds of bodies, blades not ceasing in their assault upon the air. Victoria felt like crying as Anthony and James and others jumped down, weapons blaring. Dan pulled her to

her feet, and they grabbed a couple of backpacks before they were moving, running through the wind and blood and death, running to safety. The soldiers gestured them on, but Victoria stopped to hug Anthony. She had no doubt she'd be dead if it not for his training. She squeezed tight, then let herself be ushered onto the helicopter.

It was crowded. Would they all fit? Especially with the large packs. Victoria sat on the ground next to the little girl from the castle—what was she doing here? And was that Riya and Aarav? What had happened?

It didn't matter. All that mattered was that they had survived. Jennifer was still alive. And...David? But he'd been bitten. Well, maybe he could tell them what to do before they had to put him down.

The doors slammed shut and the engine screamed as they lifted off again. Victoria let her head fall back against the wall and breathed out a long breath.

They'd escaped. They hadn't even reached the research centre they'd been trying to get to, and half of them had died, but half of them had escaped.

Victoria looked around the cabin, taking in the shock and fatigue and astonishment on people's faces.

Survivors, all of us.

Chapter Nineteen

James awoke to white-hot pain and a child staring at him. He didn't know which was worse—the agony or the creepy child-stare. He remembered passing out on the floor of the helicopter. *Fuck.* That single word somehow managed to encompass his every emotion and his entire situation.

They were still flying. James didn't know where they were going. He didn't particularly care at the moment, as long as it was away from the shit storm they had barely made it out of. His shoulder screamed at him, and he felt like passing out again, but the little girl's big eyes kept watching him, and the heavy weight of responsibility settled on his back.

He forced out a smile for her, but he wouldn't be surprised if it was more of a grimace. The girl took it as an invitation to shuffle closer. He didn't even know her name. He couldn't look after her. Would she imprint on him? *She's a child not a duck, James, fucking hell.* Still, he didn't want a child following him around. Best to give her to one of the civilians to look after.

He took stock. He was more than sure his shoulder was a lost cause, and he gritted his teeth against the wave of self-pity that accompanied the realisation. He would

deal with it. Maybe one of the scientists would help him now that Roux...

James shook his head. Good people had died. *What a waste.* They needed somewhere secure to rest and recuperate. What was stronger than a fucking castle? James didn't know how they'd gotten in. Maybe some infected got the jump on a patrol? Given the sheer numbers, James couldn't rule out the theory that they'd simply stormed the gates. The next place they settled at needed to take that into account. *Find somewhere not easily accessible.* Maybe they could find a ship and live out at sea? *That brings its own challenges, though.*

What of the scientists? Were they still alive? Maybe they could find them in Paris.

James slowly pushed himself to his shaky feet, and Trueman reached out to steady him. He had so little strength. He nodded his thanks and stumbled over to the cockpit where he tapped Teona's shoulder. She turned and smiled up at him. Warmth filled him. *Fuck me, she's beautiful.* No more pissing around. No more stalling. He was going to kiss her and thank her for waiting for him.

"Where are we going?" James had to shout to be heard over the hum of the helicopter.

"Paris," she mouthed back at him.

Paris. James only had his handgun now, but that was all he could handle anyway. He nodded and went around everyone, checking their armour and ammunition. Nobody had made it out unscathed. Blood splattered everyone, even the little girl, and James had no idea whether it was infected or not. He made a mental note to burn all their clothing as soon as they had replacements. Ota had a cut on his cheek, but Trueman was already seeing to

him. Trueman himself had a busted lip and a bleeding nose.

Johnson appeared the least affected, even less so than Aarav and Riya. The civilians had more blood on them than the soldier, and Aarav's knuckles were all cut up.

James growled deep in his throat, but it was drowned out by the helicopter. Johnson was despicable. He had no right to call himself a soldier. James turned away from him before he did something rash like attack him in the middle of a crowded, confined space while he struggled to stay upright.

After his rounds, he sat back down again. He almost fell, but he managed to maintain his dignity and lowered himself with care. The little girl was back, slouching closer as James rested his head against the wall. He'd never wanted children. He thought them noisy, smelly, and gross, and he'd never wanted anything to do with them. This girl, though, she was too quiet. It was unnerving. Hopefully when she got older, she wouldn't remember the horrible shite that happened at the castle. Hopefully she would be able to grow up at all.

He was too tired to be thinking about that. Best rest before they reached whatever awaited them in Paris. James closed his eyes again, and even though he was uncomfortable and in pain, sleep came almost immediately.

As did consciousness, what seemed like mere seconds later. Ota shook him awake, and James knew they were over the French capital from the way everyone was preparing. He pushed his weary body up as he felt the helicopter bank, and briefly saw a devastated city spread out below before the image turned back to morning sky.

James went through the motions—checking his armour and weapons. Nervousness crept through him, settling in next to his fatigue like they were old friends.

The helicopter flew around for a while before it started to descend. Coyne pulled open the door, letting a rush of cold on board to do battle with the warm, stuffy air inside. Coyne, Trueman, Ota, and the soldier they'd rescued positioned themselves and started firing. James couldn't see the extent of the madness down on the ground, but he could guess from the amount of ammunition they were using.

The helicopter touched down with a slight jolt, and James was greeted by a sight of pure carnage. Bodies everywhere, the ground drowned by savagery. And there, with their backs to a wall, were three soldiers and four civilians. All covered in blood. All exhausted. James was sure Jennifer would love a picture of this from his point of view.

He jumped down, the impact jarring enough to make him worry about blacking out again. He emptied his handgun into a few infected as Jennifer and the others ran to them, then they were up in the air again, the blades straining to carry them away from the slaughter below. He hoped there wasn't too much weight on board.

It was cramped in the cabin. James pressed up against the cockpit as Coyne shoved Danny Fuller further in so he could shut the door. His shoulder was in constant danger of being knocked, but he tried not to let anyone get close enough. Easier said than done. James watched Trueman squeeze his way to Jennifer to clean and bandage the new wounds she had. James could see three bites, all bleeding quite heavily. He hoped she'd be all right.

Alexia, Elise, and Fuller—and he supposed Victoria—didn't have their weapons anymore. *It's got to be a miracle they survived.* Roux had said they'd left with six soldiers, and only three remained. And the scientists? James could only see Evans, and was that a bite mark? James craned his neck to get a better look. Aye. *Fuck.* The doctor's blood ran in bright-red rivulets over his knuckles, dripping corrupted drops onto the floor. James thought of Martin then—he didn't know if he'd be able to kill another hapless civilian.

He turned away from the doctor. Young Dan stood at the back of the cabin close to Jennifer, and from the look of him, James thought he'd be on the floor if not for the press of bodies holding him in place. He was in shock, clear as day. But any conversation would have to wait till they landed. James hoped the boy wasn't too lost to his trauma. He watched as Dan blinked when Jennifer squeezed his hand. There was hope for the lad yet.

Everyone was still for most of the flight, staring into space, lost to memories. James noticed the frightened looks Johnson kept throwing at Jennifer, but she didn't seem to have noticed him yet, hunched in the corner as he was. James secretly hoped she went crazy at him and beat him to a pulp. He'd do it himself if not for his shoulder. He also saw Coyne staring at her with tears in his eyes. What would it be like, James wondered, to find a friend or family member again? He would cry too.

They seemed to be flying for ages, penned in the uncomfortable cabin like sheep for the slaughter. James estimated over an hour had passed since they'd taken off, but he felt Teona lower the helicopter to the ground even as the thought crossed his mind.

She shut the engine off. James listened to it power down, until silence reigned. With a sigh, the pilot hopped out of the cockpit and heaved open the door to the cabin, allowing sunlight to spill in. How long had it been since the breach at the castle? The late morning shadows stretched out, and James felt like he hadn't slept for about a week.

He stepped down carefully, his weary body protesting every movement. Where were they? Teona had landed the helicopter on a hill, and James saw rolling land stretching out for miles. He breathed in a deep breath. The air was clean and crisp, the freshness leaving him somewhat invigorated. Were they back in the UK? The rolling hills certainly fit the part.

The others filed out, stretching or simply sitting down on the grass. James wanted nothing more than to join them on the extremely inviting ground, but he held his back straight as Teona stood next to him. Calm confidence. That's what everyone needed right now. Someone who looked like they knew what they were doing.

Before he could say anything, he noticed Jennifer frowning at Coyne. She still didn't seem to have noticed Johnson, who was squatting at the back of the group out of everyone's way. James let the silence continue for a moment until the penny dropped for her.

"I'm sorry," Jennifer said to the young soldier. "You look really familiar."

Coyne, still fighting back tears, nodded. "You've never seen me with my hair grown out or with a beard."

James watched Jennifer's eyes widen. "Rhys?"

"Yep," Coyne said, grinning like a madman.

"*Rhys.*" Jennifer ran to him, and James smiled a tired smile as the two lost friends embraced, both crying freely. It was good to see some happiness amid all the shite.

"Oh my God, I thought you were dead. I thought everyone was dead." Jennifer was talking a mile a minute. "It's so good to see you, Rhys, oh my God. Are you all right? What happened?" Jennifer sobered. "Amanda?"

Coyne shook his head, and the two embraced again. "It's just us now, Jen." He let her go and smiled, clearly trying to keep the conversation happy. "I hear you're immune. Check you out, should have known you wouldn't let something like a deadly virus that's decimated humankind stop you."

Jennifer laughed, tears making her cheeks shine. It was good to hear someone laugh. "Yeah, it's just a pesky virus, I don't see what all the fuss is about," she said as blood seeped through her bandages. James snorted.

"Okay," he said. "You two can get back to your reunion in a minute. We need to know what happened. Let's exchange stories, shall we?"

James and Teona took turns retelling what happened at the castle, with the others who'd been there adding the odd comment. Everyone listened in silence, and when James told them of the deaths of the Commandant and Roux, Jennifer and Dan winced, Dan wiping away tears.

"And then we flew to Paris, picked your sorry arses up, and now we're here," Teona gestured around her. "Back in jolly old England."

England. It wasn't Scotland—far cry—but at least he was closer to home than France. James felt bolstered at being back in the UK. He hadn't wanted to leave in the

first place.

"Tell us what happened to you lot," James said. "You were supposed to go to a research facility?"

"We needed better equipment." Evans's voice came from the ground where he sat cradling his arm. He looked nothing like the egotistical doctor James had come to dislike. "We never even got close."

Jennifer nodded. "It was..." A haunted look entered her eyes.

After a tense silence Victoria sighed. She launched into one of the most detailed, horrific accounts James had ever heard. It really was a *miracle* they'd survived. It had been an absolute bloodbath.

And I thought the castle had been bad.

"Shit," Teona breathed. "We've suffered a lot of losses recently, but we'll pull through. I've had the privilege of getting to know most of you, and I know you're a tough bunch of sons of bitches. We carry on. We'll survive." She nodded, conviction dripping from her words. "We'll set up camp here, rest, eat if you can. It's half rations, mind—I didn't stock the helicopter for this many people."

A general tiredness hung over the group like a dark cloud, and James could tell everyone was pleased for a rest. He himself wanted to lie down and sleep the day away, but he remained on his feet. As everyone was settling down and passing around rations and water—James saw some people immediately start cleaning themselves—he moved over to Teona.

"Hey."

"Hey, Sunshine, how're you holding up?" She looked at him with a critical eye, her gaze lingering on his

shoulder. The damage was hidden by his clothing.

"I've been better." James smiled. "Look, there's something I've been meaning to do." He took a deep breath and spurted it out. He hated beating around the bush. "I like you, and I'm sorry I haven't acted on my feelings before now. But I'd very much like to kiss you—"

He didn't get any further as her mouth pressed against his. All thought cut off as he moved his lips against hers. Why had he put this off? Her mouth was soft and inviting, and he would gladly go without air if it meant keeping her pressed against him.

She pulled away after a kiss that was entirely too short. He distantly heard a wolf whistle from behind him, and Teona flipped someone off with a big grin on her face. She patted his cheek. "I'm glad you finally see sense. There'll be plenty more where that came from." She winked and moved off to help set up camp.

"Teona?" James said. She turned, looking at him with beautifully inquisitive eyes. "Thanks for waiting."

Her smile grew. "I like you too, James, of course I waited. Plus"—her smile morphed into a smirk—"you've got a great arse. I'm not passing that up."

James smiled as he watched her walk away and followed to help with the camp before she could yell at him to do so.

Chapter Twenty

23RD FEBRUARY

"Why do you stay here?" Heather asked, though she suspected she knew the answer. She hadn't left yet either. Where would she go? She hadn't been able to get in touch with her wife or brother, and she didn't know where they would go, either. She hoped beyond hope they were somewhere safe.

Unlike her.

"It's hell out there," Eli said. "I'd rather take my chances with one madman in here than a thousand out on the streets."

Murmurs of agreement drifted around the table. Not loud. Never loud. Brendon was outside, but it was never safe. Those loyal to him could've been listening. Hell, they could've been around the table. Heather shifted in her seat.

"What other things has he done?" Heather didn't want to know, but she had to ask. She'd been at the Red Lion—Brendon's self-styled "safe zone"—for almost a month, and she'd noticed inconsistencies in his temper

and behaviour. He ruled with an iron fist.

Five of them sat hunched around the table, including Heather. Olivia, the only other woman present, answered. "I was one of the first people here. He seemed fine at first, caring, pulling us all together and getting this place up and running with Ross, the soldier who'd helped us. But then I guess he wanted to lead on his own. Ross went missing, and we found his head bashed in, the rock lying close to the body." Eli shook his head, his jaw tight.

"How did you know it was Brendon?"

"The blood all over his hands and shirt was a big clue," Alan said drily. Heather was wary of the large man—his flippant attitude rubbed her the wrong way. Was he one of Brendon's? He fit the bill; a man who liked violence a little *too* much, his tone condescending and his morals loose.

Liam, the youngest person there at barely twenty, stood roughly from his chair and started pacing around the room they were in. It was small and bare except for the table and chairs, and he didn't have far to walk from one end to the other. "He said Ross was bitten. Load of bullshit. We have to leave. We can't stay here. He's fucking crazy, and the guys who follow him are drunk on power. They do whatever the fuck they want, and Brendon lets them so long as it doesn't go against him."

Heather wholeheartedly agreed. Surely the military had somewhere set up they could go to. She could fish and hunt, and they could avoid any diseased people. Even as she thought it, she knew she wouldn't do it. The insidious fear held her back. It was chaos outside. They wouldn't survive. They were barely surviving here, even with all the weapons and roadblocks. Every time Brendon made

Heather go out, her anxiety surged anew, especially since he'd been giving her fewer and fewer guards.

Two days ago, six of their group had died as diseased people had almost broken through. Brendon had then killed a seventh, for "incompetence". Heather had heard rumours of Brendon's instability, of his cruelty, but that was the first time she'd witnessed it first-hand. She felt distinctly unsafe in this so-called safe zone.

Liam abruptly stopped pacing. It was the only warning Heather had as the door burst open, banging against the wall with force. She almost fell out of her chair as her heart rate skyrocketed.

It was Frankie. And behind him, Brendon.

Heather couldn't utter a single sound. Her throat seized up as Brendon pinned her with one look. He smiled. Heather had long since grown used to the way it never reached his eyes.

"My friends," he said, clasping his hands together in front of him. "It has come to my attention that some of you aren't happy with the way things are around here." He wore another white shirt and set of black trousers. He was always smartly dressed, even when he killed people. Heather found it profoundly disturbing in a way she couldn't articulate. He sat in Liam's chair, resting his hands on the tabletop. Liam pressed himself into the corner of the room as if he expected Brendon to murder him there and then. Heather tried to catch Frankie's eyes, but he avoided looking at her.

Alan stood up. "Was wondering when you'd get here, boss." Heather gaped at him— He'd been in Brendon's pocket all along. She *knew* it. *I need to trust my instincts more.* Heather started to sweat. Was this the end? Was

she never going to see her wife again? No. No, she was needed. Her paramedic knowledge, her hunting expertise. He wouldn't kill her. He'd be dooming this place. Heather wasn't one for self-aggrandisement, but she knew she was the main source of food for the Red Lion. It was the other, smaller reason why she hadn't left. She would be condemning the place to starvation.

"There was a skirmish at the bridge," Brendon said. "Unfortunately, I can't be everywhere at once. But that's why I have you fine gentlemen." His arm sweep caught Frankie, and Heather's heart sank. He'd saved her, and now he'd thrown his lot in with a psychopath. "Now, down to business. Tell me your concerns, and we can try to talk through them." Heather didn't know what he was playing at. Wasn't he going to kill them?

Eli clenched his jaw so hard Heather thought he was going to crack his teeth. Olivia's hands were shaking, but that was the only outward sign of her fear. "Well?" Brendon said, an impatient note creeping into his voice.

"We just think," Eli started, but he had to pause to swallow. "We just think you need to calm down and stop killing us. We think we might leave, find another place to stay."

There was a long pause as Brendon looked around them all. Heather cursed Eli's honesty. She had no faith in Brendon's ability to think rationally. He let out a sigh. "Thank you for telling the truth, Eli." His smile was back. Heather felt sickened by it. "I can see that it took a lot of courage. But you seem to be under some false notion that I'm going around picking you all off one by one," he laughed as he shrugged. "I assure you that's not the case. I killed Ross because he was infected. He tried to hide it

and would have infected us all. It was disgraceful. I killed Tommy because his idiocy let the zombies past our defences and resulted in the deaths of six of our friends. I've protected you all, and I will continue to do so. A thank-you would be nice."

"What about Sophie?" Liam asked, his face red. Heather implored him to shut his mouth, but he only had eyes for Brendon. "Chloe? Lee? They just go skipping off into the sunset?"

Brendon's smile faltered for a second before it returned in full force. "Sophie happened to have an unfortunate accident with a zombie. And you know how Chloe and Lee were, they were always sneaking out. Probably got caught." Heather didn't believe a word coming out of his mouth.

"Bullshit," Liam spat. "We all know it."

"Liam," Eli said sharply.

The young man started laughing hysterically. "He's going to kill us all anyway. Don't you see? Mutiny, right, Brendon? Can't let that go unanswered. You'd be seen as *weak*."

Heather's stomach dropped. She supposed he was right—from what she'd seen of Brendon he was never going to let them go. She still wished Liam didn't have to poke the proverbial bear.

Brendon looked down at the table and rubbed his hands together. "You know what your problem has always been, Liam?" He looked back up, and there was no sign of his fake smile. "You're too hot-headed. And in this new world, well, that just won't do."

Heather had no warning as Brendon surged from his

chair and grabbed Liam. Her back hit the wall as Brendon's fists pummelled into Liam's face, and she found herself paralysed, frozen in shock. All her training, all her experience, and she just stood there.

It was over quicker than she would have thought. Brendon breathed heavily through his nose as he straightened, and he had a look in his eye that Heather hadn't seen before. The closest thing she could think of was euphoria. Sweat trickled down the back of her neck, and she found it difficult to breathe. She'd seen a lot of things in her time but watching someone get beaten to death was a first.

Alan was still sitting, nonchalantly picking at his nails. Frankie stood impassively by the door. What had happened to him? He hadn't been the most talkative person when it had been the two of them, but she'd never suspected his quiet had been hiding such malice.

Olivia crashed to her feet when Brendon had first moved, and she stood like Heather, rooted to the spot. Eli was the exception. He made a dash for the door, but Frankie stopped him with ease, shoving him down.

Brendon tutted. "Have some dignity, Eli. I expected better after the courage you displayed earlier." He shook his fists out. "I was going to reason with you, but I see now that won't happen. Alan?"

Alan stood and passed Brendon a gun he had hidden beneath his shirt.

"Brendon, no, we can reason, we can—"

"Shut up, Eli," Brendon said calmly. Heather was oddly fixated on the blood splattered on his shirt. "Die like a man." It was bright against the white, little pinpricks of

colour. He raised the gun and fired all in one swift movement. Heather jerked against the wall as the sound reverberated through her, smashing against her eardrums and shaking her brain. There was more red on his shirt than white now. It spattered on his face as well.

Another gunshot. *Olivia.* Heather couldn't breathe. Her vision was blurry. *Oh God.* She tried desperately to blink her eyes clear, but she couldn't focus. Seconds passed. She was still alive. She was still alive?

"Calm yourself, Heather." Brendon's voice. He'd acquired a cloth from somewhere and was wiping his face. "Have a seat."

Heather moved on autopilot. She had no memory of sitting down. She couldn't stop shaking.

"It's okay now," Brendon's voice again. "I'm not going to hurt you. I want you to clean my hands, can you do that for me?" He smiled, and something withered inside Heather at the sight. Frankie placed her first aid kit on the table. When had he retrieved that? She saw her hand reach for it, but she felt no connection to it. "Thank you, Heather. I have no doubt that you were an amazing paramedic. You have such a unique skillset—you never have to worry about me hurting you. And I know you won't do anything like this again, will you?"

Heather still sat in the room long after Alan and Frankie had removed the bodies.

Chapter Twenty-One

PRESENT DAY

Jennifer ate a bite of a cracker and passed it straight to Rhys, her stomach roiling in protest. She couldn't eat. Not after... She could still feel the heat of the fight, still smell the desperation and terror. Those memories would haunt her for the rest of her life.

She'd gone from the sadness of accepting her life was over to the euphoria of rescue to the numbness of shock to the joy of finding Rhys again. She felt all over the place, pulled in too many different directions, and a heavy tiredness settled in her bones. It didn't help that she ached from head to foot, and her five—*five*—new bites stung like a bitch. They'd all removed their armour, and her T-shirt and trousers were lighter, freer. She couldn't get rid of the smell of sweat and blood, though. *Gross.*

Rhys sat close on her right side, and Dan was on her left. She'd introduced the two, and Rhys had been so patient with Dan, tears had stung Jennifer's eyes again. The boy hadn't spoken yet, but Rhys had chatted away to him, telling him stories of Jennifer and their past, and Dan nodded along, even smiling once. Jennifer hoped he was

going to be all right. She had wished he'd stayed at the castle while they'd fought, but after hearing what had happened, she was glad he'd come with her.

Having Rhys back didn't seem real. He was *sitting right next to her*. She could scarcely believe it. They had so much to catch up on. Jennifer would have to introduce him to Alexia, although she wasn't sure how he'd take that. He'd been close to Damien, but she knew Damien had never told him of their relationship problems. As far as Rhys was concerned, they'd been going strong.

Jennifer looked to Alexia, who sat on the other side of Dan, talking to Victoria and Anthony and another soldier Jennifer vaguely recognised from the castle. Alexia's hair was loose about her shoulders, fluttering every time the faint breeze passed through. God, she was beautiful. Alexia met her eye and smiled, and Jennifer's lips curved up in response. Shit, she was going to have to tell Rhys soon. After James and Teona—she'd announced her name to the group—had kissed, Jennifer wanted nothing more than to grab Alexia and do the same, but the soldier had already been busy setting up the camp.

Jennifer sighed and leaned back on her right hand. The left still hurt too much. She looked around the group. Her second family.

Riya and Aarav were sitting beyond the trio, with a soldier Jennifer didn't know. The man was brown skinned like the two of them, and he was in deep conversation with them as they ate.

James and Teona lounged on the helicopter, the pilot's legs dangling above the ground. The little girl was there as well, sitting so close to James she might as well have been on his lap, and Charlie, the young guy who

helped Teona fly the helicopter, sat on the grass at their feet wolfing his rations down. *He's a quiet one.* Jennifer had tried to speak to him at the castle, but she hadn't gotten far.

Victoria grinned at Anthony. Alexia looked stunning drinking some water. Rhys still chatted to Dan across her. Riya and Aarav and Danny and Elise and the others she didn't know. *I'll find out their names and stories.* Poor Evans, sitting by himself at his request, stared out over the rolling hills. Jennifer couldn't do anything for him, but she'd find a safe place for the others. That goal was enough to keep her going without the prospect of a vaccine.

Looking around the group, Jennifer felt the stirrings of determination. She couldn't give people a cure, but she could give them a safe haven. Where would it be? Somewhere they could settle, so it would have to be able to support crops and stuff like that. Jennifer didn't know the first thing about farming. *This is going to be more difficult than I—*

Her mind was shocked blank.

Was that...Johnson?

Jennifer saw red.

She didn't remember moving, but suddenly she was in his face, swinging a fist hard and watching as he landed on his arse. The way he clutched his nose as pain twisted his features brought a sadistic pleasure to Jennifer.

But that wasn't enough.

She didn't know how many punches she landed before she was dragged away. The sight of him curled up into a ball was good, but not *enough*. He needed to hurt. Really

hurt. "Fucking monster!" she yelled, struggling against the people holding her back. "How is a shit stain like you still alive?"

Her captors eventually let her go after they'd dragged her to the other side of the camp. She stood still, chest heaving with every breath. No one helped him up.

"Fucking hell, Jennifer, what's gotten into you?" Teona sounded both impressed and wary.

"That piece of shit *murdered* my best friend in cold blood."

"She was *infected*," Johnson shouted back, wiping blood from his face. Pride burst through her at the sight.

"She could have been immune! I am. God, how many people have been killed who were actually immune?"

She couldn't look at him. She couldn't bear the sight of his smarmy, sneering face. With one last glare, Jennifer turned and stomped down the hill. The grass blurred around her as tears fell.

Teona shouted for her to come back but she stormed away faster. She couldn't be near that *monster.* Evelyn getting shot replayed over and over. She couldn't make it stop. She couldn't make it *stop.* Johnson's leering face, the gunshot ringing out, Evelyn hitting the ground, her blood... God, her blood. Jennifer sank to her knees at the bottom of the hill, unable to go any further.

She heaved out great sobs of air, her face wet with grief. She didn't hear the footsteps behind her. Jennifer jumped as warm arms wrapped around her, and she buried her head in Alexia's neck.

She didn't know how long they knelt there. Rhys came down at some point, and he held her hand as she

cried on Alexia. God, what a mess. *Great job, Jen, snot all over the woman you like.* She managed to pull herself around as her legs started to cramp, and she sat back and wiped away tears.

"Sorry," she mumbled, gesturing vaguely at Alexia's wet neck.

Alexia tutted gently. "It is fine, Jennifer. You never need to apologise for this." She smiled, and Jennifer felt the world get a touch brighter again as she gazed into her soft brown eyes.

The moment was broken by Rhys. "I'm the one who's sorry, Jen. When I found out what he did, I didn't do anything. I should have beat the shit out of him like you did."

Jennifer had only ever seen Rhys truly angry twice—once when they'd been driving and some dickhead had cut across them almost causing an accident, and once when they'd gone out for drinks for Rachel's birthday and a random guy wouldn't leave her alone. Now, his quiet anger at himself only left her feeling sad.

"No amount of rage is going to bring her back, Rhys," Jennifer said, knowing full well she'd never be able to completely let go of her hatred of Johnson. She didn't care that she was being hypocritical. "I miss her so much. Every day. *God*, seeing him again, I just wanted to rip him apart."

"From what you have told me of Evelyn she seemed like the best of friends," Alexia said, rubbing Jennifer's back. "I'm sorry I never had the chance to meet her."

Jennifer nodded, pushing back fresh tears. "She was more a sister than friend to me. Growing up we were around each other's houses all the time." Jennifer smiled.

"My mum used to say she was her second daughter."

Rhys also smiled. "Remember that time she spilled coffee down her white shirt just before she went in for that interview? And she still got the job?" He shook his head. "Amazing."

Jennifer's smile widened as she turned to tell Alexia. "Yeah, she applied for a job at a shop, and she went in all frazzled and stressed and we didn't think she'd get it. Turns out she was their best applicant."

Alexia smiled, her hand never ceasing in its movements across her back. Jennifer could see the cogs turning in Rhys's head. "I wish I had that skill and luck. My first job interview was also at a shop, a food shop, and I stuttered my way through it. I was not surprised when I didn't hear back from them."

"You've got a good job now, although you're not getting paid for it," Jennifer joked, trying to make the situation lighter. She felt better after sitting with them, away from Johnson. She wanted to stay down at the bottom of the hill a little longer—she didn't know what she'd do when she re-joined the group.

Alexia shrugged and laughed. Warmth spread through Jennifer, and she knew Rhys could see the heart eyes she launched at Alexia.

He extended his hand to Alexia. "I don't think we've been properly introduced. I'm Lance Corporal Rhys Coyne."

Alexia shook his hand. If she was surprised by the more formal tone Rhys used, she didn't show it. "Alexia Lécuyer."

"It's nice to meet you." Rhys smiled.

"You too." Alexia returned his smile.

"So," Rhys drew the word out, and Jennifer internally sighed. "How long have you two, y'know?"

Alexia frowned. "I am sorry, I do not think I understand?"

Jennifer sighed. "We aren't dating, Rhys."

"Ah okay, because, y'know, Damien might still be alive—"

Jennifer cut him off. "I'm sorry, Rhys, you know the odds of that are small. And even if he was alive somewhere, we'd been having trouble for a while. It was over."

"So, it's only taken you two months to get over him? I thought you guys were in love, you were going to get married."

"Woah, no." Where had he gotten that from? "I liked him, but I was never in love. It was over weeks before all this shit happened, we just hadn't gotten around to officially ending it." Jennifer looked at Rhys sadly. "We've just found each other again, Rhys. Don't taint this by being angry at me for something that finished ages ago."

Rhys held her gaze for a beat, then nodded. "Sorry. I just...I miss him. I miss them all."

Jennifer nodded. "Me too."

Alexia stood up. "I will leave you alone to catch up."

Did she seem sad? Jennifer quickly thought back through what she'd said. That they weren't dating? Did Alexia take that to mean Jennifer didn't want to? *Shit.*

"Alexia, wait." Jennifer winced as she pushed herself to her feet, her new wounds loudly reminding her they were still there. Alexia stopped and turned, and Jennifer

did something she'd never done before. She made the first move.

She tentatively reached up and slipped a hand behind Alexia's neck, letting it get lost in her loose hair. She'd had more than one daydream about playing with her hair. She looked at Alexia, a question in her eyes, and saw permission granted. With a faint exhale through her nose, Jennifer brought her mouth to Alexia's and the rest of the world bled away to nothing. All Jennifer was aware of was Alexia's lips gliding over hers, her hand tangled in her hair, Alexia's hands slipping around her waist. Alexia's scent wound its way around her, and Jennifer pulled her closer. She didn't know how long they stood there breathing each other in, hands moving, lips moving. Elation burst up and chased the anger and melancholy away.

They eventually parted. Jennifer grinned and received a beaming smile in return.

"I'd like to, erm." Jennifer had to stop and clear her throat. "I'd like to keep getting to know you better. Keep being with you, y'know." God, was she being awkward? She felt like she was being awkward.

Alexia was still smiling, so maybe she was doing something right. "I would like that very much," she said, and pulled Jennifer in for another kiss.

This day has been a hell of an emotional rollercoaster.

Chapter Twenty-Two

Victoria was exhausted. She was pretty sure she'd fallen asleep on the helicopter, but she still felt like she needed about ten more hours. She'd been sitting with Alexia and Anthony and a soldier called Edward, eating and chatting and struggling not to fall asleep. At least she wasn't thirsty anymore.

Her body ached. Muscles she didn't know she possessed ached. Riya had seen to her cuts and bruises, and her knuckles were bound in thick bandages that made it difficult to hold things. Still, Victoria wasn't complaining. She was fed and watered and all cleaned up. It had felt unspeakably good to ditch the blood-soaked armour. Her shirt was stained with sweat, which was revolting, but other than that, she was cleaner than she had been in what seemed like forever.

Victoria's mind was blessedly blank. She wasn't thinking about the past few hours, she wasn't thinking about how many people she'd killed, she wasn't thinking about almost dying. She wasn't thinking about anything at all. It wasn't shock; she was just too tired.

Anthony's voice was a nice balm, even if the topic wasn't. "It was horrific. Never in the entirety of my service

have I seen soldiers lose control so quickly. It was embarrassing."

"I know," Edward agreed. "How do you think they got in? And how did they overrun us so quickly?"

"There were a lot of them," Anthony said. "Maybe the sheer number? How did they get so close? Do you think they overwhelmed some scouts and were on the castle before we could do anything?"

"It's definitely possible," Edward replied. "The simplest explanation is often the right one. I think they overran us so easily because people panicked. A lot of those soldiers had been based there since the collapse and didn't really have any exposure to infected people."

Anthony shook his head. "All that loss of life, it's such a shame. Have you had a chance to write that poem?"

It was Edward's turn to shake his head. "Not yet, but I have some ideas of how it's going to go."

Victoria perked up. "You write poetry?"

Edward frowned for some reason, and Anthony quickly spoke. "It's okay, she's an English teacher."

Victoria was not a teacher any more. Hearing someone say she was made her want to hit something. Teachers built up the young, educated them, and helped them prepare for the future. What kind of future was there now? She no longer built people up, she tore them down in bloody fashion. *Murderer.* That was what she was. Someone who destroyed instead of created. She was surprised to realise it didn't bother her as much as it once did.

She was a fighter. Someone who killed, yes, but to protect the larger group. She leaned back on her elbows as she basked in the warmth of contentment, a small smile

tugging at her lips. It felt a lot like acceptance.

She sat bolt upright as Jennifer flew past her in a mad rush. Victoria was on her feet a second later, running after her and wishing she had a weapon. What was going on? She couldn't see anyone other than their camp. No infected, no immoral assailants.

Jennifer cracked a soldier across the face, then she dived on him and started beating him up. Alarm erupted through her. *No, she's immune, she hasn't gone crazy. Has she?*

Victoria and Teona reached her at the same time, and together they hauled her away from the man.

"*Fucking monster*," Jennifer cried, and the word reverberated through Victoria. It was something she'd called that part of herself she hadn't wanted to acknowledge, the part that had frightened her. But it *was* her. The monster was simply one aspect of the whole that made her who she was, and Victoria was done suppressing it.

Once Victoria and Teona had pulled Jennifer to the other side of the camp they let go. "Fucking hell, Jennifer, what's gotten into you?" Teona said, eyeing her warily but also with pride. Both emotions warred in Victoria too—caution in case the virus had finally caught up with Jennifer, and impressed she could beat a man so soundly.

"That piece of shit murdered my best friend in cold blood," Jennifer snarled. A rush of relief almost buckled Victoria's knees. She wasn't insane after all, just upset. Victoria looked at the bloody-faced man still half-sitting, half-lying on the ground, and saw a scared, pitiful creature. Jennifer had talked about her friend Evelyn who'd being killed by a soldier called... Jackson? Johnson?

Whatever. He looks like a cowardly idiot.

"She was infected," he shouted back, wiping blood from his chin.

"She could have been immune! I am. God, how many people have been killed who were actually immune?"

Jennifer had a point. Victoria wondered again if she was immune, and again decided against ever finding out. She tried to think back to what Mike had said about immunity, but she couldn't remember. Most of her ex-fiancé's work had gone over her head. Besides, she hated thinking about him. Memories of Mike led to memories of her sister, and she didn't want to relive the murder over and over.

Jennifer stormed off and Victoria didn't stop her. She wasn't stupid, she wouldn't go far. From the tears streaming down her face, Victoria guessed she'd want to be alone. *Or maybe not.* Alexia hurried past, soon followed by Rhys. *She'll be all right.* Victoria returned to her seat on the grass next to Anthony and Edward. She made herself relax but kept an eye on Jackson or Johnson or whatever his name was, just in case.

Edward scowled. "He *is* a piece of shit. He wouldn't even be here if I had my way."

The soldier told Victoria things James had left out of his recounting of London, of the things what's-his-name had done, and distaste rose fast, rushing through her like a flash flood. She agreed—he shouldn't be part of the group. Should she get rid of him? It would make people happy. Yes, she was a murderer, but she'd always killed in self-defence. Could she murder someone in cold blood? Straight up shoot them, no fighting for her life, no fear or adrenaline. Victoria didn't know.

"Anthony," she asked hesitantly, unsure how her question would be taken. "You've killed people before. How did it make you feel?"

His brow furrowed, but it was an inquisitive frown, not an angry one. Victoria couldn't recall ever seeing him angry. "Well," he said slowly. "The first time I ever killed someone it didn't really register until about a week later. I remember acting all tough and blasé in front of every-one, but inside, I guess I was having what could be de-scribed as a crisis of faith, even though I'm not religious. I wondered if heaven and hell were real, and which one I'd be going to." He shrugged. "I got over it. Throughout the years it became something I don't dwell on for too long. It makes me feel dirty, so I think of other things. I'm sorry if that doesn't really answer your question."

"No, that's fine," Victoria said. Would she one day shy away from thinking of her murders? She didn't think so. Death was a subject that demanded time spent contem-plating it. Especially murder. Could she kill whatever-his-name-was? Victoria concluded that she could. She'd feel strange for a while, dirty, as Anthony put it, but in the end, she would rationalise her actions away.

Schoolteacher Victoria would be horrified by her thoughts, but that woman had yet to kill her sister. Victo-ria realised her old self had died that day as well—it had taken her a long time to figure it out.

Killing the disgraced soldier would benefit the group. They wouldn't have to worry about his loyalties, his ability to protect, or his mental state. It would make Jennifer and the soldiers who'd gone to London feel better. Victoria didn't feel comfortable having such a liability around an-yway.

I'm already rationalising it and I haven't even done anything yet.

She stood up and went to James and Teona at the helicopter. "Hey, Hot Shot," Teona greeted her with yet another nickname. Victoria wasn't sure she had ever called her by her actual name. "How're you holding up?"

She was surprised by the question, and by the genuine concern in Teona's eyes. But then, they were a family, so it wasn't really that surprising at all. Victoria suspected Teona revealing her name after so long was her way of fully committing to them.

"I'm as good as can be expected," Victoria said, not thinking about Paris. "Do we have any weapons left? And ammunition?"

"Straight to business I see," Teona grinned. "Yeah, but not a lot. You want a weapon? I get it, you feel naked without one, right? We'll make a soldier out of you yet." She winked and jumped into the helicopter, where she retrieved an L85. "Here." She handed Victoria the animal. "You don't have to worry, though, there's no one around for miles. Just hills, grass, and more hills."

Should she tell her what she wanted it for? Victoria hated liars and lying, could she become one herself? *No. I'm never going to keep secrets from any of them.* "I'm going to kill him—" She pointed because she still couldn't remember his bloody name.

Teona and James both visibly became more alert. "Fuck me, you do get straight to the point. He's a piece of literal shit, but we can't let you kill him, Victoria. Do you even understand what you're saying?"

"Of course I do." Victoria frowned, annoyed at the

assumption she wasn't in her right mind. "I'm not going to be constantly looking over my shoulder, worried he's going to do something or miss something and harm the group. And don't worry about me, it's not going to torture my soul or anything," She took a deep breath in. She'd never said this aloud before. *Just say it. Like ripping off a plaster.* "I murdered my sister. I was a killer before the world fell apart. I can cut down some lousy man who is a potential threat to us."

James looked shocked. "I didn't see that coming."

Teona snorted. "I didn't either. So much for a sweet schoolteacher." She eyed her sharply, clearly reassessing her. Victoria didn't care.

"Look, I'm not asking for your permission. Over the past couple of months, I've come to see you all as family, so as a courtesy I'm telling you what I'm going to do. I'm never going to lie to any of you, and everything I do will be to protect us, I can promise you that."

"You know what the road to hell is paved with, right?" Teona said.

"I've already been to hell, Teona," Victoria sighed. "I'm doing this, and I'll bear the looks and the judgement. I've done it all before."

"I can't just let you execute a person," Teona said forcefully. "No matter how shitty he is."

Jennifer returned at that moment, holding hands with Alexia. Her look of happiness melted away at the sight of Johnson or Jackson, and Victoria felt bolstered. She could do it.

She came to a realisation that had been playing on her mind for the past couple of days. "You soldiers aren't the

only ones in charge any more. I'm sorry."

Teona and James both frowned and followed her gaze to Jennifer. "Miss Immune? When did that happen?"

"Slowly," Victoria said, and turned away before the pilot could say anything more. She made her way over to Jennifer who had stopped and waited when she saw Victoria approaching.

"Should I say congratulations?" Victoria asked, nodded at their linked hands.

They both smiled, and Jennifer shrugged awkwardly. Victoria laughed. Funny she could still do that, given what she was about to ask. "You two have pined after each other long enough. I'm happy for you both."

"Thanks, Victoria, it means a lot." Jennifer's smile widened as she looked at Alexia, and Victoria was reluctant to make it disappear. But it had to be done.

"Listen," Victoria said, hesitant. She had never been tentative about saying something before, but she knew Jennifer was going to struggle with this. "I need to talk to you about him." She gestured to Jackson and Jennifer's face immediately darkened. Alexia squeezed her hand.

"Johnson? What about him?"

So that's his name. "Can I speak to you privately?"

Jennifer frowned and Victoria knew she was going to say Alexia could stay, but Alexia excused herself first. "I will sit with Anthony again. I did not finish my food. Come when you are finished." She kissed Jennifer's cheek and strolled over to join Anthony and Edward.

Jennifer sighed, a half-smile curling her lips. It vanished as she turned to Victoria. "What's up?"

Victoria opened her mouth to ask but realised she didn't need words. It was a strange sensation as an ex-English teacher, but she felt this was better asked non-verbally. Instead, she hefted the animal in her arms, and she saw the moment Jennifer understood. Her eyes widened, and she breathed in heavily.

"Why are you asking me this?" Jennifer said quietly, traces of alarm in her voice.

"You're one of our leaders," Victoria said simply. "If you don't want me to do it I won't, as Teona doesn't want me to do it, although some advice? He's a problem that needs to be removed."

"*I'm* a leader?" Jennifer shook her head. "Victoria, I know you've protected us before, but you're not a killer." She stopped, and Victoria had a front row seat to the penny dropping. "You are, aren't you? I've seen the way you use that weapon, the ease with which you fight. But you were a teacher."

"I killed my sister," Victoria admitted for the second time that day. It was easier to say. "I was on my way to Holloway prison when everything kicked off. If not for a guard releasing my handcuffs, I'd probably be dead now. I never found out her name." A strange sorrow stole through her at the memory. She hoped the guard had made it. Jennifer stared at her, her lips parted in shock, and Victoria didn't like it. "Look, nothing has changed. I killed her in self-defence—she had the virus. It doesn't matter now anyway. Do you want me to remove Johnson?"

"Everything has changed," Jennifer said, and Victoria's stomach plummeted. *It's okay, I've put up with the judgement before. It's all right.* It stung to come from

Jennifer, though. "And nothing at the same time." Victoria frowned, the hurt retreating. *Talk about emotional whiplash.* "You're my friend. Looking back, I guess I've always seen it." A weight lifted she didn't know she'd been carrying.

"Thank you."

Jennifer smiled, but it fell away quickly. "You may be comfortable being a killer, Victoria, but I'm not."

"I'd be the one pulling the trigger."

"But I'd be the one who gave permission. Don't ask this of me. I don't know if I can handle it."

Victoria nodded. "Figure it out," she said, not unkindly.

Jennifer squeezed her eyes shut tight. Victoria waited patiently. Eventually, Jennifer opened her eyes again. "A leader is someone who knows how to delegate. I delegate this decision to you." Victoria could see the pain in her eyes, and she knew Jennifer would always think herself responsible. She knew Victoria would prefer to kill him, and so her words had been empty air.

She'd given her permission.

Victoria nodded again, sadness in her eyes as she held Jennifer's. She wished Jennifer didn't feel so conflicted. She turned on her heel and marched across the camp toward Johnson. Better to get it over and done with. She noticed Teona still by the helicopter, and James had a hand on her arm. He must've held her back. Victoria looked away and continued forward.

He was at the edge of the camp, clearly wanting to be part of the safety it offered but pushed out by the others. Victoria felt a flash of pity for him—this viral apocalypse

was always going to either make or break people; he was one of the unfortunate broken ones. Still, the pity didn't last long. Johnson killing Jennifer's friend could be excused—in all likelihood, he'd been operating under strict instructions to kill bitten people on sight—but the cowardice and terror he'd displayed in London signed his death warrant in Victoria's eyes. Nothing excused terrorizing people. Victoria hated bullies. She'd seen enough of them at school to know how irreparable the damage could be.

She stopped in front of him, her shadow passing over his bloodied face, a physical metaphor of his finite life.

"What do you want?" he spat, not looking at her.

Victoria realised she hadn't really thought this through. Should she kill him here, in front of everyone, or someplace else? How would she get him to move somewhere else? Should she talk to him first, or just shoot?

"Hey, you dumb bitch, are you deaf? What the fuck do you want?"

In the end, his rudeness decided for her.

She brought the animal up in one swift movement, relishing the thought that it seemed almost eager to tear into this pathetic excuse for a human. She witnessed the widening of Johnson's eyes as he realised what she was going to do, and she squeezed the trigger.

The roar of the animal drowned out his cry, and silence settled as his body slumped back. That was that.

Victoria stood still, examining her emotions. She was more annoyed he'd called her a dumb bitch than anything else. She felt calm, at one with the monster, as it always had been. She was concerned about the rest of the group,

not that she'd killed a man. *No second guessing myself.*

Turning on her heel sharply in a similar way she'd seen Teona do, Victoria braced herself for the judgement. Everyone was on their feet, all the soldiers bar James and Teona alert for an attack. Victoria watched as they slowly relaxed, taking in what she'd done. Edward nodded to her, something like gratitude in his dark eyes. Anthony was more closed off, but she could see that he wasn't going to lose any sleep over it.

Teona looked livid. Even as Victoria watched she stood up and marched over to Jennifer. Victoria picked up her pace. She wasn't going to let Jennifer face the sergeant's anger on her own.

Chapter Twenty-Three

Jennifer's mood nose-dived into miserable after her conversation with Victoria. She stood rooted to the spot as she watched Victoria stride away, and she fought down the sick feeling threatening to overwhelm everything. This was what she wanted. Johnson had killed Evelyn. Evelyn. Her best friend. Her sister in all but name. So why couldn't she stop the growing nausea?

She'd signed his death warrant. She knew Victoria wouldn't see it that way, but in Jennifer's eyes she may as well have pulled the trigger herself. The responsibility was almost too much to bear, and she tore her gaze away from Victoria's retreating back before she called out to stop her. Johnson dead was what she wanted. No one would care, right? God, how sad was that? Now she was almost feeling sorry for him. *Get a grip,* she chastised herself. *He killed Evelyn. He's a shitty person.*

What was this going to do to Jennifer's morality? She was still her—the thought of killing was abhorrent, even in Paris when she'd been fighting for her life, she hadn't killed anyone. Was this going to change her? She hoped not. What if she had to give the order to kill again? Would it be easier? Thoughts and emotions swirled around in her

head, but nothing became any clearer.

If this was what leadership was then Jennifer wanted no part in it. This tangible weight was too much to carry. But it was too late—the civilians looked to her, as did half of the soldiers. Why? Why did she have to be immune? Why did they think that granted her some kind of special power to know what to do? All she wanted was a safe place. That was all she'd ever wanted. Somewhere they could all settle, without fear, without the threat of the virus hanging over their heads. She wanted to give that to all of them.

Jennifer squared her shoulders. If being the leader was what it took to make that a reality, then she could do it. She could take responsibility for one person's death if that meant saving the rest of them. A flicker of doubt flashed though her mind, but it was gone before it could take hold. She *could*. For Evelyn. For her new family. God, that weight wasn't getting any lighter, but maybe, just maybe, she was strong enough to carry it.

Jennifer turned to James and Teona to find them both watching something to her left. Victoria. Jennifer couldn't watch. She was about to become a murderer. What was she going to say to everyone? Hell, what was she going to say to the two sergeants? Jennifer remembered that time in the trees after the helicopter had run out of fuel when she'd tried to tell them what to do. Teona had shot her down so easily.

The sound was like the crack of a whip, and everyone leaped up, alert, eyes darting every which way. Jennifer stayed still. She slowly let her eyes fall shut for the briefest of seconds before she steeled herself and opened them to questioning gazes. Straight away they looked to her for an

explanation. *When had this all happened?*

She saw Teona striding toward her, James following a step behind, and Victoria, even further behind, half-jogging toward them all. She didn't look at Johnson. She couldn't. Did she feel relief he was dead? Was her thirst for vengeance sated? Was that sadness she felt at the thought they'd fallen to killing one another? Maybe a mixture of it all and more.

Teona stopped in front of her, fury in her eyes. "Explain, Jennifer," she ground out through clenched teeth. "What the fuck? He was a loathsome arsehole of a person, but we can't go around shooting people we don't like. Is this about getting vengeance for your friend? Because that is a very dark path, Jennifer, one you don't want to go down."

Jennifer clenched her hands into fists, and quickly relaxed them when she realised what she was doing. *Show no weaknesses. You are calm, you are in control.* "It's not about revenge," she said firmly. "It's about protecting this group. Keeping them safe. He was a danger. Can you say, with absolute certainty, that you could rely on him if push came to shove?" She didn't wait for a response. "It's done. He's dead, and we're all better off for it."

Teona tilted her head to the side, clearly reassessing her. What did she see? Jennifer kept her expression neutral, careful not to display any of the turmoil raging inside. He was dead. Jennifer had given permission to kill someone, and the world was still spinning. Nothing had really changed, yet everything had as well.

"When did you become so hard?" The question was whispered, and Jennifer's façade almost collapsed.

"When my friends and family were torn from me.

When I first saw people die. When I was bitten. When we ran for our lives, fought for our lives. When safety was snatched away, again and again. When I decided that I wasn't going to rely on others to provide that safety anymore. When the hope for a cure died in Paris."

Jennifer looked around the group, saw exhaustion and pain, fear and heartache, but also resilience and strength, and, above all, hope. Even now, hope. She raised her voice. "I'm sorry you all witnessed that. Johnson was a coward. I will not let your protection be the responsibility of someone like that.

"I will do everything I can to keep you all alive. To find a safe place for us all, away from the horror of the infection, a place we can finally relax and rebuild our lives." She raised her arms so the bandaged wounds were visible. "I will put myself in harm's way so no one else gets this infection. We're a family, and we'll look out for each other. I promise you." She didn't look at Evans. She hadn't reached him in time, and she knew she would never forget the desperate panic she'd felt as she saw all the scientists fall.

No one clapped or anything, not like she was expecting it. But they all—except Evans—looked bolstered. Encouragement thrummed through her in a crescendo.

The doctor himself stepped forward, his eyes dulled with the knowledge his life would be ending soon. The pristine white bandage Riya had wrapped around his arm was a stark reminder of the death now invading his body, and shame sparked anew in Jennifer at the sight of it. *I couldn't have reached him in time. I couldn't have reached any of them, not when I was fighting my own infected. Not when I was protecting Dan.* Guilt's hold

didn't slacken, regardless of the truth.

"I don't know where you can all settle down, but I do know there are a lot of hydroelectric plants in Wales and in Scotland in particular," he said without his usual arrogance. "If you found one suitable enough and could get it working, you would have renewable power."

"We could go to Scotland," James said, attempting nonchalance but not quite reaching it. "I know where a few of them are."

Teona snorted. "Pining for the motherland, Sunshine?"

He gave her a deadpan look. Teona winked.

"That's a good suggestion," Jennifer said, the idea taking root in her mind. The last thing she wanted was to go back to the stone age with no electricity. The lack of internet alone over the past two months had been killing her, never mind something as simple as no lights or heating.

"Is there anything we need to know about the virus that we don't already?" Victoria asked.

Evans shrugged. "I don't think so," he said, in his new dead way of talking. "You've all seen what it does to people. I wanted to check Jennifer's blood for antibodies, and then perhaps try to synthesise a vaccine based on our new knowledge. It would have been a long, difficult process, and perhaps nothing would have come of it." He smiled, and it was a horrible sight, all lifeless and dull. "Well, nothing did come of it."

"Is that why you've been taking so much blood?" Jennifer asked.

"Partly. We had some stored in cool bags for the

journey—the best we could do—but those were lost in Paris. We tried growing the virus in cell cultures at the castle, but that wasn't particularly effective, and there was always the danger of an accident and getting infected—"

Victoria snorted, the sudden sound cutting Evans off. "Sorry," she apologised. "That's exactly what happened to my fiancé."

Jennifer blinked. *Victoria had a fiancé?* "I didn't know you were engaged."

Victoria waved her off. "I've done my grieving, it's all right. Besides, he was cheating on me with my sister."

Jennifer blinked again. *What the fuck?* "Okay, enough about dead, cheating fiancés. Doctor, is there definitely nothing else we need to know?"

Evans frowned, clearly thinking. "I don't think so, no."

"Okay," Jennifer said again. "Thank you. I'm sorry." She stopped, unsure of what to say. "You did your best to give us a cure, and I'm sorry everything went so wrong. I truly am." She tried to say with her eyes what she couldn't with her words, but the doctor was looking at Victoria, not her.

"Are you to be my executioner?"

Victoria nodded slowly. "I'm sorry."

Evans barked out a humourless laugh. "Everyone's sorry now, aren't they?"

"Wait," Jennifer said. "I'm immune, it stands to reason others will be as well. Do you think you could be?"

The doctor shook his head sadly. "I can already feel it creeping through me. My head is pounding, I feel

nauseous and tired, although that may be due to recent events."

"I had all those symptoms too. They don't mean anything."

Jennifer saw a spark of hope flare in his eyes before he ruthlessly quashed it. "I can't think like that. What if I'm not? It would crush me even more."

"Well, no one is killing you until we've at least seen some necrosis," Jennifer said firmly. "Is that fair?" Evans nodded. "Good. Now I suggest everyone go back to eating and relaxing, it's been a very hectic few hours and I want you all to be able to pause for breath. We'll stay here for the night and decide on our course of action in the morning. Danny and, sorry, what's your name?" Jennifer asked the soldier who'd been chatting to Aarav and Riya.

"Hiran," he said with a posh English accent.

"Hiran, could you and Danny move the body, please? It doesn't have to be far, just, away." Jennifer sucked in a discreet breath. "Anthony, go with them and cover them. I know we're in the middle of nowhere, but better to be safe than sorry."

Teona maintained eyed contact for a beat as the three men moved off and everyone settled back down, and Jennifer thought she was going to protest. *Come on, come on, please.*

Teona clenched her jaw and nodded once. "This isn't over, Jennifer. We need to talk about this. And I'm definitely still in charge of military matters." She pivoted smartly, took the gun from Victoria, and marched back to the helicopter. Jennifer released the breath she had been holding slowly, not wanting to draw attention to how

nervous she was.

She didn't want to be in charge. Even co-leading with Teona sounded like too much responsibility. *Get everyone to safety. Then relax.*

She turned and walked to Alexia, who rested with Edward. Rhys, Dan, and Victoria weren't far away. She was now partly responsible for the group. *How do the soldiers do it?* That weight was beyond heavy, but she held her head up anyway and painted on a smile she didn't feel as she sat down between Alexia and Edward.

Chapter Twenty-Four

Victoria was freezing when she woke up. She'd slept outside with only her clothes, coat, and thin blanket for protection against the elements, and it had been frosty. There weren't enough tents to go around, and she'd stupidly offered to go without. She wouldn't be doing that again in a hurry.

She was one of the first people up, probably because she was cold to the bone and plain uncomfortable. Along with Anthony, and Edward—who'd been on guard—she watched the sunrise over the rolling hills.

The dawn was muted behind grey clouds, but Victoria still found the beauty in it. Faded pinks and reds greeted her as she stretched, trying to work some warmth back into her body.

She shivered, and Anthony smiled at her. "We're definitely back in England, aren't we?"

"It's bloody freezing," Victoria complained, prompting a chuckle from the two soldiers.

She moved through the camp quietly so as not to disturb people and grabbed some toothpaste and a tampon from her bag. Her period was almost finished, which was

good. She jogged around the helicopter and down the hill to the designated toilet area, did her business, and jogged back to the group before the reality of what she was doing repulsed her too much. *I'd never in a million years thought I'd be peeing outside regularly. Disgusting.*

They didn't have any toothbrushes, so she made do with her finger. *Better than nothing.* She was going to try for some semblance of hygiene, no matter what. *Only one tube of toothpaste between all of us, though. It's not going to last long.* A shudder raced up Victoria's spine. She did *not* want to think about when it eventually ran out.

Hiran was awake when she returned, and together they relieved Anthony and Edward. They stood watch as the rest of the camp slowly shook off the cobwebs of sleep, the silence falling away as more people woke up.

Victoria still shivered occasionally, but she felt more comfortable now she'd moved around a bit. She noticed Hiran hunching down in his coat and smiled briefly. She'd spoken to him last night after they'd discussed guard shifts, and he seemed like a nice man. From Cambridge, where Victoria's father had been from. She hadn't known her father—her parents had divorced when she and Katherine had been little, and he'd moved away shortly after.

The camp was a bustle of activity—water boiling, food rations being passed around, people chatting and shivering in the brisk air. Victoria stood still on the edge of it all, keeping a careful watch on their surroundings. She narrowed her eyes when they landed on Evans, who was sitting where he'd slept, cradling his arm with a defeated look on his face. Victoria sighed. *Three guesses what that look means.* It seemed her peaceful start to the day was over.

Jennifer had also noticed him. Her brow was pinched as she walked over to Victoria, and Victoria smiled when Jennifer failed to stop a yawn.

"Sorry," she said as Victoria fought her own after watching Jennifer. "I didn't have a good sleep."

Victoria knew she blamed herself for Johnson's death, and she suspected nothing she said would change that. "It's all right. How are you feeling?"

"Like shit, to be honest," Jennifer sighed. "Cold, tired, the bite wounds ache like mad, and y'know..." She stared out over the hills. "Do you think I can do this? Keep the promises I made yesterday?"

Victoria knew she was looking for reassurance, for validation. She'd seen it countless times from kids in her classroom. "I do," she said confidently. Any wavering in her tone would make Jennifer doubt her. "I've seen you take charge, Jennifer, I've seen you protect people. Dan's alive because of you, *I'm* alive because of you. You can do this." She smiled at Jennifer and received a tentative one in return. *Good enough.*

Jennifer took a deep breath. "Let's do this."

Victoria followed her over to the doctor. Jennifer opened her mouth to speak, but whatever she was going to say died on her lips. Victoria edged round her and saw why. Evan had removed his bandage, and black necrosis was already curling through the wound, which looked *awful.*

A rush of sadness took Victoria by surprise. They were going to have to kill him. As if there hadn't been enough death already.

"I'm so sorry," Jennifer said, and Victoria saw she

meant it.

Evans shrugged and barked out a laugh. "I came to terms with this yesterday."

By now everyone had cottoned on to what was happening, and a solemn air hung over the camp like the frost that gripped the hills. Victoria was fast becoming tired of the dreary atmosphere that seemed to follow them everywhere. She tutted at herself. *Death isn't sunshine and rainbows. It requires seriousness.* Still, she hoped things would improve, and she wouldn't have to kill another member of the group after the doctor.

It was all over quickly. Evans didn't say anything as several people expressed their sorrow. Victoria wasn't sure how much he heard. She supposed if she knew she was going to die she wouldn't waste time listening to empty words.

James looked like he was going to step in and do it, but Victoria shook her head at him. He could carry Martin, she'd carry Evans.

In the end, he still didn't say anything, and it was over in a heartbeat. Danny and Hiran carried his body over to where they'd put Johnson, and that was it. Victoria felt subdued as they packed everything away, and the low mood stayed with her for the rest of the morning.

*

They decided on Scotland.

James had stayed mostly quiet during the discussion about what to do and where to go, but he'd been silently rooting for Scotland. It would be beyond brilliant to go home. They decided to follow Evans's last bit of advice

and find a hydroelectric plant for power, and since Scotland had the most, it was the logical choice. James had still been nervous they'd pick Wales.

The debate hadn't lasted long. Teona told everyone about the original plan with the safe zones, how the military had set them up to house potentially hundreds of people, and how it was highly unlikely any were functional since everything had fallen apart before mass evacuation had been attempted, so they were quickly dismissed. Jennifer had asked people for advice and if they had any preferences, but everyone seemed happy with the thought of their own self-sustaining power source, and no one complained when she and Teona settled on Scotland. Most of the conversation had been taken up with discussing the pros and cons of hydroelectricity, if other renewable energy sources were better, and if they could possibly run a plant when they settled. The latter point had caused the most upset, but they would have to cross that bridge when they got there.

James braced himself for his bandage change. Riya looked at him sympathetically. "This is going to hurt."

James nodded and gritted his teeth. He'd stripped from the waist up, and the cold was already numbing his body, which could only be a good thing.

Riya started peeling away his blood-crusted bandages from the previous day. Burning heat flooded out from his shoulder but it offered no comfort. James clenched his jaw so hard he was surprised he didn't crack some teeth.

After what seemed like a lifetime, Riya pulled away the bandages. She smiled at him. "All done. Now I will clean it and reapply fresh bandages."

James knew they didn't have many left. Hopefully

they could raid a hospital or pharmacy for more. Hopefully the reopened wound wouldn't get infected.

He held himself still as she worked, thinking of anything but the pain, and she was finished faster than he thought she would be. "Thanks," he grunted, inspecting his shoulder. "You've done a good job."

She beamed at him. "Thank you. I would never have thought I'd take to it—nursing was not something I ever considered. But it feels good to heal, especially in this torn world. I feel like I'm helping more than I ever could with a gun."

She helped him back into his top, prompting another flare of pain. "Maybe I should learn as well," he gritted out. "I can't be a soldier any longer." He knew he didn't hide the resentment as Riya looked at him with pity.

"I'm sorry, James," she said sadly. "If it's any help, we all appreciate the sacrifice you made. You helped us escape."

It was a help. It truly was. It was just a *small* help. He knew he'd never regain full use of his arm. He'd never hold a rifle again. He'd never play the drums again. He'd never be able to properly hold Teona. He shut his eyes against a wave of bitterness that threatened to drown him, but he didn't give in to it. Yes, he'd never be a soldier again, but he could still help. He'd take them to Scotland, they'd find a power plant that was defendable, and he'd help everyone settle. He'd teach the civilians survival skills, and he'd help find food and water. It was going to be all right.

It was going to take time, but he would adjust.

James gave Riya a small smile and nod, which she

returned. "We'll help you. We are a family now, like Jennifer said."

James stayed silent as she bound his arm in a sling, his mind on Jennifer. She and Teona would make a good team. In a way he was glad. Responsibility was a heavy fucker, and it had only grown more cumbersome with one working shoulder. He immediately felt guilty for the thought. As far as James knew, Jennifer had no experience leading people. People gravitated to the person who was immune, expecting them to keep them safe and offer direction in this new, directionless world. He supposed he should have seen it coming. Danny and others at the castle had looked at her with reverence.

Teona would help her. Of that he had no doubt.

Riya finished up and handed him a packet of antibiotics. "Take these. They are what Louis gave you originally, and I don't want it to become infected. What is it you say? Stay safe instead of sorry?"

"Better to be safe than sorry," James said, distracted. Antibiotics. He was no doctor or scientist, but he *was* practical, and he knew these were going to be the new currency. He didn't want to waste such a precious commodity on his shoulder, not when they didn't know if it even was going to become infected. It might be fine. James nodded and Riya moved off, but instead of taking one of the tablets he shoved the packet into his trouser pocket and sealed it away.

I'll be fine, he told himself, trying to will the pain away. It was a shame she hadn't given him any painkillers. Well, James could handle it. He gritted his teeth and stood up, pulling his coat on one-handed and zipping it up against the cold. Not allowing himself to think of his

fucked-up circumstances, he strode forward to help dismantle their transitory camp.

And to get his rations because he was *starving*.

Chapter Twenty-Five

Packing everything up took almost no time at all, and they were on the move faster than Jennifer could've hoped for. Teona had taken her sweet time saying goodbye to the out-of-fuel helicopter—she'd talked to it like people talked to their cat or dog, she'd even *petted* it. Jennifer wasn't the only one to roll her eyes—but they were still moving before the sun had fully cleared the horizon.

She didn't know how she felt about being back in England. London wasn't *that* far away. Her home. The place where she'd had her parents and Evelyn and everyone. God, it seemed like a lifetime ago. She didn't think she could go back. She said a silent goodbye to the city and her past life there. Her new home lay north.

She was in the middle of the group, leaving the orientation to the soldiers, namely Danny and Hiran, who seemed to have bonded over carrying dead bodies. Victoria was up there with them, no doubt learning all about navigating and tracking and so on. She was becoming more of a soldier with every passing day.

Dan and Rhys ambled along beside her. Rhys chatted away to Dan, still trying to bring him out of his shell. Jennifer had never realised how good he was with kids. But

then, none of her old friends had younger children in their families.

Behind her walked Aarav and Riya, conversing in their mother tongue. They seemed to be all right—Jennifer even heard the odd chuckle from them. In front of Jennifer strode Teona and James with Charlie and the little girl. Teona and Charlie were talking about flying from what Jennifer was able to overhear, and James kept stride silently next to them while carrying the little girl on his good arm. It was a bizarre sight—he didn't strike Jennifer as particularly paternal, but the girl wouldn't leave his side.

To Jennifer's great disappointment, Alexia was behind them guarding the rear. Alexia, Elise, Anthony, and Edward formed a rough circle around the group, and they carried the only weapons left with ammo in them, along with Victoria, Danny, and Hiran up ahead. They'd counted everything last night, and in total they had one magazine for each gun, and enough food and water to last five days. On their trek up to Scotland they were going to have to scavenge and hunt.

Jennifer fiddled with her camera for a while, but inspiration never struck. She was still too numb from everything. She glanced back at Alexia for what felt like the hundredth time, hoping she'd come and help her out of her melancholy, but she was a good soldier and wouldn't compromise the group like that.

Her mind stuck on Alexia. The memory of their first kiss threatened to make her giggle like she was some stupid teenager with a crush, but she managed to keep her composure. Jennifer's thoughts revolved around her, around the way Alexia's breath hitched when they kissed,

the way her hands roamed her body, what her—

"So, Miss Immune," Teona's loud voice smashed through her thoughts like a sledgehammer, and Jennifer almost jumped out of her skin. "*Five* new bites?" She seemed impressed.

"Yeah," Jennifer replied with a cough. God, she hoped the pilot hadn't noticed anything. "They all hurt like hell."

The one from the other day protecting Elise, a new one on her lower right arm, one on the junction between her left shoulder and neck and two more on her upper left arm. Riya had done her best bandaging them, but blood seeped through, particularly from the one on her neck. They were going to run out of bandages soon.

"I got this one on my hand a few days ago when our truck was attacked. I got the first one in Paris as I tried to block a man. Naomi killed him," Jennifer said with sadness. Naomi had made her uncomfortable with her constant awe-filled looks, but she'd only been trying to protect her. "Two got through the line and charged straight for Dan and Owain, so I jumped in front of them. Alexia killed those two." Owain's death had hit her harder than Naomi's—he had always been kind to her and had often tried to blunt Evans's haughtiness. "Then when the line collapsed, four rushed me at once. I fought one off—" she was super proud of that—"and Danny killed two and Alexia one, but not before I was bitten again."

Teona whistled lowly. "Sounds fucked up." Jennifer nodded. "Listen, Immune, bit of advice. You've got the protecting and the putting yourself in harm's way thing down, but you really need to work on your image."

"My image?"

"Yeah. Take just now for instance"—*great, she did notice something*—"I don't know where you went in your head, but you were clearly not present. You looked distracted, and that's weakness. Always be alert and ready to act at a moment's notice. This world has always been fucked up, especially for women, and even more so for black women like me and queer women like you. Now it has only gotten worse. We have to stick together. Always be present, and even if you're not, at least *look* like you are. Half the battle is image. Get that right and the rest will follow."

Jennifer nodded slowly. "Thank you," she said. "I'll work on it."

Teona grinned. "Good, because you need to."

Jennifer laughed with her. "Always straight to the point."

"Never saw the point of beating around the bush."

"Speaking of getting straight to the point," Jennifer said. "How are we going to work this? I know people are looking to me because I'm immune—stupid, I know—but you are far more qualified to lead."

Teona shrugged. "Like I said before, I get final say on all military matters." Jennifer nodded. She certainly wasn't going to give Teona orders on things she knew more about. "But other than that, it can be a partnership." Her eyes hardened. "No more making decisions without me, yeah? We discuss everything."

"All right," Jennifer said. "Let's do this, together." She almost raised a hand for a high-five but thought better of it.

Teona laughed. "Yeah, yeah, don't get all mushy on

me." She winked. "Partner." Teona sauntered off to join James and Charlie without waiting for a reply. Jennifer chuckled, glad Teona had agreed to work with her. Straightening her back and keeping her chin up, Jennifer tried to exude an air of relaxed vigilance, not unlike Teona herself. She didn't know how well she pulled it off, if she even did at all.

*

They'd been walking all day. Victoria was shattered—even all the training with Anthony hadn't prepared her for the way fatigue wormed its way under her skin and fed on her energy. She didn't even want to contemplate the blisters on her feet.

They hadn't encountered a single other person. The lack of people both pleased and perturbed her. There hadn't been so much as a brief glance of someone in the distance. Victoria decided it was a good thing—no people meant no infected, so she'd take it as a win.

They'd thought about finding cars and driving, but they'd need several to carry them all and the supplies, and they'd come across one too many roadblocks that put the idea to bed for good. Still, Victoria wished they had been able to drive. Her poor feet were crying out for rest, but she kept pushing forward, determined not to show the slightest hint of weakness in front of these people who thought her so strong.

She carefully stepped over a child's broken push-chair, making sure her animal was secure in her grip as she scanned the surrounding trees and lake. She didn't have a clue where they were. She wasn't as well versed as she perhaps should have been on Britain's geography.

They came upon buildings, sudden in their appearance, and she halted the group. Danny and Hiran moved forward quickly and quietly, and Victoria barely had time to rest her numb feet before they were strolling back.

"Place is empty," Danny said.

"There is a hill around the bend." Hiran pointed through the trees. "It would be a good place to camp for the night."

Victoria silently urged Jennifer and Teona to agree to call it a day. They'd been ruthless in their drive to keep going, stopping the group only for toilet breaks and bandage changes. They'd even made them eat while walking. Victoria was sure Jennifer suffered as well—she'd seen her moving from foot to foot during the last toilet break. In fact, Victoria was sure *everyone* was hurting—even the soldiers were looking a little worse for wear. She didn't want to think about what James was going through. His skin glowed sickly pale and sweat dampened his face, but he offered up no complaints. When Jennifer had pulled him aside to ask how he was, *he'd* been the one to insist on pushing forward.

"Yes, we'll stop." Teona nodded. Victoria could almost hear the collective release of breath from the group.

They rounded the bend and climbed the hill, and Victoria finally shrugged out of her backpack. It had been fine when she'd picked it up that morning, but it seemed to have mysteriously gained a few hundred pounds as the day wore on.

She listened to the bustle behind her as she took in the view—a small park in front of her with slides and swings, picnic benches dotted around to the left and right, and the glassy lake through a thin screen of trees. It was a

good a place as any to camp.

Victoria's coat soon followed her bag on the ground. She was *sweating*. Aching and hot, she made herself help with the camp, and before she knew it, tents were erected and a fire crackled happily in the middle of it all. Jennifer and Dan were handing out the evening rations, and Victoria was surprised to realise how famished she was. Lots of exercise and little food was not a good combination.

Elise, Edward, and Anthony took first watch as everyone settled down in a loose ring around the fire. Elise hadn't spoken much all day, but she had briefly moved up to James and the little girl for a quick chat. Victoria didn't know what they'd discussed, but she'd caught Elise shooting glances at the girl a few times.

Edward and Anthony were pretty much inseparable from what Victoria could see. They pulled the same guard shifts, they walked and chatted together when they weren't guarding the perimeter, and now they were off securing the camp site. They must have bonded in London. She couldn't remember seeing Edward at the castle.

After a quick rinse in the lake that was nowhere near cleansing enough, Victoria settled herself between Jennifer and Teona and accepted her food with a quiet "thank you". She ate in silence, opting to watch and listen instead of talk. James sat on the other side of Teona, and Riya buzzed around him like a bee, removing his shirt and bandages and cleaning his shoulder. Victoria winced in sympathy—his injury looked dreadful.

"Have you started the antibiotics?" Riya asked as she cleaned around the wound with one of their dwindling antiseptic wipes.

"Aye," James grunted.

Riya muttered something under her breath and sighed. "I wish Louis was still here."

"Aye," James said again, softer this time.

Victoria frowned at the thought of Louis and the Commandant. This world had taken too many good people.

Riya huffed as she began to reapply his bandage, a worried crease appearing between her brows. "I hope I can keep this clean and help you heal, James."

"I know you can." James smiled. It was strange to see the gruff soldier being so gentle.

"We'll keep helping you, James," Teona chipped in. "We're still going to get back to your physical therapy."

James looked almost panicked. "That's going to have to wait till it's healed a wee bit more." At Teona's frown he elaborated. "I tore it all again at the castle."

Teona's frown deepened. "And when the fuck where you going to tell me that?"

James rolled his eyes. "I'm telling you now, Teona, don't worry. Just let it heal again, it'll be fine."

Teona eyed him suspiciously. "If you say so."

Victoria snorted. They'd shared one kiss and they were already behaving like an old married couple. She tuned their bantering out and focused on the other new couple in the group. Alexia helped Jennifer change her bandages as Riya was busy with James.

"Does it hurt?" Alexia asked as she gently pulled away a bandage from Jennifer's arm. Victoria thought Jennifer's grimace was answer enough, but she replied anyway.

"No, it's fine."

Victoria almost snorted again. Jennifer was clearly trying to impress Alexia, and judging from the affectionate yet amused glance Alexia gave her, she saw right through it.

Jennifer shrugged sheepishly. Alexia laughed and swooped in for a quick kiss before refocusing on her task. Jennifer's cheeks were tinged pink as she smiled.

"You two are adorable," Victoria said, unable to keep the mirth from her voice.

Alexia laughed again as Jennifer scowled at her. "Shut up, Victoria."

Victoria chuckled along with Alexia, and she was reminded of Jennifer's youth. She forgot sometimes, amid all the fear and fighting and how easily everyone turned to Jennifer, that she was only in her early twenties.

She bumped shoulders with Jennifer and winked at the two of them, a thought popping into her mind that made her smirk. "I've never had to give *the talk*, but always use protection—"

"Oh my God, *Victoria*." Jennifer blushed hard.

Victoria laughed as Alexia's cheeks coloured as well. "Like I said, adorable."

"Sorry about her," Jennifer said to Alexia. "Sometimes she's like my older sister and sometimes she's like my mum."

"Hey," Victoria rebuked, pushing aside thoughts of Katherine. "I am nowhere near old enough to be your mother."

Now Jennifer was smirking. "Older sister then.

Protective and embarrassing."

Victoria rolled her eyes. "I'm just trying to keep you safe from infections." She put on airs, raising her chin and flipping her hair. "Some of them can be quite nasty, you know."

The three of them shared a chuckle, then Victoria left them together. She finished her food and stood up, stretching as she tentatively walked a few steps. Her feet hurt, but they held. She thought about doing some kick-boxing moves and getting some practice in, but the bone-deep tiredness was still there. It had entered her body after Paris and seemed to have taken up permanent residence.

Instead, she stood at the edge of the hill and watched the sun set in the sky. Dan and the little girl played on the swings under the watchful eye of Elise, and it was nice to see them both smiling. *He looks like a big brother.* He pushed her higher on the swings. The sound of the girl's laughter was like sweet music, their joy framed by blazing orange.

Victoria smiled as she watched, content with the day's ending.

Chapter Twenty-Six

Charlie held the little girl. James had tried, and succeeded, for most of the morning, but he was too weak to hold her for long. It gnawed at him, the worry, the fear, until he was sure everyone could hear the strain on his heart.

He had been mortified when Jennifer asked if he wanted to slow their pace yesterday. He'd never felt so fragile in his life, and he did *not* like it. Not one fucking bit.

So, he did what he did best. He powered through it.

He didn't stray too far from the girl—they really needed to find out her name—as she would start crying if he wasn't close, but he moved just far enough so he was walking side by side with Trueman. Chatting to the man would distract him from the gnawing ache, and it would be nice to get to know him better. James had been remiss in not doing it sooner.

"Sir," Trueman said in way of greeting.

"Trueman." James nodded. "How's it going?"

"Quiet, sir, nothing to report."

"Good." James looked around, taking in the scenery.

There wasn't much to comment on—they'd been walking down country roads for hours, bearing witness to fields, trees, more fields, and the occasional built-up area they avoided like the plague. *Which I guess it kind of is. Another horrible plague to decimate humanity.*

"How are you?" James asked, somewhat gruffly. He felt a little awkward—*after everything we've been through together, we should know each other more than we do.*

Trueman blinked, the only indication James's question had surprised him. "Fine, sir. Well, given the circumstances. And yourself?"

James grunted. "As good as I can be, given the circumstances." There was a pause, and he pushed on. "There was a training exercise up in Scotland where I had to survive for a week in the wilderness with just the supplies on my back. This kind of reminds me of it."

"Yeah," Trueman agreed. "We'll have to start hunting soon. No doubt Victoria will want to learn as well. I'm still keeping up her training. We'll make her into a fine soldier yet."

We lose one soldier, and we gain another. James ignored the bitter taste in his mouth. He trusted Victoria with taking his place. *And I can still help.* He had a feeling he was going to be repeating that to himself for a long time.

"I used to enjoy training out in the countryside," Trueman said. "The air always feels so clean out here. I was born and raised in London, so it's nice to be out in the open. Freeing almost. Cities can get so claustrophobic. I've always found the country to be beautiful."

James couldn't agree more. "I'm not a city man myself, and whenever I visited, the air did taste dirty. Particularly London. I've always loved the outdoors, though, when I was younger me and my friends used to run through the fields and forest near our houses and imagine we were cavemen fighting off mammoths and sabre tooth tigers."

Truman grinned, his chin stabbing down as he chuckled. "When I was younger, we used to hang out in high-rise flats. It would have been amazing to run through trees and big open spaces. Although, as I got older and could go further afield, I remember playing football at Hyde Park. There was one game that got really rough really fast, and two of my friends had to go to hospital." Trueman shook his head, a nostalgic look on his face.

"What happened to them?"

"One broke his arm, the other his ankle. It was the same boy who tackled them both." Trueman shook his head again, this time angrily. "After Steve hobbled off to the sidelines, we were going to call it off, but Corey started taunting us, calling us names, so we decided to play one more match, get our own back and then take Steve to hospital. Not five minutes in, Corey broke Billy's arm. Him and the rest of his bully friends ran off after that, laughing as they did."

"What a bastard," James said. He wondered if this Corey had been the one to bully Trueman at school. "I'm sorry. At least the boys were all right."

"Yeah." Trueman was smiling again. "Steve definitely milked it. He got a lot of sympathy from a girl called Beth, which he thought was great because he fancied her."

The two soldiers shared a laugh. "The things we do to

impress women," James said. "Speaking of, you've been spending a lot of time with Victoria. Do you like her? I've been told I'm a brilliant wingman. I introduced one of my friends to his wife."

Trueman looked uncomfortable, so James quickly backpedalled. "Sorry, man, I didn't mean to make you feel awkward. It doesn't matter. If that seemed a wee bit too familiar—"

"No, it's all right. It'll be nice to be friends," Trueman relaxed then tensed again, hunching up in a way that seemed defensive. "It's just, erm, I don't like Victoria that way."

James held up his hand in a placating gesture. "That's fine. Are you okay?"

Trueman released a long breath. "I'm twenty-eight, and I've only told two people. Not even my parents. Never found the right time. And when I joined the army, I don't know, I guess I was scared. Still am. But, seeing how society came crashing to a halt, and seeing the way you're all fine with Jennifer and Alexia, I think it'll be all right. It's upsetting that I won't ever be able to tell my parents or friends, though. Or my aunt, but I suspect she knew. I used to love going around hers on weekends—"

Trueman was rambling, but James had understood as soon as he'd mentioned the two women. He didn't push him though—he would come out to them in his own time.

Instead, James clapped him on the shoulder and cut his babble off. "Did you like playing football?"

Trueman blinked, his mouth still hanging open. "Oh, yeah, I love football. I support Chelsea."

James scrunched up his face. "Celtic could take them

any day."

"As if," Trueman scoffed.

"Aye! How about we have a match when everything's settled down?"

Trueman smirked, a glint entering his eye that made James worry he was going to get thrashed in the hypothetical game. "Definitely. It'll be good to play again." He paused, a more serious look settling over his face. "And, erm, thank you."

James waved him off. "You don't have to thank me, man." He would never forget the grateful look the corporal sent his way as they continued chatting about football, and he wondered at the abuse he must have faced as a kid to make him so skittish and want to hide a huge part of himself. James cursed the prejudices of the old society and hoped they'd do better a second time around.

*

"The place is quiet," Danny said, that unnerving awe-filled shine in his eye. "We haven't seen any sign of infected or otherwise."

"Thanks, Danny," Jennifer said. "You've done a good job securing the area."

Danny nodded once, a little proud smile gracing his lips. "We'll keep everyone safe. I give you my word." His tone was serious, like he was one of the old knights he so often gushed about.

"I know you will. I trust you."

His smile widened and he strode away with his head held high.

Jennifer knew the power of positive reinforcement, which was her motivation to try to be upbeat and compliment everyone as they settled for the night. They'd had another long day hiking mile after mile after mile. She knew exhaustion was enough to foul anyone's mood—she'd pulled enough all-nighters at university to know that intimately.

So tonight, even though all she wanted to do was curl up in her sleeping bag, she made it a point to speak to them all. Even just a few words, like with Danny.

She made her way over to Riya, who was taking stock of their medical supplies. "How's it looking?"

Riya glanced up and gave her a tired smile. The pace had been particularly brutal for her. Jennifer assumed she'd been a bit out of shape when everything went to shit. She'd come a long way, there was no denying that, but she was still the first to flag. Her thick black hair was tied up, but strands broke loose around her face, giving her an unkempt look. Not that Jennifer fared much better. She knew she had dark bruises under her eyes, and if the fresh cramp in her stomach was anything to go by, she was going to start her period soon. It was a wonder Alexia didn't run at the sight of her.

"Not good," Riya sighed. "At the rate I've been changing everyone's bandages, we only have enough left for two more days. We have no antibiotics left. I gave the last to James." She lowered her voice even though no one was close enough to listen in. "His shoulder is really bad. *Really* bad. I don't think he's going to get his movement back, and he may be in pain for a very long time, maybe even the rest of his life."

On some level, Jennifer had known, but it was still a

shock to hear. *Shit, James.* Her eyes found him across camp, showing the little girl how to boil the kettle, which was something children her age should not be doing. An intense wave of sorrow hit Jennifer at the thought of his pain. He would have been medically discharged had the world kept spinning, but they needed all the help they could get, and Jennifer knew she was going to ask him to keep going. And bless the man, she knew he would.

"Stop giving me fresh bandages," she told Riya. "And any whose wounds are healed enough to go without them. Focus on James."

"But, Jennifer," Riya protested. "Yours and James's are the most serious. I'll ration the others for James, but you need more as well."

Jennifer briefly let herself feel the pain pulse through her before she roughly clamped down again. "No. My wounds are healing well. Dan still needs the cut on his arm seen to, and Victoria's knuckles as well."

"Victoria's hands are healing better than your wounds, and while I agree Dan needs fresh bandages for another day, *your* need is greater." Riya's tone was no nonsense, and Jennifer had to stop herself from relenting.

"What if something happens and we need those bandages? No, Riya, stockpile mine for future emergencies. I'll be fine." Jennifer grinned at the long-suffering expression on Riya's face.

"Have it your way then, but let me keep putting one on your neck, that one is bad."

Jennifer thought for a second, but she knew Riya was right. Besides, she didn't want her top rubbing against it. "Okay. And thanks." Jennifer broadened her grin, and

eventually Riya cracked and smiled a fond smile back. "You're doing such a good job here, Riya, honestly."

"Thank you," Riya said warmly. "I will carry Louis' lessons on and help wherever I can. I can teach you. It will be better if more people know."

"That's a good idea," Jennifer agreed. It was past time to learn. "In fact, teach everyone who doesn't already know, will you? It's an essential skill, and everyone should know at least the basics."

"I will." Riya nodded.

"Thanks."

Jennifer settled next to Rhys for the meal as she had for the past couple of days. Alexia, Dan, and Rhys were the people she spent most of her time with. It was difficult to be far from Rhys. He was a tether to her past self, the one with no troubles, no duty to keep people alive. It was dangerous in a way—Rhys represented her lost innocence, and she couldn't get that back even if she tried. She had responsibilities now, and she wouldn't risk that for a taste of simplicity again.

Still, it was hard not to revert to *Jen* around Rhys.

So, she let herself be physically close to him, but she found herself keeping him at arm's length emotionally. They still hadn't talked about that night. About their friends. About anything really, beyond the reunion. She also sensed Rhys hanging back, but then she would in his place as well. She had Alexia, she was immune, and she was leading a group of survivors through an infection-ravaged world. Jennifer hardly believed it herself.

The meal was a quiet affair. Jennifer played with her camera for a while until movement caught her eye and she

watched as James sat himself down in front of the little girl.

"James," James said, pointing to himself. He then pointed at the girl, his eyebrows raised in a question. She looked at him blankly. Jennifer could feel the whole camp holding its breath.

"James," the soldier repeated, pointing at himself again.

The girl licked her chapped lips and pointed to herself, and, in a voice so small Jennifer had to strain to hear, said, "Ismay."

A large smile bloomed on James's face, and Jennifer could see it reflected around the fire. The happiness permeating the atmosphere clearly boosted Ismay's confidence as she gave a toothy grin back. "Ismay," she said again, louder this time. She pointed at James. "Jams!"

James laughed, a sound echoed by the camp. "Close enough, lass, close enough. Come on, let's get you tucked in."

The camp filled up with people chatting and laughing, something Jennifer hadn't heard before. Ismay's voice had given everyone a little bit of their confidence back, it seemed, and something like satisfaction seeped into Jennifer's skin.

She moved to sit next to Dan, who'd been on the opposite side of Rhys. She gently bumped shoulders with him. "Hey, you," she said softly.

He gave her a small smile but didn't meet her eyes. *Paris really knocked his progress back. What happened there was enough trauma to last a lifetime, never mind all the other shit he's gone through.*

"How are your feet with all this walking?" Jennifer decided to ask him something benign to try to get him talking. "My feet are like two blocks of pain on the ends of my legs." She wasn't exaggerating.

"Erm, they're fine," Dan mumbled. "I mean, uh, they hurt, but erm, I can keep up."

"I don't doubt that for a second, Dan," Jennifer reassured him. The last thing she wanted was for him to feel like he was a liability. "You're strong. Amazingly so. Both physically and mentally. I mean," she laughed, "you're definitely fitter than I am." That earned her another tiny smile. "You've been through so much, Dan, yet you've held on to your compassion and kindness. I saw you playing with Ismay, helping her be a child again." She paused as a thought hit her. *He must want to feel like a big brother again.* She bumped his shoulder again. "You helped me when we first met, and you've been helping me ever since. It takes a strong person to go through as much pain and loss as you have and still be kind. I'm proud of you."

There was a beat of stillness, then Dan smiled shyly, but wider than before. "Thanks, Jennifer, that means a lot." He looked up and met her eyes briefly, and she grinned. Oh, how she'd missed that shade of blue.

"You don't have to thank me for speaking the truth," Jennifer said, bringing him into a one-armed hug. "You gonna be okay?"

She felt him nod. "I'm gonna be okay."

She squeezed him then let go. She winked at him as she stood up and he ducked his head shyly, but she could see his smile. She walked back to sit next to Alexia, her heart lighter than it had been in days.

"Hey," Alexia said softly.

"Hey."

"What you did was wonderful."

Jennifer waved it off. "I just told him the truth."

"Still," Alexia said, her eyes bright in the fading light. "I don't think I've seen him smile so much."

Jennifer turned to look back at Dan, and she could see the faint upturn of his lips as he continued eating his rations. "He's going to be okay."

Alexia nodded. "Oui, he is. How are you feeling?" Jennifer didn't miss the glance at her bandages.

"I'm fine," she said. "They hurt, but they're healing. I've actually told Riya to stop bandaging them." Jennifer felt more than saw Alexia frown, and she rushed to continue. "It's fine, honestly. They're healing, and we never know when we'll need spare bandages."

Jennifer could tell Alexia wasn't happy. "If you think it's the best action then I support it. But I am worried about you, of course."

Jennifer smiled, warmth filling her up. "I'm okay, I promise."

Alexia hummed, the faint crease between her brows proof of her concern. Jennifer wanted to smooth that crinkle away, so she changed the subject. "So, there's one thing I've been wanting to ask," she said cheekily, and Alexia raised an eyebrow in question, a smile playing about her lips. "When did you start liking me?" Jennifer asked with an eyebrow waggle.

Alexia laughed, and Jennifer couldn't keep the grin from her face. Joy flitted through the air, through *her*, and

she wanted to keep Alexia laughing for as long as possible. "Was it instantaneous, or did you need to warm up to me first?"

"I thought you were beautiful right away," Alexia said. "When I got to know you, I started really liking you. It was only when Teona said you were bisexual that I let myself think I could maybe have a chance. And that time in your room at the castle, I almost kissed you when you told me about the things you want to photograph. I was scared, though, so I left."

Jennifer had asked as a joke to rid Alexia of her worried frown, but her thoughtful answer moved her. She leaned in and Alexia met her halfway, their lips meeting softly. It wasn't a kiss filled with heat and passion, but one heavy with promise and future, and Jennifer didn't want it to end.

Eventually they parted. "You definitely had a chance," Jennifer whispered, her lips still close to Alexia's. She started smirking. "I thought you were hot the moment I saw you," she laughed as Alexia pushed her away. "Instant attraction."

Alexia tutted. "You are so romantic," she said sarcastically.

Jennifer's laugh died down. "When we were at the hospital, I started hoping you were interested in women, interested in me, but it wasn't really till the castle when you told me that I started to let myself think *I* had a chance."

"We would have saved ourselves a lot of time if we told each other sooner," Alexia laughed, shaking her head.

"Yeah," Jennifer agreed. "At least we're together

now."

"Oui." Alexia trailed her hand along Jennifer's jaw. "Get some sleep now. I'll see you in the morning."

Jennifer noticed everyone tidying up and climbing into their sleeping bags and tents. She'd been so lost in Alexia she hadn't noticed anything else. *Great. So much for heeding Teona's advice.*

Jennifer sighed, disappointed she couldn't spend more time with Alexia. She had first watch, though, and Jennifer really needed to sleep.

She curled up in her sleeping bag with a smile on her face. She hoped she'd dream of Alexia instead of the nightmares that had plagued her since Paris, robbing her of proper rest. Part of the reason she pushed everyone so hard was her desire to fall asleep and be too exhausted to dream.

Luckily, sleep came quickly, and with it, peace.

Chapter Twenty-Seven

The day had dawned bright and crisp but had since descended into an overcast gloom that threatened rain but failed to deliver. Victoria missed the sun, and she hoped spring and summer would hurry themselves along. Summer had always been her favourite season, not just for the summer dresses or the summer holidays—although she wasn't going to lie to herself, that break from school was a large part of it—but also for the happiness that seemed so universal when the sun shone. This winter had been horrible, and Victoria wanted some warmth to pick everyone back up again.

They'd walked so far these past few days, Victoria was sure her blisters had blisters. Her feet were long since past hurting, and she was glad they'd grown tougher. She used to love getting manicures and pedicures, but those days were long gone. At least her knuckles were healed enough that she could wield the animal with little difficulty.

They were in Cheshire. Victoria had been to Chester Zoo when she was ten, but she couldn't remember much from the trip, and it had been her one and only foray into the area. She knew footballers and rich people lived here, so she hadn't expected it to be so...country-like. So empty.

Their rations were running low, so they'd ventured close to one of the few built-up areas. They hoped to scavenge for food, water, and medical supplies.

Teona had decided their needs outweighed the threat of infected. Victoria agreed. They hadn't seen anyone in days—which didn't mean she was going to let her guard down. All in all, it had been a nice respite from the chaos.

Victoria gripped her animal, the familiar weight comforting, and edged around the corner of a building. The red brick was crumbling, and Victoria had to step over the body of an old man. Seeing dead bodies had become commonplace, which was usually fine—*never thought death would be my new normal*—but this one was rotting, and it was *revolting*. Victoria almost gagged, but she somehow kept her repulsion in check.

There was nothing around the corner. They continued down the street past trees and houses and cars, some of which looked immaculate while others had windows smashed, doors wide open, blood staining the glass. The violence looked random. Several more bodies like the old man's littered the street, all in varying degrees of decay. The breeze carried the smell away.

"It should be at the end of this long arse street," Teona said. She and Victoria were up front today, and Teona had stolen a phone that had some charge from a fresh corpse and gotten a map of the area up, which showed a supermarket and shopping complex nearby. The new body had alarmed everyone, and they were all on edge as they crept through the town.

"Okay, let's keep moving. I want us to be in and out and on our way again in less than an hour," Jennifer said.

They made it almost to the end of the street before a

repugnant smell assaulted Victoria's poor nose.

Teona twisted her face. "Smells like something crawled up someone's arse and died," she muttered. Victoria had to agree.

More dead bodies? But no, this didn't have the sickening sweetness of rotting flesh. It was more the stale, acrid scent of unwashed bodies.

Victoria gripped her animal as Teona halted the rest of the group. The two women shared a nod, then they inched forward on light feet, Teona a step ahead of Victoria. She tried to see over the hedge that blocked the view to the right, but the bloody thing was too tall. They made it to a set of traffic lights when Victoria heard faint shuffling and one muffled groan, quickly cut off. Teona signalled Victoria to cover her—Anthony and Edward had been teaching her the proper hand signals—and darted out from behind the hedge with all the grace and power of a feline, leaving Victoria feeling clunky as she burst out after her.

Neither of them discharged their weapons. Pity stirred in Victoria and mingled with distaste at the sight before her. There were four people, sitting or lying on the pavement, all in different states of undress. One man was in a pair of shorts and a ripped top that looked like it used to be a shirt, while a woman wore a coat fastened over a jumper. The other two were children, no more than ten Victoria estimated, and they wore what looked like the tattered remains of a school uniform.

The man in shorts blinked blearily at them and made a pitiful keening noise as he tried to crawl away, his weakened body unable to move far. The woman didn't give any indication she'd seen them at all. Victoria looked more

closely at her. Her chest was rising and falling, but slowly, infrequently. Death would take her soon.

The children were much the same. Two girls, both lying on the curb where road met pavement. One watched Teona and Victoria and the other stared at the sky.

The man stopped crawling as his energy ran out. Victoria thought he was crying, but she couldn't get a good look at his face. Was this what happened at the end of the infection? Falling into this stupor, body too emaciated to carry on? Victoria suppressed a shudder. She'd never seen this end stage before. *If I get it, someone better kill me before this happens.* They seemed so helpless, so pathetic. Victoria hated the thought of experiencing a loss of agency, never mind this horrible wastage that came after.

"Should we...?" Victoria gestured at them with her animal, unsure of what to do. They weren't a threat, but should they put them out of their misery? The noise would attract anyone close, and Victoria was loath to waste precious bullets.

Teona shook her head and relaxed her stance. She waved the rest of the group over. "I think we should leave them," she said to Jennifer, who nodded slowly, a pained expression on her face. "They're going to die soon anyway, poor fuckers, and we can't waste the ammunition."

"Okay," Jennifer said, still staring at the infected. "Let's continue then."

Victoria and Teona were the first ones to see the shopping complex. They edged into the car park slowly, taking every precaution not to be seen. Victoria frequently glanced behind her to make sure the others were all there. They hadn't come this far to get jumped now.

No movement. The place was a ghost town. Victoria had yet to get the watched feeling she'd had in Paris, which she took as a good sign. They weaved through the few cars that were dotted about and walked right up to the doors of the supermarket without seeing anything. Victoria was both suspicious and relieved.

They bunched up at the entrance, the automatic doors jammed open by a pram designed for twins.

"Okay, people," Teona said in a stage whisper. "I suggest a few of us go in and sweep the area while the rest stay out here with a couple of soldiers for cover, yeah?"

James nodded, shifting Ismay higher on his hip. The little girl stared about the deserted car park. Her silence unnerved Victoria. She'd frequently thought kids were too loud, especially in her classroom, but this level of quiet was plain eerie.

"You know you're in charge of military stuff," Jennifer said.

"Good," Teona said with a smirk. "Since I'm the military leader now, I hereby take the title Supreme Commander." Her announcement was met with eye rolls and good-natured tutting. "Don't tut at your Supreme Commander," she said haughtily, sticking her nose in the air. "Right, Victoria, Trueman, and Ota with me, the rest stay with the group here. Any sign of infected or other bastards, call out 'Komodo Dragon vulnerable'."

"Komodo Dragon?" James raised an eyebrow that looked like Teona's signature move.

"Shut up, Sunshine. Komodo Dragons happen to have very good immune systems. You'd know that if you'd paid attention at school."

James snorted but didn't say anything more.

"Be safe, everyone," Jennifer said. "We'll be waiting here."

Victoria moved behind Teona and settled her animal. "We'll be back soon," she said, then they were moving through the doors and into the supermarket proper.

The temperature dropped slightly. The chill was pervasive as they crept through the aisles, and Victoria had to keep unfurling her fingers on the animal lest they become numb. She did *not* want to be caught off guard because her finger couldn't pull the trigger fast enough.

The lights were off, plunging the interior into a perpetual gloom. Her eyes adjusted quickly, but she still wished for extra illumination. The others didn't turn their torches on, though, so she didn't either. The moving beams of light would give them away.

The smell was on par with the dead bodies. It was a mixture of what she thought was curdled milk, rotting food, and sweet decay. It was times like this she wished she didn't have a sense of smell. *Bloody hell this is disgusting.* She started breathing through her mouth, but then it felt like she was tasting everything instead of smelling it. *Absolutely vile.*

The shelves were all empty. She knew supermarkets had been struggling in the months leading up to the outbreak due to the food recall, but the shelves had still been more or less fully stocked. Everything here had been picked clean. Victoria ruthlessly quashed the frustration that threatened to rush through her. *We're too late, there's nothing here. We're going to have to start hunting.* People were easy, it was her or them, but Victoria didn't know if she'd be able to kill an innocent rabbit or

something. *And what about our dwindling medical supplies?* They were fast running out of everything. Was Scotland the wrong option? They *were* right next to Wales.

In the end, the whole foray into the supermarket was wildly disappointing. It housed nothing but spilled food and dead bodies and didn't have so much as a box of paracetamol on a shelf. The four of them made their way back to the entrance, regret roiling off them like clouds breaking around a mountain.

*

There was a sharp clatter from beyond the car park, like a shelf falling over. The sound reverberated through the air, and the hairs on the back of Jennifer's neck stood up. No other sound followed, but everyone was on high alert, the soldiers arranged in a semi-circle around them, not unlike Paris, their heads swivelling, and their weapons held aloft.

Jennifer's breathing quickened. Teona's advice came back to her, and she held her back straight as she tried to exude a vigilant aura. James had given Ismay to Charlie, and he and Dan both stepped closer to her. She'd protect them if anything went wrong. *God, after a few calm days, of course it ends now. We can't ever catch a break.*

Jennifer slowly scanned around them. Buildings and shops, cars and bodies. The silence was oppressive. Everyone glared around with tension that held their bodies rigid. Jennifer eased her shoulders down from their hunched position, her backpack feeling heavier than it was.

Still no movement, still no noise. Had something just randomly fallen over? *No, we can't make that assumption. Presume it's infected.* Her eyes roamed the car park,

the buildings. She wished Teona and the others would appear. The sky was bright and clear, not a cloud or bird in sight.

Several minutes passed with everyone in a heightened state, but nothing more happened. Jennifer watched the soldiers relax as the silence stretched on. Danny turned around and gave them a quick smile to no doubt reassure them, but Jennifer still felt on edge, the adrenaline refusing to drain away. *Maybe it* was *something falling over. Not everything has to have sinister connotations.* Still, relaxing didn't sit right with her.

"Stay on guard," she said, her anxiety making her tone snappish. "We remain on high alert until the others come out. Then we'll discuss scouting the rest of the buildings."

We should have done that before we split up. Made sure the area was secure. She would not make the same mistake again.

At least the soldiers had straightened up. They were back to scanning the area, so Jennifer felt better. If anything did come, they'd see it.

More time passed and still nothing happened. Jennifer began to think nothing would. *Better to be safe than sorry.* She gave the car park yet another look, and if it wasn't for her paranoia, she was sure she would have missed it.

Behind a battered jeep to their left, she was positive she saw something move. The jeep was a dark-green colour, and the boot and driver's door were open. She could have sworn...

"Did anyone see anything behind that jeep?" Jennifer

whispered, pushing Dan and Charlie behind her. Hiran was closest to the vehicle, and he pointed his weapon at it as he edged closer. He halted next to it, and Jennifer saw him take a deep inhale before he darted around.

Jennifer's breath caught in her throat.

Chapter Twenty-Eight

Victoria and the others were almost at the doors when she heard it. The sharp pop of gunfire followed by a strangled, "Komodo Dragon vulnerable!"

They moved before the first syllable ended. Bright daylight slammed into Victoria's eyes as she absorbed the scene in the car park.

Three dead people littered the ground to the left, and one was shot by Elise as they tried to run away. Victoria's heart raced a mile a minute, but it seemed like everything was under control. The faint smell of gunfire lingered as the sound died off, and all was still again. *They needn't have shouted. They had it all under control.*

"We have to get out of here," James said, eyeing their surroundings warily. "That will have been heard for miles."

"Yeah," Jennifer agreed. She turned to them. "Did you find anything?"

Teona frowned. "No. Biggest waste of time ever. The place has been cleaned out."

Disappointment rippled through the group like a disturbed pond. "Sorry," Victoria said. "We'll find

somewhere else."

"Yeah," Jennifer said again. "Don't worry, everyone, this place was big, loads of people will have come here. We'll find somewhere small that still has stuff. Let's get out of here."

They made their way quickly back through the car park and onto the road, where Danny and Hiran took the lead. They turned the group left, and everyone settled in for another long stint of walking.

Victoria covered the right side. Her eyes never stayed in one place for too long—she was all too aware of the racket they had made. She wanted the group to walk faster so they could get as far away as possible before people—infected or otherwise—came sniffing around, but she knew everyone was tired. She was too. The thought of walking for hours again made her feet ache more than they already did.

She needn't have worried. They got as far as the second roundabout down the road.

An animalistic yowl crashed through the air as a young woman dashed across the road from the houses and trees opposite and jumped up onto the bonnet of a crashed car. Her momentum carried her far as she launched herself from it, and she managed to sail right over Victoria like a deranged bird. Victoria spun as she kept her eyes on the woman, and she watched as she landed on Jennifer, who'd shoved Aarav out of the way. The two collapsed in a tangle of limbs on the roundabout, and fear spiked in Victoria's blood at Jennifer's pained cry.

The infected woman's momentum turned against her. She crashed into Jennifer, but she kept going, rolling

free and skidding to a halt a little way away. Teona quickly put her down before she got the chance to rise.

"Ow..." Jennifer mumbled as she slowly struggled to her feet. Alexia and Rhys were by her side in an instant, carefully helping her back up.

"Are you all right?" Rhys asked, alarm clearly written all over his face.

"Yeah." Jennifer winced. "Just a few more cuts and bruises to add to the collection."

"Did she bite you?" Alarm was clear in Alexia's voice.

"No," Jennifer said. "No. I'm okay."

Victoria sighed with relief as she scanned the treeline for any more infected. They didn't have the bandages left for more injuries. "Let's keep moving."

They wasted no time. Aarav gave Jennifer a reluctant nod and they were off, jogging down the road away from where the woman had come from. Victoria didn't understand his dislike of Jennifer. He was a lovely man—Victoria had spent several lunches and evenings with him and Riya and they were easy to get on with—but Aarav seemed to be holding on to his distrust of Jennifer's immunity even in the face of clear evidence. Maybe they simply didn't like each other. It happened.

Again, they didn't travel far.

They came up to some traffic lights and turned right onto what appeared to be a main road, with tall trees on the right and buildings and more trees on the left. They didn't make it halfway down the road before they were stopped. Not by infected this time.

Victoria breathed hard as she pushed her tired legs

forward. She was still on the right, so she should have seen them. She should have *seen* them. They burst out of the tree cover like avenging angels, clad in full military gear—armour, helmets, rifles, the works. One had a wicked-looking shotgun and a couple had grenades strapped to their belts. Victoria barely had time to blink before they were surrounding them, shouting to drop their weapons, pushing them closer together. Victoria bumped into Dan as she was pressed back with a barrel in her face.

The others handed over their weapons. Victoria gritted her teeth. *There's not a lot else we can do.* Fury curled around the thought, offering no comfort. With great averseness, she handed over her animal, feeling naked without its reassuring weight.

"What—" Jennifer started, but she was cut off.

"Come with us," one of them growled, a squat, broad man with a face that looked like it had been intimately acquainted with a shovel. *"Quickly."*

Victoria almost fell over as she was roughly pushed forward, and she shot a glare at the man behind her. He grinned toothily at her, and she scowled as she once again forced her weary legs on. They continued down the road, the trees flanking both sides looking more sinister than before. Victoria glared at them. She should have *seen them.*

They passed another set of traffic lights, more abandoned cars, more bodies and blood. Victoria's lungs started to burn. She glimpsed Riya out of the corner of her eye, the poor woman struggling to keep up. A man kept shoving her, and Victoria saw Aarav get more and more wound up. *Don't snap.* Victoria wished she could somehow tell him to keep his cool. *They have guns, they'll*

shoot you!

They came up to a large roundabout and swerved left around it, barely slowing. The only good thing Victoria could think of was that she couldn't hear any pursuit. Not like Paris. She risked a glance behind and saw nothing but Elise getting chivvied along. She had a face like thunder, and Victoria hoped beyond hope everyone could keep it together until they got to wherever they were being taken.

They skidded to a halt. A blockage in the form of a bus cut off their access to a small bridge. Two more armed people were lying atop said bus with what looked like an assault rifle and a sniper rifle each. Victoria frowned. Could this abrupt kidnapping be a good thing? These people seemed well prepared.

One of the people in front trotted up to the bus and pried open the doors. Victoria and the others were once again shoved forward, and even if this was a rescue, she did *not* like it. A little civility went a long way.

She was pushed onto the bus after Jennifer. "What are we going to do?" Victoria whispered furiously as they shuffled down the aisle.

Jennifer spared her a brief glance as she jumped out of the emergency exit on the other side of the bus. "Keep your head down for now," she muttered back. "We'll see where this goes."

They were bunched up until everyone was through and the doors were firmly shut again. *I can admire their caution whilst hating their manhandling.* Victoria glared fire at the man who pushed her forward, but he just sneered at her and fingered his gun. *I bet he doesn't even know how to use it. Idiot keeps his finger inside the trigger guard.*

Blue railings lined either side of the bridge, with yet more trees on the right and a river on the left. They were shepherded up to a large white and brick building, The Red Lion emblazoned across the front in big letters. *A pub?*

They had to go around a black railing on the path to get to the entrance. All the windows on the ground floor were boarded up. The shovel-faced man stopped them in front of the building.

"Line up along the railing," he gestured. Victoria thought he sounded like he was from Liverpool, but the accent was far from thick.

They did as they were told, and Victoria made sure she was next to Jennifer. She'd protect her if things went south here. Shovel-face disappeared through a bright-red door, and Victoria took the opportunity to look around. More roadblocks were in place around the pub. A row of vans and sandbags spanned the road to the right of the building, and she counted four people there.

The other side of the roundabout was more difficult as it was wider, but again they'd blocked part of the road with another bus and filled the gaps with more cars and manpower. Victoria counted five people patrolling there. One of the guards looked like they didn't know which end of their weapon the bullets came out of. *They certainly look the part here in their fancy armour, but can they hold their own?* She had doubts.

She whipped back around when she heard people come out of the pub.

Chapter Twenty-Nine

Two men emerged into the daylight. One was Shovel-face, but it was the other who drew Victoria's attention. He was tall. Easily over six feet. Hazel eyes set in a handsome face. Sandy brown hair swept back in a way that looked effortless. His strong jaw was clean shaven, and he wore a dark-grey shirt with black trousers, like he'd stepped out of an office.

But it wasn't his appearance that made Victoria stare. As soon as she'd laid eyes on him her skin began to crawl, like she instinctively knew something wasn't right about him but couldn't put her finger on what. Part of her wanted to get as far away from him as possible. It was confusing. He stood there looking at them all with a pleasant smile curving his lips, yet Victoria struggled not to squirm as his gaze swept over her.

"Hello, everyone," he said in what Victoria assumed was a Cheshire accent. His voice was soft. "My name is Brendon, and this here is our little safe zone. I apologise for keeping you all out here a little longer, but we need to check you haven't been bitten. I'm sure you understand."

He continued smiling at them, and Victoria saw the others relax. Couldn't they feel what she felt? They still

had weapons trained on them.

"We understand your caution," Jennifer said with a frown as she eyed their armed guards. *Does she feel it too?* "But I can assure you those guns aren't necessary. My friends haven't been infected."

Brendon gave Jennifer his full attention. "With all due respect, for all I know, you're a masterful liar and the whole lot of you have been bitten." Jennifer opened her mouth to no doubt protest, but Brendon kept talking. "I'm sure you haven't." He held up his hand in a placating gesture. "You all must be adept at surviving, otherwise you wouldn't have made it this long. The reason *we* have made it this long is because we're meticulous when it comes to safety, and I've always been a stickler for the rules." He flashed everyone that charming grin again. "Can I get your name?"

"Jennifer." Jennifer was still frowning, but Victoria thought she seemed more relaxed.

"Jennifer," Brendon parroted, giving her a little nod. "You said your friends haven't been infected."

Jennifer nodded. "Yeah, they haven't."

"And what about you?" Was it Victoria's imagination, or did Brendon stare at Jennifer a little too closely? Nerves thrummed though her and coiled in her stomach, making her feel nauseous. *That bloody bandage on her neck. Everyone can see it above the coat.* What if their assurances of Jennifer's immunity fell on deaf ears? What if they shot her without giving them a chance to explain? Victoria shifted closer to her.

"You mentioned your friends. You didn't say *we* haven't been infected. You said *they* haven't been infected.

What about *you*? Don't think we haven't noticed your neck."

Jennifer tipped her chin up and stood straighter. "I'm immune," she said shortly, without preamble.

Her statement was met with silence. Victoria saw several guards shift and finger their weapons, and she glared around at them all. Brendon's pleasant smile hadn't wavered. *It doesn't reach his eyes,* Victoria realised. That's what was wrong. His face was warm and welcoming, but none of it touched his eyes.

"Immune," he repeated slowly. "We had a man claiming the same thing not a week ago. He'd been bitten twice that we could see. He said he had an older bite on his stomach, but I couldn't let him get too close. I couldn't jeopardise the safety of the rest of us. You understand."

His smile morphed into something that looked like a mockery of sympathy, and again, his eyes didn't change. It was unnerving. He waved a hand and Shovel-face stepped forward, raising his gun. Voices rose around Victoria all at once, but she tuned it out as she calmly stepped in front of Jennifer and stared down the barrel. She was dimly aware of Alexia stepping up next to her.

She hadn't been able to save Katherine—she couldn't honestly say she would've if she'd been able to—but Jennifer, Jennifer she could save. She had vowed to herself that she would protect her, and Victoria didn't do things half-heartedly. She planted herself like an oak and didn't budge even though Jennifer tried to push her aside.

Brendon touched Shovel-face's shoulder, and the man retreated, lowering his gun as he did so. Victoria didn't flinch as those dead eyes landed on her, calculating, appraising. He opened his mouth to speak, but Victoria

didn't give him the chance.

"She *is* immune. She's been bitten seven times. We had doctors and scientists working with her to find a cure, but they're dead now." She could hear rustling behind her, and it took her a moment to realise Jennifer was taking off her coat. "You can see for yourself how well she's healing. I understand the need for caution but shooting everyone before you have all the information is just plain idiotic."

Victoria enjoyed the way Brendon's jaw clenched at the insult. She moved to the side at Jennifer's tap on her shoulder, but she kept her gaze pinned to Brendon's. After a couple of seconds, he turned back to Jennifer, his eyes immediately dropping to her bare arms. The fresh bites were coming along nicely, and even if he still didn't believe, well, the older ones from almost two months ago were well and truly healed, leaving scarred teeth indentations.

After several stressful seconds his smile was back, and he held out his palms. "Immunity. So, people are immune. That's *incredible*. This isn't the end of humanity after all. Maybe we can salvage our society." He said all the right things with all the right inflection, but Victoria saw through his act.

"Yeah," Jennifer agreed. "This virus won't beat us. We can claw civilisation back." She gestured down the line. "You can search everyone for bites—it's only right that we stick to safety precautions. I would appreciate it if you got your people to lower their weapons, though. And we would like ours back."

Victoria thought for a moment that he was going to flat out refuse, but it seemed he'd decided on the role of

gracious host. "As a show of good faith..." Brendon gestured, and Victoria could breathe a little easier as the weapons were lowered. "As for *your* weapons, well, you don't need them right now. You are all welcome here, and guns aren't necessary inside the perimeter."

Jennifer opened her mouth again to say something, and again he rode right over her. "Now, please excuse our forwardness, but we had to be thorough, you understand. Can you all strip so we can check you for bites?"

Victoria sighed inaudibly. For the second time in as many months she found herself in her underwear, outside, in front of a crowd of people. *Bloody fantastic.* She stared straight ahead with her arms folded, glaring at the pub's red door as a man and woman worked their way into the middle of the line from each end. Jennifer didn't strip, and Victoria envied her. She wished *she* was immune so she wouldn't have to keep enduring this farce every time they encountered a new group.

It didn't take as long as when Evans did it, which Victoria was more than happy about. She put her coat back on when Brendon spoke again.

"Excellent! I apologise for not believing you earlier, but trust is hard to come by these days, as I'm sure you understand." He smiled that charming smile of his, and Victoria saw most of the others smile back. The only exceptions were James and Teona. What about James's shoulder? Weren't they going to ask about it?

Apparently, Brendon was a mind reader. He clapped his hands together. "Welcome! You are free to stay here, except for you, my friend." Brendon was looking at James. Victoria saw Teona bristle as her face darkened with anger. "I'm afraid we're going to have to keep you outside a

little while longer and go over that shoulder of yours. How do we know it's not hiding a bite?"

His mild tone made Victoria's teeth hurt. "He was fucking shot," Teona snapped. "That's why it's so heavily bandaged. Do you think we'd use that many bandages on a fucking bite?"

Brendon blinked at Teona's tone, and Victoria smothered a smirk. She had never appreciated Teona's straightforward attitude more. *What you see is what you get with her. She could meet the Queen and still swear her head off.*

"Nevertheless, we have to check, you under—"

"If you say, 'you understand' one more time, I'm going to fucking scream."

"It's okay," James said, putting a calming hand on Teona's arm. "They're just being careful." He turned to Riya. "Can you help me?"

Riya looked torn, glancing from James to Brendon to Teona. "Help him," Jennifer said, although she clearly wasn't happy about it. They were down to their last bandages. Hopefully this place had more.

Victoria saw James clench his jaw as Riya unwound his sling and bandages. She flashed him a sympathetic look. *He must be in so much pain. All my cuts and bruises won't come close.* When his shoulder was finally bare Victoria had to hold back a grimace.

She would describe it as half-healed at best, and that was being too generous. His whole shoulder was bruised, and even through the entry wound itself was small, it still looked bloody awful. Red and angry and swollen. It was a wonder he could move his arm as much as he did.

Riya tutted. "Are you taking the antibiotics?"

"You have antibiotics?" Brendon cut in before James could respond.

"Not many," Jennifer said quickly. "And they're for James." Victoria didn't like the greedy glint that had entered Brendon's eyes. Jennifer was right to downplay their medicine. Not that they had much, but the less Brendon thought they had the better.

He nodded his head politely. "Of course. That wound does look nasty."

"Aye, thanks," James said sarcastically.

Riya started to wrap his shoulder back up. "Well," Brendon said. "I think you've all proved you're safe. Why don't we move this conversation inside? We have warm food, and we use the river to wash. With guards present, of course. You can never be too careful."

Washing sounded like absolute bliss to Victoria. As did warm food. After days living off cold rations, she almost threw caution to the wind and dashed inside. But she didn't trust these people. Objectively, there was no reason not to. They seemed to run a good operation. But appearances could be deceiving, and if Victoria had learned anything these past few months, it was to trust her instincts.

They all headed inside the large pub, and Victoria kept her guard up and stuck close to Jennifer. Hopefully they'd get some time alone and Victoria could voice her fears.

Chapter Thirty

The moment Charlie set Ismay down, she ran to James. *Poor lass.* She'd begun to cry silently when they'd been checked for bites, and her tears hadn't let up since. James patted her head gently. He didn't know what else to do.

Inside the pub was warmer than outside, and James relished the feeling of heat seeping back into his bones. He spared a quick glance at his surroundings—walls with weird art adorning them, a few rooms sprouting off from the main one, the open floor cleared of tables, the square bar empty of drinks. He was more focused on Teona.

She glared about the place like it had personally offended her, her mouth set in a thin line that cried disapproval. James didn't know what the problem was. This seemed like a great place, and Brendon looked to have his head screwed on when it came to security.

James was about to pull Teona to one side and ask her what was wrong when he caught sight of Victoria. She and Teona wore mirrored expressions. *Why do I feel like I'm missing something?* James watched as the two women shared a look he couldn't begin to interpret.

Brendon was one of the last through the door, and it shut behind him with a soft thud, blocking out the natural

light. Torches and candles and battery-powered fairy lights were dotted about the place, and James's eyes adjusted quickly. Brendon smiled that easy smile of his, and James thought again that he couldn't believe their luck. Of course, he still wanted to go to Scotland, but this place... He sighed, feeling more tension leave his body. It would be brilliant to rest here for a while. Let his shoulder heal again.

"We have rooms upstairs that we'll put you in," Brendon said. "When we first moved in here it was full to the rafters," he continued, his smile fading as sadness entered his tone. "We've lost a lot of people. But"—his smile came back suddenly—"that was all before we put all the roadblocks and safety precautions in place. We haven't lost anyone since. It's good to be so full again."

Brendon gestured to the man who'd led them here. "This is Frankie. He'll help you all get settled. I don't mean to be rude, but I was in the middle of a guard meeting when you all showed up. Before I go, though, let me reiterate that you are all welcome here. Please make yourselves at home." With one last grin in their direction, he strolled through one of the many doors leading from the main room.

"The next bath is in half an hour," Frankie started, looking like he'd rather be out fighting infected than here with them. James frowned at him. He had the appearance of a brawler, not a talker. "Evening meal is in two hours. Meet here for both. Follow me and I'll show you to your rooms."

They made their way upstairs, and it became clear to James that they would still be sleeping in their sleeping bags. He didn't see a single bed. Not that he minded per

se, it just would have been nice for his shoulder to rest in a proper mattress instead of on the hard floor. Most of the furniture had been cleared out of all the rooms, so he couldn't tell what they'd been before. Not that it mattered. *At least we've got a roof over our heads again.*

"I'll leave you to sort rooms out. Remember, bath time in half an hour." Frankie stomped back down the stairs without waiting for a reply.

There was a beat of silence as his footsteps receded, then Jennifer released a long breath. "What a mad day, right?"

James grunted as Danny snorted.

"I thought we were going to be killed when they surrounded us," Hiran said, taking his bag off and propping it up against a wall as he explored in one of the rooms. Aarav and Riya and Elise followed him, also removing their bags and coats.

"Rest here, guys," Jennifer said, smiling as Dan yawned. "Go down to the river and wash, and we'll have some food and sleep indoors tonight." Her smile dimmed as her tone got serious. "Tomorrow, I want everyone to discuss what we're going to do now. Do we stay here? Do we continue on to Scotland? Think about it tonight."

They split into the two rooms, and not a lot was said as bags and coats were dropped and sleeping bags were unfurled. The once bare room was now home to organised chaos, and James sighed happily at the thought of being protected behind barricades again. He frowned at himself. When the fuck did he start needing barricades to breathe easy? Shaking his head, he dismissed the thought. It was only natural to feel safer behind walls these days.

"Dan," Victoria said. "Why don't you take Ismay downstairs for a bath?"

Dan looked alarmed at the idea. Elise saved him from responding as she wandered over to their room. "I will take her," she said with a smile directed at the little girl. James almost did a double take—he couldn't remember the last time he'd seen her smile. Had he *ever* seen her smile?

She held out her arms and Ismay ambled over to her, a little smile gracing her lips as Elise picked her up. James knew Elise had spoken to Ismay a few times in French after she'd opened up, and he'd once caught her pulling faces at the giggling girl as he carried her, but he hadn't realised they were so close.

"Thanks," Victoria said to Elise's retreating back. She shook her head with a slightly exasperated look on her face. "Dan, go down with them."

He looked at her suspiciously. "Are you trying to say I smell or uh, are you trying to get me out of the room?"

Victoria paused. "Both?" Dan's lips pursed and she grimaced. "Sorry, Dan—"

"It's okay. I get the adults want to talk without the kid present."

James detected no small amount of bitterness in the lad's voice.

"C'mon, Dan," Coyne said with a soft smile. "I'll go with you. If it's important they'll tell us later."

"Exactly," Victoria said. "I don't mean to belittle you or make you feel like a child. It's just that I need to discuss something with Jennifer and Teona."

Dan nodded, still looking slightly dejected. He and Coyne left the room, Coyne trying to cheer Dan up as he shut the door quietly behind them.

Jennifer looked confused. "What is it?"

James was curious as well. He certainly wasn't leaving until he found out what was going on.

Victoria dived straight in. "It's Brendon. I get a...strange vibe from him." She held up her hands quickly as James and Jennifer frowned. Alexia watched passively as she leaned against the wall with her arms crossed. "I know how it sounds, but Teona feels it too. He... I don't know, but I don't like him. I don't think we can trust him."

"Yeah," Teona agreed. "His eyes look dead, it's creepy as fuck."

"His eyes look dead," Jennifer deadpanned.

"Yeah," Teona repeated. "Didn't you see it?"

"I don't think we should stay here, Jennifer," Victoria said. Could James almost detect *pleading* in her tone? Surely not.

Jennifer's frown deepened. "I don't understand. This is a good place here, how badly has he freaked you out? Is it because of the way they brought us here? Because yeah, that was shitty, but understandable, I think. And when he realised we were all right, he stood down. Gave us rooms, welcomed us in."

"I *know* all that, I do," Victoria said beseechingly, "but there's something not right about him. I know it's not much to go on, but *please* consider continuing on?"

James was certainly not opposed to still going to Scotland. And while he hadn't seen anything off with

Brendon, it didn't mean *they* hadn't. "He seems like a normal man to me," he said. "But I trust the opinions of you both." He nodded to Victoria and Teona. "If you say something's not right, then I think we should be careful."

Jennifer blew out a noisy breath. "He's right. I trust your instincts. God knows they've kept us alive in the past." She shook her head. "How about this—we stay here for a few days, rest, get our bearings, check the place out. If you still feel the same way, then we'll leave."

Victoria pulled a face, but she nodded. Teona sighed. "That's fine," she said. "We do need the rest. We *have* been pushing hard."

Jennifer rolled her eyes. "It's nothing the *Supreme Commander* can't handle."

Teona smirked. "I knew that title would stick." James joined Jennifer in rolling his eyes. Teona noticed. "You don't like it, Sunshine? Because you better get fucking used to it, it's here to stay."

James gave her a dry look. "If it's decided that we're staying here for a while, I'm going to the river to wash."

"Ooh yes, I'm joining you," Teona said, all but bouncing on the balls of her feet. James tried not to let his wandering mind show on his face. Given Teona's knowing smirk, he knew she'd seen straight through him. "After you, Sunshine." She smacked his arse on the way out of the room.

"See you down there," Victoria called after them, but James was too focused on the way Teona's hand hadn't left his backside. This was going to be the most stressful bath he'd ever had.

*

"Thanks for listening, Jennifer," Victoria said. Jennifer nodded. She was still baffled about where it was all coming from, but she was more than willing to hear them out.

"You don't have to thank me," she said fondly. "James was right, I do trust your opinions. We'll stay alert over the next few days, and we'll leave at the slightest hint of trouble."

Victoria smiled at her. "Watch Brendon as well, see if you can see what Teona and I do." At Jennifer's agreement, Victoria continued. "I'm going to wash as well. I'm bloody filthy."

Jennifer laughed at the look of disgust on Victoria's face. "We'll see you down there." Victoria gave her and Alexia a wink as she walked out the door.

"Do you think Brendon is bad?" Alexia asked, stepping over to Jennifer and running her hands up her arms, careful of the wounds there. Jennifer couldn't suppress the shiver that raced through her at the soft touch.

"I think there must be something not right, especially if both of them feel it," Jennifer replied, leaning into Alexia. "We'll keep our eyes and ears open in the meantime."

"Ears open?" Alexia had such an adorable look of confusion on her face that Jennifer chuckled.

"It means we'll listen for anything that seems weird," Jennifer explained.

"Ah, okay. English is a strange language." Alexia smiled, stepping closer. Jennifer grinned as well, and suddenly there was no more space between them. Jennifer

got lost in Alexia's warmth, her taste, her feel. It was only when things started to get a little more heated that she reluctantly pulled away. Alexia's sad pout almost had her stepping in again, but she laughed instead.

"Come on, we need to wash as well."

Alexia sighed dramatically but agreed with a nod of her head. "My hair is very dirty," she said as she pulled it out of its tie and ran her fingers through it. Jennifer had to swallow as she tracked those fingers. She caught sight of Alexia's smirk and knitted her brows together suspiciously.

"You know exactly what you're doing, don't you?"

Alexia had such a look of forced innocence that she could only be guilty. She laughed as Jennifer gave her a little shove. "You like my hair. You always put your hands in it."

"Come here." Jennifer smiled, and once again Alexia's mouth was on hers. It didn't last as long this time, as a cough interrupted them.

Brendon stood in the doorway, smiling politely. "Sorry, I don't mean to be rude."

Jennifer shook her head. "It's all right," she said as she eyed him more closely. What was it Teona had said? Dead eyes?

"I came to ask," he started, "after everyone's been washed and everyone is settled, would you care to join me for food?"

Alexia's hand came to rest firmly on Jennifer's lower back, the heat of her seeping into Jennifer's skin. It was almost like she was jealous. Not that Jennifer minded— she felt a strange sense of glee at Alexia's possessiveness,

but she was confused. Alexia gave Brendon a look that was just shy of outright hostility. *Can she feel what Victoria and Teona does? Why can't I?*

"Food?"

"Yes." He was still smiling politely, and Jennifer didn't see anything untoward about it. "I gather you are in charge of your group, and it would be nice to chat."

"Chat," Jennifer repeated slowly. She supposed it would be a good opportunity to see whether what Victoria and Teona said was right. "Okay, sure." She tried to ignore the way Alexia's hand tightened on her back.

Brendon's smile widened. "Excellent! I'll come get you when food is ready." He nodded at them and left as silently as he'd arrived. She didn't get the chance to tell him Teona was as much in charge as she was.

There was a beat of silence, then Alexia released a breath she'd clearly been holding. "I don't like him," she announced, sliding her hand around Jennifer's waist to settle at her hip.

"Yeah?" Jennifer asked. "Are you okay?"

"I am fine," Alexia said shortly. "I think maybe Victoria and Teona are right."

"I'll be on guard during the meal with him," Jennifer reassured her. "I'll try to see if I can spot anything weird."

"You will be okay?"

"Promise."

Jennifer basked in Alexia's obvious concern and slid her arms around Alexia's neck. She leaned in for a quick kiss. "Last one to the river is a rotten egg?"

Alexia looked confused for a second before her

expression cleared. That was all the warning Jennifer had before Alexia dashed out of the room.

"Hey!" Jennifer shouted after her, laughing as they ran down the stairs.

Chapter Thirty-One

Jennifer felt like a new woman freshly washed and dressed in clean clothes. She'd been given soft, black leggings that fit perfectly, and a slightly oversized light-blue shirt. Everyone had all but ripped Brendon's hands off taking the new clothes. Alexia wore jeans that fit snugly and a green checked shirt with the sleeves rolled up. Jennifer had almost started salivating at the sight of her.

Her hair was loose about her face, no longer limp and lifeless. Her skin was free of grime. It was the cleanest she could remember feeling since the castle. The only thing that spoiled it was the fact she'd started her period. Her mouth twisted in distaste. *Just when I feel good again, Mother Nature slaps me in the face. Thank God Victoria brought all those pads and tampons.* She'd had to cut her wash short because of it, but she'd watched Teona wind James up as she'd dried. It had been beyond hilarious.

She sat with her back to a blocked window in a room next to the main door. A cold brick fireplace covered the wall to her left and the empty bar was directly ahead of her with LED lights and little candles dotted across it, twinkling in the gloom. The room was tiny, and the red

walls and seats made it seem even more closed in.

The food tasted like heaven. Her taste buds were throwing a party in her mouth after days of rations that were mediocre at best, and downright inedible at worst. The group here had stockpiled food from the supermarket and hunted wild game from the countryside. The kitchen didn't have power, so they cooked with fire outside.

Jennifer did her best not to shovel chicken into her mouth, but given the amused glint in Brendon's eye, she wasn't sure how well she succeeded. It was just *so good.*

She savoured her last bite, partly because of the divine taste and partly because she didn't want the small talk to become serious. She still felt like she didn't know what the fuck she was doing. *Teona should be here as well.* When she'd mentioned the meal to Teona, she had told Jennifer to eat with him and try to gauge what he was about.

He was being amicable and charming, chatting away about how they got the bus in place on the bridge, and Jennifer had yet to see what the others had. Still, she kept her guard up.

"So," he said once they finished their food. "Tell me your story, Jennifer. I imagine it's quite the tale."

And Jennifer did, albeit in broad strokes that left out a lot of detail. Just because he seemed fine to her didn't mean the others were wrong, and she didn't want to compromise the group by giving too much away. She didn't mention Evelyn or her friends, didn't mention Johnson or Martin. She skimmed over Paris—that disaster was still far too fresh—but she did talk about the castle and the scientists. He looked sad when she spoke about their deaths and the abrupt end of the possibility of a vaccine.

"I'm sorry," he said, tilting his head to the side as sympathy painted over his face. "No doctors or scientists have come through here, the closest we have is Heather, who used to be a paramedic. You haven't met her yet—she's been away hunting since the early hours of the morning."

"Your paramedic is away hunting?" Jennifer asked, surprised. What if something happened and they needed her?

Brendon chuckled. "I know what you're thinking—why take unnecessary risk in sending our only paramedic away? Well, she's also our best hunter. Our *only* hunter, although she is training others." Brendon shrugged. "The tinned food won't last forever, and I had to weigh up the pros and cons of keeping her here or sending her out. Food won over first aid. We run a tight ship here, and the number of diseased people in the area seems to be dying down."

Jennifer nodded. That was reasonable, if risky. What if something happened to her and she never came back? Tough decisions.

"I didn't know people could be immune till you came along," Brendon confessed. "I've seen so much death that the idea people could be safe from the disease never even crossed my mind." A shadow passed over his face, and Jennifer wondered at his story. How much death had he seen? She thought of the others' unease around him. How much death had he potentially dealt out?

She never got the chance to ask, as he continued talking. She huffed out a breath. He'd talked over her a few times already. She got the impression he liked the sound of his own voice.

"I always thought this was nature's way of cleansing the Earth. That humans were the virus, and we were being eradicated. Just look at all the damage we've done—all the wars and all the harm to the environment. Perhaps this has been a good thing. Perhaps the Earth can heal from the stresses humanity has put it under." Brendon shook his head slightly. "But you're immune, so I guess others will be as well. Maybe humans aren't meant to be wiped out. Maybe just culled. Weed the weak ones out so the strong can start afresh."

Jennifer agreed that people had been laying waste to the planet, but she didn't agree with the idea that it was all so nature could remove the weak. Humans weren't strong or weak, they were a mixture of both. *I've made it this far in this fucked up world, and I didn't have any real survival skills. Hell, people think I'm weak just because I'm a woman. But I'm not weak. Nobody is. Johnson was more weak than strong, but he was a soldier, and he survived the initial outbreak, so he must have had some resilience at some point.*

"I can see where you're coming from," Jennifer said slowly, "but I don't think you're right."

"No?" Brendon looked confused, like no one had ever disagreed with him before.

"I don't think nature is *culling* us," she said. "I think this is just a random thing that became more disastrous than it should have been because of the food recall and the media blackout. It's not some orchestrated thing to eradicate people. Humanity will survive this. I think they would have even if no one was immune. We can start anew, yeah, but it's not just *strong* people who've made it. Some people might just be lucky. Others you might see as

weak but have lived because they showed strength when they needed to. It isn't black and white."

Brendon held her eyes for several beats. Jennifer refused to look away. "Can I ask about the camera?" He gestured to the object in question, perched on the end of the table. The change in conversation topic startled Jennifer for a moment.

She opened her mouth and closed it again, dropping the previous subject. He obviously didn't want to get into a debate with her.

Instead, she grinned, unable to stop the gusto that always leaked into her voice when she talked about photography. She told him about the moments she'd frozen over the past couple of months and about her desire to document the outbreak. He nodded along politely throughout her gushing, but Jennifer got the distinct impression he didn't really care.

She picked up her camera. "Can I take your picture?" She needed to be careful with it—it was only half charged now, and this place didn't have any power. She didn't know when the next charging opportunity would present itself.

"Of course," he said with a charming smile. Jennifer grinned back as she raised the camera and framed him in it, making sure his face filled the lens and the background was just that—background.

"All done," Jennifer beamed, twisting the camera round to show him. He studied his image critically for a few moments before nodding appreciatively.

"You have a good eye."

"Thanks," Jennifer said, her grin still fixed on her

face. She turned the camera off to save the battery. "Can you tell me your story? Got to have something to go with the picture."

He laughed as he nodded. "Of course. I heard about the outbreak in London on the news. I'd just gotten in from work, so I was pretty tired, but when I saw all the riots and then the army moving in, well, let's just say it woke me up. I sat glued to the TV for hours. When news of Paris's fall shortly after London broke, I knew this was serious and was going to change the course of history. My brother rang then, and we talked on the phone as updates came in throughout the night. Chaos sweeping across America, the deadly riots around the world, China shutting its borders down. It was amazing how fast it all happened, but I guess when civilisation collapses, it does so with a bang."

Jennifer had learned all that and more at the castle. God, how badly had this virus affected the world? Had it totally decimated humanity? She couldn't quite suppress the feeling of being in the dark about the rest of the planet.

"Is your brother here?" she asked tentatively, knowing there was a good chance he was dead.

Brendon looked down and away, and Jennifer had her answer.

"After that first night," he continued, looking back up again, his smile present but dimmer, "there was a mad rush to get supplies, food, water, medicine, you understand. Everyone and their mother had the same idea. I grabbed what I could. Things turned violent fast. Then the news started reporting that other quarantine zones were breaking, but it cut off before we could get more information. Before I knew it, this little town was

embroiled in chaos and death and insanity. The power failed shortly after." He shook his head, a grimace twisting his mouth. *He must hate being in the dark as much as I do.* "A group of us banded together, and this place is the result." Brendon gestured about the room proudly. "We've lost people and gained people, but we're still here. We're survivors."

His grin was infectious, and Jennifer smiled right along with him. *Survivors. That's what we are.* Jennifer thought of her group, of all the shit they'd been through, of all the shit they'd probably still have to go through. *Survivors.* It had a good ring to it.

"I hope you don't mind but..." Brendon said. "Can I ask you something...personal?"

The hesitation in his voice made Jennifer pause. Something akin to trepidation slowly inched through her, even though he appeared totally nonthreatening. She knew exactly what he was going to ask. She'd gotten it enough times when she'd dated Robin.

"Yes," she said, wishing she wasn't going to regret it.

"You and the other woman, what is her name again?"

"Alexia."

"Alexia," he repeated slowly, and Jennifer didn't like the way her name sounded in his mouth. Was he going to be yet another typical man when it came to two women dating each other? "Are you two"—he waved his hand around vaguely—"together?"

As if he hadn't walked in on us kissing. "Yes," she said shortly.

"Ah, I see." He nodded like he knew all the answers to everything. Jennifer tried to curb her irritation. "You're

gay." He said it in such a matter-of-fact tone that Jennifer didn't know whether to be pleased he wasn't making a fuss or annoyed he'd assumed incorrectly. She hated lying, but more often than not when she'd told men she was bisexual they immediately became horrible and harassed her, demanding threesomes or that she make out with a girl in front of them. *Although, I suppose it doesn't matter what he assumed. Lesbians get the same treatment. Straight men don't care either way.*

She *hated* lying, though. And being bisexual was a big part of her identity. She almost held out, but the truth clawed at her like an animal trying to escape.

"I'm not gay, I'm bisexual." The itch dissipated immediately only to be replaced by regret as a glint she recognised all too well entered his eyes. She'd seen it reflected in men who regarded her sexuality as a challenge.

He hummed, and Jennifer steeled herself. She was beginning to see what the others saw, albeit for different reasons.

"So, you like men as well," he said. Jennifer tried to cut in, but he ploughed straight on like a battering ram, silencing her protests before they even left her mouth. "You know, from the moment I saw you I recognised your beauty. Your fierceness." Jennifer barely stopped herself from rolling her eyes. "We'd make a great team, I think."

She jumped in as he took a breath. "Stop right there, I'm not interested. I'm with Alexia, and that's that. I would appreciate it if we talked about something else."

He clearly wasn't used to rejection if the way his face fell in on itself was anything to go by. It was the first time she'd seen him look angry. She didn't like it. She had to remind herself that her friends were on the other side of

the door, eating their own meal. She only had to shout and they'd be there in a heartbeat.

"Think about it, Jennifer," he implored, his smile back in full force. "Think about *us*. I'm in charge here, I can make life very easy for you and your people. I can give you things she can't—"

Jennifer couldn't hold back a scoff at that. His face darkened, but she couldn't find it in herself to care. "Listen," she snapped. "You've been very accommodating, and I thank you. But *shut up* about *us*, because there is no *us*, nor will there ever be. Not only am I happy with Alexia, but you and I literally just met a couple of hours ago. Like, what the fuck? Get it out of your head, because this is the only time I'm going to tell you."

He stood with no warning, and Jennifer sucked in a deep breath as he loomed over her. *The others are outside, it's all right.*

"If that's how you feel, I think we're done here." Brendon's voice was cold, and Jennifer wondered if he was going to kick them out. She suddenly saw what Teona meant by dead eyes. "Have a good night. And no more pictures, or I'll take your camera off you."

"You try to take this camera off me, and I'll kick you so hard in the balls your voice will go high again."

He sneered a little before he turned and walked swiftly out of the door without saying anything more, leaving Jennifer sitting at the table glaring after him. *What just happened?* What an arsehole, not taking her relationship with another woman seriously. Everything had gone downhill so fast Jennifer was left reeling.

She released a long breath. She was firmly in the

Scotland camp now. She had to convince the others that continuing was the best option.

Chapter Thirty-Two

Evening descended quickly, wrapping around Heather like a well-worn coat. The weather had taken a turn for the better, the mild warmth soothing as she sat by the rushing river. The trees around her were still shaking off winter's touch, the branches more bare than leafy, but if the recent warm spell was anything to go by, that would change soon. The scents of winter faded as those of spring took root, and while there was a cold beauty to winter, Heather longed for the wild colour of spring.

She sighed as she began to pack up her fishing gear. Slowly. The longer it took to get back to Brendon, the better.

The river was dark, reflecting the sky above. Her boots crunched on the gravel as she strolled down the path next to the cold water, but she wasn't concerned about the noise. There were no diseased people around here for miles. She had last encountered some two days ago on the other side of the town, and they'd been dying of dehydration. It seemed this zombie apocalypse was winding down, leaving only the human monsters behind. Brendon had even stopped giving her guards.

His mood swings were getting worse. Yesterday he'd

defused a dangerous situation where Dale and Pete had stolen guns and food to leave this horrendous place with smooth words and an easy smile, only to take Frankie's gun when everyone had lowered their guard and shoot them both dead.

Frankie was well in Brendon's pocket. A grimace twisted her face at the thought of it. He'd saved her life, and he threw in with Brendon the first chance he got. She'd thought he was better than that.

If she tried to leave, would Brendon go back on his word and kill her too? Where would she even go? These thoughts had crossed her mind often, and they always ran in the same circles. *What would you do, Kallie? I miss you so much.* Thoughts of her wife were painful, and that agony hadn't dulled in the months since the outbreak. She *had* to be alive somewhere, with a better group than Brendon's.

Heather hiked her gear higher on her shoulder. *Kallie would leave. That's what she'd do.* Nothing was stopping her really. She could hunt and fish. She would avoid diseased people. They seemed to be dying off anyway. She'd almost left so many times before. Maybe this time she would do it. Maybe she'd finally be away from Brendon.

He'd hunt her down. She knew it for a fact deep in her bones. Keep her trapped in the pub, only letting her out when he needed her skills. She'd be watched like a hawk, her every move recorded and relayed back to him.

How is it that he's got so many loyal followers anyway? Another question she'd asked herself a lot. He could be charismatic, but his mood always flipped. Everyone had seen it. Could it be something as simple as fear? That was certainly what was keeping her rooted to the spot.

Then there were people like Frankie who didn't mind a bit of violence, who liked that sort of thing.

Heather sighed, and there was no sign of her breath misting in the air. It really was getting warmer.

She halted her thoughts before they could tread the same well-worn paths, instead turning her mind to her catch. It was a good haul. Five rabbits, *nine* chickens—they must've escaped from a farm somewhere—and a good half-dozen fish. Coupled with the tinned food they had it would be more than enough for a few days. Maybe when she had to go out again, she'd find the courage to leave. *Maybe pigs will fly backwards. Get a grip of yourself, woman.*

No matter how slow she walked that damn pub always rose out of the dusk shadows, looming over the river like an executioner about to drop his axe. The blow was yet to come, but it felt as unavoidable as the sun rising in the morning.

Just three days ago Brendon had killed a young girl seeking refuge, claiming she was too weak to have survived for so long and that she *must've* been infected. Heather had examined the girl herself and had found no such wounds. And a little further back he'd shot that man who'd claimed to be immune.

Heather was a paramedic, not an immunologist, but she assumed at least a small proportion of the population would be immune. That was how it worked, right? At least with some diseases. The man had had two bite wounds, but he'd seemed in good health otherwise, and they'd been healing. She'd tried to tell Brendon afterward that they should have heard him out, observed him for a day or two. Brendon had chewed her head off and threatened

to kick her out. His eyes had been so crazed she'd thought he was going to attack her there and then, in the middle of the pub's main room in front of half a dozen witnesses.

Once again, she turned her mind away from the unpleasantness of the past few days. *Huh. Past few months more like.* Brendon might be in a good mood tonight. She'd certainly brought in a decent amount of food.

Heather shook her head as she walked up to the Red Lion. Steve and Shane were on guard tonight. The two cousins were nice young men, not the brightest, but certainly sincere. Heather felt comfortable around them. She didn't feel comfortable around a lot of people these days. Maybe they would come with her? *Don't be thick, woman. Just because they're nice to you doesn't mean they're willing to give up the relative luxury of this place. Deal with Brendon or deal with the madness outside? It's a simple choice, really. At least Brendon is familiar.*

"Caught us lots of food, Heather?" Shane called quietly as she got closer.

She flashed him a smile. "Oh yeah, we're gonna eat like kings."

It was the same exchange they had every time she came back from a hunt, even when she hadn't caught much. But they waved her in, and all too soon she was walking into the lion's den. Literally.

It was hot in the pub, bordering on sweltering. They didn't have heating, so it must have been from the sheer number of bodies in the room. Heather paused in the doorway, looking around with wide eyes.

There were more people than she could ever remember being there. New faces she didn't recognise, lounging

around the place, eating and drinking. *How am I going to feed this many people?* Heather thought with something akin to despair in her stomach. And was that a *child?*

As she moved further into the room, she caught sight of a pale man with his arm in a sling and a black woman going up the stairs, the man grimacing and the woman rubbing his back. A blonde woman was also watching them, a concerned look on her face as she turned to talk to an Asian woman. Heather saw *another* child—teenager really—wolfing down food like he hadn't seen any in weeks. She was about to grab Beth and ask her what the hell had happened while she'd been away when Brendon burst out of the red room. Heather wet her dry lips. He had a face like a smacked arse, which didn't bode well for anyone. Was he going to kill some of the newcomers? He'd done that before to prove he was in charge.

He caught sight of her and her haul, and he relaxed. His face transformed completely when a couple of the newcomers started talking to him. Heather had seen him play this game before too. Ever the amiable host until he snapped and made an example of alleged bad behaviour.

Heather caught sight of the blonde woman frowning at Brendon with steel in her eyes. Could she see through his bullshit? Heather watched as she stood and marched over to the door he'd slammed open. Another woman emerged, this one with brown hair, and were those *bandages*? Heather counted one on her neck and one on her arm—

Were those *bite marks*? Heather's blood ran cold.

She watched the two women have a hushed conversation. Why had Brendon let an infected woman into the pub? How had he not shot her when he saw the wounds?

Heather's breath caught in her throat. *Could she be...immune?*

She made a quick trip to the kitchen to store her catch and hurried back out into the main room. Everyone was still there. With a quick glance at Brendon—he still chatted with the two men who'd gone up to him—Heather strolled as casually as she could up to the blonde and brunette.

"Hi," she said tentatively, unsure of what to say now she'd reached them. She'd seen the distrustful looks they'd shot Brendon, but that didn't mean they were going to do anything about it. What if they were as spineless as Heather herself, and they weren't going to stand up to his tyranny? And what about the bite wounds? Should she outright ask or work up to it? What if—

"Are you the paramedic?" the brunette asked. Her direct voice cut through Heather's spiralling thoughts, and she jolted back into the room.

"Yes." How did she know that? Brendon must have told her. He did like to brag to newcomers that they had a trained medical professional. Heather looked at her properly. Past the bandages and bites. She was around the same height as Heather herself, and she was younger than she'd originally thought, maybe mid-twenties? The blonde was the older of the two, so Heather addressed her instead. "Have you just arrived?"

The blonde threw a quick glance at the brunette, a faint smile curling her lips. "We got here a couple of hours ago," she answered. She had an accent that Heather thought was maybe from London. They both did, come to think of it. Not cockney and not posh, but certainly London.

"My name's Jennifer," the brunette said. "And this is Victoria."

"Heather." She smiled at them both.

"It's nice to meet you, Heather." Jennifer smiled back. "I take it you've just gotten back from hunting?"

"Yeah, I caught a lot of fresh meat, but I'll have to go out again sooner than I'd thought because of all the extra mouths," she said good-naturedly. She kept her smile on her face in case Brendon looked over and saw them all frowning. Heather cursed silently. She'd put her back to him.

Both women grimaced at her words, and Heather quickly thought over what she'd said. Nothing unusual? Maybe they had weak stomachs and didn't like the thought of killing for their supper.

"Thank you for the food, Heather," Jennifer said, her face once again smooth. "It means a lot that you'd risk yourself out there so people won't go hungry."

Heather reevaluated her earlier assumptions. She'd presumed Victoria was in charge due to her age and the way she'd marched over to Jennifer, but it seemed the younger woman was the one running the show. *Of course she is.* Heather could have smacked herself. *Brendon was in the back room with* Jennifer *not Victoria.*

"It's nothing," Heather chuckled, brushing off the compliment. Brendon thanked her all the time. So much so it had lost all meaning.

"I mean it," Jennifer insisted. "It must be hard going out there with infected. And you do it alone?"

Heather quickly quenched the warmth in her stomach. It *did* feel nice to get a sincere thank-you as opposed

to Brendon's false gratitude. "Yeah, we can't spare a lot of people. They would just get in the way anyway."

Victoria stepped forward slightly. Not a lot, but just enough to get into Heather's space a little bit. "Would you be willing to teach me?"

Heather leaned back a touch. *She's intense.*

"Victoria," Jennifer said softly, and Victoria pouted as she stepped back.

"Never mind," she said. Heather wondered what that was all about. She was glad though—she hated teaching.

"Is everything all right?" Heather asked.

Jennifer smiled. "Yes. What can you tell us of this place? What's Brendon like? How long have you been here?" She changed the subject, but Heather picked up on the digging for information straight away. It wasn't exactly subtle.

"I'll answer your questions, but first you answer one of mine." Heather waited for Jennifer's nod to continue. "Are those bite wounds from diseased people?"

Jennifer's mouth twisted as she raised her arms to show off the marks. "Yes, I'm immune," she said simply.

Well, fuck me sideways.

"You're actually immune?" Heather breathed, staring at her arms. She could scarcely believe it. All this time, all this death, and people were immune? Long-forgotten hope stirred in her chest, and she did nothing to dampen it. Could doctors and scientists find a cure? The world may not be doomed after all.

"Yep," Jennifer said, popping the "p".

Heather's eyes grew hot. *Immune.* She couldn't

believe it. *Kallie could be immune. I have to believe she's out there. I have to find her! Why have I stayed here so long? That man Brendon killed probably* was *immune.* She felt an abrupt, powerful urge to hug the woman in front of her.

"Are you all right?" Jennifer asked, concern clear on her face. Heather couldn't remember the last time someone looked at her as anything more than a means to an end. She started to blink rapidly. Maybe things would change around here now these new people had arrived.

"I'm fine, it's just..." She had to stop and collect herself. "It's good to know people can be immune."

The two women smiled gently at her. Heather was going to have to excuse herself lest she burst into tears in front of these strangers. Or worse, Brendon. How was he taking all this? He'd be scheming up ways to use it to his advantage. Heather's heart sank at the thought that he was probably going to keep Jennifer caged here indefinitely. She almost warned them, almost told them to get out while they still could, but a heavy hand settled on her shoulder, and Heather squeezed her eyes shut at the pressure.

"*Heather.* It's good to have you back. I see you've met our newest guests."

She opened her eyes to Brendon's gleaming smile, and her stomach was so twisted she half thought she was going to throw up all over him. Latching onto the amusing yet terrifying image, Heather took a deep breath and let the warm rush of air calm her.

"Yes." She smiled, locking down her fear. "I've brought back a lot of meat, but I think I'll have to go out again sooner rather than later. I wasn't expecting so many

people."

Jennifer and Victoria weren't smiling. Heather wanted to kick them. Victoria was openly glaring at him, and Jennifer's face could have been a mask for how still it was. *He's going to kick off. He's going to kill someone.*

He didn't do anything. Instead, his smile melted away and was replaced by a look of remorse. "I would like to apologise for earlier," he said to Jennifer, doing his best kicked puppy impression. "I'm sorry for my assumptions and forwardness, and I'm sure you and Alexia are very happy together."

Victoria snorted and folded her arms. Brendon spared her a brief glance filled with annoyance, and Heather was heartened by his lack of response. *He really wants to make a good impression.* Heather looked around the room again. There were more of Brendon's people than newcomers, but the balance had been shifted. There could even be more newcomers upstairs. Maybe he didn't think he'd win a fight with these people if he pissed them off.

Jennifer was silent for a beat. "I don't ever want to hear it or anything like it again. Alexia and I *are* happy, and I'd appreciate it if you stayed away from us."

Heather had to stop her jaw from dropping. A muscle in Brendon's cheek twitched, and she saw his eyes darken. It wasn't just what Jennifer had said that shocked Heather, it was the way in which she'd said it. Like she was in charge and not Brendon. Like she expected him to do what she said.

Brendon smiled, his teeth shining as he notched the charm up. "You seem to be under some false impressions

here. Let me put that right for you. You are *my* guest, under *my* roof, and I *will not* be spoken to like I'm a child being scolded by his mother. *You* answer to *me,* and if you don't like that you know where the door is."

He didn't wait for a reply as he turned and thudded out of the back door, slamming it after him. Heather's brain short circuited. When he got angry things were destroyed. Plates, furniture, people. She didn't know what to make of his newfound self-restraint. *He must really think the new group could win in a fight.*

"What an *absolute* piece of shit," Jennifer said harshly, glaring at the door Brendon had disappeared through.

"We should leave as soon as we can, Jennifer," Victoria said. "That man's a ticking bomb."

Both women seemed to remember Heather's presence then. They started and looked over at her. "Don't worry, I won't tell him you plan on leaving. On one condition."

Victoria frowned at her. "And what would that be?"

"Take me with you." Heather didn't even try to stop desperation from leaking into her voice. Now that Brendon was out of the room, she felt like a gag had been removed, and she spilled everything that had happened from the moment she stumbled into the Red Lion. All the murders and intimidation, all the emotional blackmail and threats, all the food withheld until compliance was the only option if you didn't want to starve to death. On and on, until Heather's throat was sore from talking so much. It was the most she'd spoken at any one time since the outbreak.

The women listened well, only interrupting to get her to elaborate on certain points. Heather felt deflated by the end, but also lighter, as if talking about it had made it more bearable. Jennifer and Victoria exchanged an unreadable look, and Jennifer nodded once.

"We'll leave in the morning," Jennifer said determinedly. "Pass the message on to everyone. I want people to get a good night's sleep first. We've got more walking ahead of us." Victoria nodded once before walking away, determination in lockstep with her. "Of course you can come, Heather." Jennifer smiled at her again, and Heather almost broke down crying. She was *getting out*. "We'll go at dawn, so be up early."

Heather nodded eagerly. "What about the meat I brought? Should we take it?"

Jennifer looked torn. "I don't like the idea of stealing from everyone here. Take some. About a quarter. That way they still have the lion's share, so to speak."

Heather nodded as Jennifer smiled and moved off. She found another dark-haired woman and wrapped an arm around her waist. Heather barely registered it. *I'm leaving*. Leaving. *I'm finally getting out of this shithole.* Hope crashed through her system like morphine, lifting her spirits to soar amongst the clouds.

She didn't let herself think of Brendon, or of the high chance everything would go sideways in the morning. Right now, Heather was living in the moment, and the moment was fucking amazing.

Chapter Thirty-Three

James woke to the sounds of people shuffling about. He blinked blearily, sitting up as the fog of sleep dissipated. Everyone was packing up their sleeping bags and shrugging into coats. *What?* James came instantly alert as he looked around for danger, but nothing jumped out. The predawn light filtered through the thin curtains, and while people moved quickly, they also moved calmly. *What's going on?*

He didn't have time to speculate. Teona crouched in front of him, and his frown loosened as he smiled at her.

"We're leaving," she said in a hushed voice. "Apparently it was decided after we'd already gone upstairs. I, for one, am fucking glad about it—Brendon gives me the creeps." She shuddered. "Get your lazy arse out of bed, Sunshine. How much pain are you in?"

James grunted as he stood up, and Teona's look of concern deepened as he rolled his good shoulder, working out the kinks from another night spent on the floor.

"I'll get Riya and she can have a look at your shoulder and bandages." She was gone before he could say anything.

With a fond head shake, James went back to stretching. His back cracked pleasurably, and he felt better than he had since the castle.

He quickly packed up his sleeping bag, which was the only thing he had bar the clothes on his back. He'd gladly taken a new grey T-shirt and faded blue jeans, throwing his old blood-stained uniform in the river. It had been nice watching it float away. The jeans fit all right, but the top was a couple of sizes too big, though it helped with his sling, so he wasn't complaining. He padded over to talk to Jennifer, who yawned as she stuffed her own sleeping bag into her backpack.

She smiled at him when he got close. "Hey, James, how are you?"

"Aye, good, thanks," he replied. "Hurts a wee bit, but that's nothing new."

Jennifer snorted. "I suspect that's an understatement," she said as she gave him a droll look. "Listen. We're leaving for Scotland. Do you know whereabouts we should go? Which power station, where has the best farmland, access to water, shelter, that sort of thing."

James had been waiting for these questions, so he had his answer ready. "I think we should go to Loch Sloy or Loch Lomond. They're right next to each other. They're to the north of Glasgow in the middle of a national park, so it's pretty remote. Very little chance of infected. There's a power station there, but I don't know how to work it."

"We'll figure that out somehow."

"Aye. We can hunt there, maybe try some fishing if we can find equipment. We can maybe even raise livestock at some point. Loads of little freshwater streams

feed the lochs, so we'll have plenty water."

Jennifer nodded. "That all sounds amazing. Is it good farmland?"

He shrugged his shoulder. "I don't know to be honest. Hopefully we'll be able to figure something out."

Jennifer looked worried. "I hope so. I don't want to drag everyone up to Scotland only to find out we can't sustain ourselves there." She sighed. "Oh, and don't worry about fishing. Heather is coming with us."

"Heather?"

"Yeah, she's the paramedic Brendon mentioned yesterday. She's how this place feeds itself."

If Teona and Victoria were right about Brendon, he wasn't going to like them poaching the paramedic. "Why are we leaving anyway?" James asked. "Were Teona and Victoria right?"

Jennifer's face twisted in distaste. "Not only were they right, but it was just the tip of the iceberg. Heather told us what really goes on here. God, it's awful, James." Her face distorted further. "Brendon's killed people. Lots of people. He fucks with people and tortures them by withholding food and water. Heather said he didn't like a man's teeth, they were crooked or something, so he starved him then shoved him out of a moving van into a bunch of infected. He has pretty bad mood swings, which I had a little taste of yesterday."

"What did he do?" *Starved and murdered a man because he didn't like his teeth? What kind of crazy is he?*

"Propositioned me and made me feel uncomfortable. He was homophobic and didn't take me being with Alexia seriously. Then he got angry when I turned him down. It

was like a switch had been flipped."

James nodded, his own face twisting with anger. He hadn't picked up on any of it. *What the fuck has happened to your observational skills, huh?* "I'm sorry," he said, still berating himself. "If he'd done anything I would have been straight in." *Why the fuck don't some people understand the meaning of the word no?*

She smiled at him. "I know, don't worry. He didn't get physical or anything, just stormed out."

Teona chose that moment to return with Riya. "Let's get you fighting fit, Sunshine."

"I'm going to check on the other room," Jennifer said, giving his good arm a quick squeeze and smiling at his grimace.

James shrugged out of his T-shirt and let Riya do her thing. "This isn't healing as well as it should be," Riya admonished, as if he could personally control his healing process. "You're definitely taking the medicine?"

James thought of the little bottle of tablets sitting unopened in his pocket. He didn't think he could lie to them both, but luckily, he was saved from doing so by raised voices next door. The three of them shared a look as Riya fixed fresh bandages around his shoulder as fast as she could. Teona helped him back into his T-shirt, and together they went to see what the commotion was.

*

Victoria was fast running out of patience. The two of them were like unruly schoolchildren in dire need of discipline.

"Keep your voice down," she hissed. They did *not* need Brendon and the others waking up and trying to stop

them from leaving. "We've told you—"

"You've told us a lot of things that we can't prove," Aarav cut in, not lowering his voice in the slightest. "You have a *feeling* about him? What does that even mean? He's taken us in, given us food and water, and asked for nothing in return. Why should we leave?"

Jennifer clenched her fists. "Do you not trust Victoria and Teona? They've kept us alive this long," she ground out, clearly annoyed. "And we've told you what Heather told us—"

Aarav scoffed, and Jennifer's scowl deepened.

"I know you have a problem with me, but don't let that cloud your judgement," Jennifer spat. "This place is bad news. We have to *leave.*"

James, Teona, and Riya walked through the door then, and Victoria met Teona's dark gaze. The irritation she saw there was reflected in her own eyes. "I thought we'd been through all this?" Teona said, exasperation clear on her face.

"Apparently not," Victoria sighed.

"Aarav," Riya said, going over to him and grabbing his hand. She switched to their language, so Victoria didn't know what they were saying, but it was clearly an argument. She walked over to Jennifer instead.

"What is it between you and Aarav?"

Jennifer let out a long breath. "Well, first he didn't trust my immunity, but we got over that when I didn't go crazy. But then he found out about my sexuality, and he's only gotten worse now I'm with Alexia."

"Your sexuality?" Victoria was confused. What did

that have to do with anything?

"I guess Aarav is homophobic," Jennifer explained. "A lot of people are. Aarav can't let go of his *stupid* prejudices."

The proverbial light bulb went off over Victoria's head as their dislike of each other suddenly made sense.

Alexia strolled in and immediately stopped at the anger permeating the room like a bad smell. "What is wrong?"

Jennifer made a vague gesture. "*Some* people," she said with a pointed look at Aarav, "can't seem to understand that people can be anything other than straight."

Alexia narrowed her eyes at Aarav, who was still arguing with Riya. The two of them were both red in the face, and Victoria couldn't tell who was winning the row.

Teona tutted. "Who gives a fuck about who people fuck? I've never understood people who take offense at things that don't affect them. It's the same with racism— the colour of my skin has nothing to do with anything, yet people still hurl abuse at me. Fucking ridiculous."

Hiran stepped up to them. "I just want to say that my parents emigrated from India, and we do not hold the same views as Aarav."

Jennifer smiled at the soldier. "It's okay, Hiran. I'm not going to generalise an entire country based on a single person. Besides, I know Britain brought homophobia to India when it was colonised. So, if anything, I'm angry at Britain."

"Excuse me," Alexia called over to Aarav and Riya. The couple broke off their argument and turned to her. "If you have a problem with me or Jennifer, come here and

we can talk about it."

Riya's mouth twisted and she looked away, but Aarav raised his chin and glared at Alexia. "Homosexuality is not right," he said, his words short and clipped. "You can both choose to be with men, I don't understand why you insist on this wrongness."

Victoria could see fury winding up Jennifer's spine with every syllable he uttered.

"I am going to stop you there," Alexia said, her voice steel. "It is not a choice. Do you choose to be attracted to women?" She didn't wait for an answer. "No. Just like I do not choose to be attracted to women. There is nothing wrong with us—the only thing that is wrong is the intolerant world we lived in. I have grown up with homophobic comments and slurs shouted at me. I hid who I was for a long time. I *will not* do that now. I *will not* stand here and take your hate. I am proud of who I am, and nothing you can say is going to change that."

"A man and a woman is right," Aarav insisted. "Nothing else. A union between man and woman brings children—"

"What fucking century are you living in?" Jennifer cut in incredulously. "If same-sex couples want to have kids they can, thanks to science. Humanity has long progressed past that stupid argument, Aarav. Love is love, and it is *beautiful,* regardless of gender. Why can't you see that? What does it matter to you if Alexia and I are in a relationship? It doesn't affect you."

"It is disgusting, and I will not follow a woman like you."

Silence rang through the room. Victoria didn't know

what to say. Clearly Jennifer and Alexia had been subject to this before, and Victoria's heart broke for them.

"The old society fell," Alexia said quietly. "I hope this new one we build will be more open and accepting."

"It will," Jennifer said with such finality that Victoria couldn't imagine anything else. Jennifer sighed. "I can't let you stay here, Aarav. Brendon is a horrible person, and he'll hurt you. No matter our dislike of each other, I won't let that happen." Her kindness left Victoria reeling. If she were in Jennifer's shoes, she would have left him without question.

"I don't believe you," Aarav said, and Victoria bristled.

"You don't believe Jennifer?" Victoria took a step forward and watched with glee as he took one back. "*Teona and I* were the ones with the creeped-out feeling. *I* was there when Heather told us some of the things he's done. Do you not believe me either? Or Teona?"

She watched Aarav's eyes dart between her and Teona, but she never got a chance to hear his reply. Frankie barged into the room, all stomping boots and smashed face. "Jennifer, Brendon wants to see you downstairs."

Oh crap. Victoria shared a wide-eyed look with Jennifer. "I'll be down in a minute," she said.

"He wants to see you now."

James stiffened at that, but Jennifer shook her head at him. "Fine, I'm coming."

"I am too," Victoria and Alexia said simultaneously.

"This isn't settled, Aarav," Jennifer warned as they made their way out of the room. He sneered at her, and

Jennifer shook her head.

The three of them followed Frankie down the stairs. A heavy weight settled in Victoria's stomach the closer they got to the bottom.

Chapter Thirty-Four

Jennifer's body thrummed with rage. How dare he? How fucking *dare* he say that? Her fists clenched, her nails digging into her palms, and she only relaxed at Alexia's soft touch. Alexia ran a hand down her arm, and some of her tension leeched away.

She should be used to the homophobia by now. God knows she got a lot of it with Robin. It still hurt, especially coming from Aarav. They didn't get along, but Jennifer had thought they were above such nastiness. She was so *angry*. As if her sexuality affected her judgment. And calling her a *liar?* Jennifer had half a mind to leave him here, but she couldn't do that to Riya.

They made their way down the stairs and into the main room, and Jennifer's swirling thoughts ground to a halt. There, in the middle of the room close to the back door, were three people. One was Frankie, leaving their side and strolling over to the other two. The other was Brendon, grinning that shining smile of his. The third was Heather, silent tears rolling down her face as a gun pressed hard against her head.

Jennifer sucked in a deep, steadying breath. This was turning into a *really* shitty morning. "What's going on

here, Brendon?"

His smile didn't falter. "I'm an early riser, never did like sleeping in much. As I made my way to the kitchen for some breakfast, I discovered a nefarious plot." The gun didn't waver. "Heather here was already in the kitchen. Stealing the food she'd worked so hard to bring back for all of us. I imagine she was trying to be stealthy. Is that right, Heather?" He turned his blinding smile to the paramedic, who tried to flinch away, but Brendon's grip was too strong. "Now, I cannot *stand* thievery. It's barbaric. Uncivilised. And we are still civilised people, aren't we, Heather?" She whimpered in response, and Brendon's smile twisted for a moment. "Pathetic."

"Enough, Brendon," Jennifer said, trying to project authority into her tone. God, how did they get out of this? She'd never felt so out of her depth in her life. "Let her go. You're scaring her."

"I've told you before, Jennifer—I'm the one in charge here. You don't give me orders." His smile was still perfect, but Jennifer saw the maliciousness underneath. He'd never looked so ugly. "Now, when I asked dear Heather here about what she was doing, she spilled the beans quite readily." He pursed his lips. "It was quite sad to watch. No loyalty."

"We are leaving," Jennifer said. There was no use trying to deny it. Heather was terrified of him, so of course she'd told him everything. Jennifer didn't hold it against her. *Poor woman.* "You can't stop us. Heather wanted to join us, and I said she could. I told her to take some food." Brendon opened his mouth, but Jennifer pressed on, raising her voice over him. Sweat prickled along her forehead. "Not a lot, but just enough to keep us going for a bit. You

would keep most of it."

Brendon's eyes bored into her own, but Jennifer refused to be the first one to break. *Don't look away.* She caught sight of Heather's pleading gaze in her peripheral vision, and she had to swallow against the emotion that rose in her. *I can't break.* She pushed aside the nagging voice that said she was going to fail. Brendon's signature smile returned, and Jennifer had to suppress a grimace at the sight of it. "And to think I extended sanctuary to you people. I rescind that offer."

"We're leaving anyway," Jennifer said, lifting her chin. She somehow kept her voice steady. "We'll be taking our weapons back and Heather will be coming with us."

"If you think, for one second, that I'm going to let you take my hunter and paramedic, you truly are delusional."

Heather let out a sob at Brendon's words. He yanked her close to him and she screwed her eyes shut. "*Shut up,*" he snarled, the ugliness inside him finally bubbling to the surface. He released a long breath and fixed his smile back on his face. "Heather is mine, and she's not going anywhere."

"Heather is her own woman, and she can go wherever she wants." The anger that had been simmering away in the background from earlier rushed to the surface. Jennifer let it burn away some of her fears. She was tired of men trying to control women. She was tired of men butting into her business, telling her she was wrong and disgusting. She was so *tired* of men thinking they could tell her what to do. "And she wants to come with us. I said she could. I don't go back on my promises."

"I don't trust the word of a thief," Brendon hissed. "Whatever she's promised you, Heather, I wouldn't

believe any of it."

Heather twisted in his grip, but again failed to get away. Her tears showed no sign of drying up. "Just get it over with, you *motherfucker*," she cried. Brendon's eyebrows shot up in surprise.

"I didn't know you had a spine in you, Heather. And such language," he tutted. "I'm not going to waste such a valuable resource like you. Don't be silly." He sounded like he was reprimanding a small child. *Condescending piece of shit.*

Jennifer felt more than saw Victoria move. It was subtle, but it boosted Jennifer's confidence. Victoria was ready for anything. Jennifer knew the odds were stacked against them, but she trusted her to save Heather. Alexia pressed closer to Jennifer.

"You're not going to hurt her, so put the gun down," Jennifer said, raising her palms toward him.

"You're right," Brendon nodded, his smile widening. "I'm not going to shoot *her*."

Victoria moved. She was a blur in the corner of Jennifer's eye. Even as Brendon started turning the gun on Jennifer, Victoria was there, grabbing his arm and punching him in his stomach. The gun went off, a deafening sound that hit Jennifer like the bullet that shot out of the barrel. Luckily, said bullet embedded itself in the wall behind her. Jennifer ducked automatically, and Alexia grabbed her hand and pulled her down the narrow corridor behind the stairs.

The explosion of noise brought shouts from upstairs, and Jennifer heard the pounding of feet on the floor as the familiar feeling of adrenaline loosened her limbs and

silenced her racing thoughts. God, she hoped the situation wouldn't devolve further. Couldn't they catch a break for once?

*

James was idly listening as Teona, Trueman, and Hiran berated Aarav. He thought about getting involved as well, but the three soldiers tag-teamed well. He knew it was personal for Trueman. The man could fight his own battles without James butting in and trying to talk about something he had no experience with.

The argument was getting heated again and Trueman almost outed himself when a loud gunshot rang up from downstairs. It was so unexpected that James went rigid, his mind flashing back to France, his mind freezing, a bullet tearing through his shoulder, his blood pouring out, his body going cold, so cold, so cold, so cold—

Heat. Glorious heat. Teona cradled his face in both her hands as his eyes slowly focused on her. "Hey, James," she was saying softly. "It's all right, you're all right. You're in a pub in England, you're not getting shot, okay?"

"I'm okay," he gasped out. He was sure she felt his heartbeat through his skin. "I'm okay."

"Come on," Teona said. "We have to see what's going on. Are you going to be all right?"

"Aye." He nodded, more in control of himself with every passing second. She gave him a dubious look. "I promise. Let's go."

Together they stumbled down the stairs. The rest of the group were already there, even the kids. They pushed their way to the front, where Jennifer and Alexia stood.

Jennifer had her arms extended, and James took in the sight in before them.

Victoria pointed a handgun directly at Brendon. Frankie and three other people—one man and two women—had guns pointed at Victoria and Jennifer. Brendon held Heather in front of him, and his grip on her hair made James wince in sympathy.

"This doesn't have to turn violent," Jennifer said beseechingly. "We can still talk about this."

"We are *way* past talking," Brendon snarled. He turned to his people. "Kill them."

With two simple words James's world exploded.

*

Victoria managed to get two shots off as she dived for cover. She had no idea if they hit their targets or not, and she didn't stand around to find out.

She followed Jennifer and Alexia over the bar, Hiran following close behind. The deafening pop of gunfire drowned out all other sound as bullets tore up the space around them. Victoria's mind flashed back to the forest with Jennifer as splinters of wood and glass rained down like tiny daggers that cut into exposed skin. Victoria had accepted the new clothes they'd offered, and as she crouched in some black jeans and a white sleeveless top, she wished desperately that she'd put her armour back on. At least she still had her boots.

The onslaught on the bar stopped abruptly, but the sound of gunfire still echoed around Victoria's skull. She leaned out to try to get a better understanding of what was going on. Brendon and Heather—and the rest of the group

for that matter—were nowhere to be seen.

She had to duck back as two people spotted her and opened fire again. *Bloody hell! How do we get out of this?*

Alexia grabbed her arm. "We need more guns," she whispered, her words tripping over themselves in their rush out of her mouth. "Cover me while I get his."

Victoria followed her finger to a man who was walking past slowly, firing up the stairs. He must have thought they were pinned by the others and not a threat. He was an idiot. Once again, she was struck by the thought that they looked the part but didn't know what they were doing. They certainly weren't soldiers. She nodded once and let the part of herself she'd referred to as the monster bleed free.

Her world burst alive with colour and movement.

*

Alexia surged over the top of the bar in a whirlwind of energy and motion, and Jennifer stared with a mixture of fear and awe crawling up her throat. She disarmed the man with ease and shot him with his own gun. Jennifer didn't know whether to be impressed or scared. *Alexia* could have been the one getting shot.

Victoria was close behind, shooting one man and disarming another with a well-placed punch before shooting him as well. She passed the handguns to Hiran and Jennifer, who held hers loosely. The last time she'd had a weapon it hadn't worked.

"Be careful, the safety is off," Victoria said, like a mind reader. "Don't shoot us accidentally."

"I'll do my best not to," Jennifer gasped. How did the

soldiers appear so damn calm?

"Let's get out of here," Hiran said.

"We have to make sure everyone gets out," Jennifer said, determined not to leave anyone behind. Not even Aarav. Where was Dan? Panic began to curl its icy fingers up her spine, but she shook it loose. She needed a clear head, now more than ever.

"We'll get you out first, Jennifer," Victoria said in that no-nonsense tone of hers. "Then I'll come back in for the others."

They darted out of the back door into crisp morning light. Alexia led them around the side near the river as a few more of Brendon's people came around the opposite side of the pub. They didn't seem to have seen them, and Jennifer crouched against the rough brick as her lungs drew in greater amounts of oxygen with each breath.

*

James punched a man in the throat. Elise and Coyne had grabbed Dan and Ismay and dragged them upstairs, and this bastard had gone to follow them. *Who the fuck hurts kids?* Not on James's watch.

The bastard stumbled back, loosening his grip on his L85—James thought it was one of their weapons—and he seized his opportunity. With a swift kick between his legs, he yanked the weapon out of the man's slack grip and brought it round in a heavy arc that connected solidly with his head. He went down like the sack of shite he was.

James couldn't properly hold the weapon himself, so he tossed it to Teona who'd dropped a woman in the narrow corridor that led to a fire escape. She passed him the

handgun she had with a feral grin.

"We need to get out of here, sir." Trueman appeared from nowhere, cracking open the front door they all moved to. He slammed it shut again immediately. "Not that way, they're lining up outside. They have grenades, sir, and I'm sure I saw a shotgun."

"Shit," Teona cursed. "At least we cleared out the few who came in here. Brendon must have escaped out the back in all the chaos."

"So, we hold the pub and they're outside," James clarified. "I say we grab what supplies we can carry and make a break for it out the back. They have more firepower than us, we can't hold them off here."

"Okay, let's gather the others and get the fuck out of here," Teona said, already moving to the stairs.

*

Victoria signalled for everyone to keep low as she crept round the side of the building to check on Brendon's people at the back. Crouching down, feeling the familiar burn of energy in her muscles, she peered around the red brick.

She counted five people, all armed with an array of weapons. All had handguns, two had knives, two had assault rifles, and one had three grenades strapped to his belt. *Where did they get all this stuff from? They must have pillaged a military base.*

She leaned back and held up five fingers for the others. Hiran and Alexia nodded back, and Victoria gave Jennifer a look that said *hang back*. She did *not* want anything happening to Jennifer. There was always the possibility they might run into other scientists.

On Victoria's signal the three of them rushed out, guns blazing. Victoria managed to drop two of them as they readied themselves to storm the pub. Hiran got a woman as they started to hastily retreat, and Victoria was almost shot as she darted back behind the wall. She quickly checked her arm for any injuries, and thankfully nothing but smooth, pale skin greeted her frantic search. She blew out a breath. *Focus!* They'd gotten three out of the five. That was good. They'd lost the element of surprise, though.

Alexia came to rest beside her, her chest heaving. "They are right next to the back door. If you can keep their attention here, I will sneak around."

"I'll do it," Victoria said, catching Jennifer's wide-eyed look of horror at Alexia. "You keep their attention here." She didn't wait to hear a response.

She ripped off the frankly shoddy boards over one of the windows and smashed the window as Alexia fired to cover the sound. Conscious of the broken glass as she climbed back into the pub, Victoria didn't let her brain fully compute what she was doing. The moment she stopped would be the moment she died. That wasn't going to happen.

She stole back through the pub, quiet as a mouse. Stepping lightly on the fragmented debris that littered the floor, Victoria strained her ears. If they were in the pub she'd know.

A hand clamped down on her shoulder and Victoria reacted. Spinning away from the touch, she brought her fist down in a fast arc, powerful enough to knock her assailant clean out.

It was blocked. Expertly.

By Teona.

"Whoa there, Bruce Lee, calm your tits."

Victoria could have laughed. She wasn't being attacked. "A little more warning next time would be great." *Bloody hell, all that time I was boasting about my training, she could do it all and more.* She felt like a child playing at being an adult.

"I'm not going to go around wearing a fucking bell at a time like this, am I?" Teona retorted. "Where are the others?"

"Outside. They're pinned by two attackers. I'm flanking them through the door."

"Let's do this then."

Victoria saw James leading Elise and the kids back down the stairs before she turned and led the way to the back door. On Teona's signal she jerked it open and burst out, her little animal roaring with a ferocity to match its larger cousins. She hit Grenade Man in the stomach, but it was Teona who finished them both off with shots to their heads.

Silence reigned again. Hiran poked his head around the corner and Victoria waved them out. The ground soaked up the blood, and once again, Victoria's boots were smack in the middle of it all. Only this time, there was no nausea at all.

*

Jennifer found herself back in the main room of the Red Lion. Everyone was grouped together next to the bar, and the worst injury was a graze to Danny's arm that was more burn than gunshot wound. She stood close to Dan, who

had gravitated toward her the moment their eyes met.

"Hiran and Danny, take two backpacks and fill them with as much food as you can," Teona ordered. "Storming the pub?" she asked James.

"Aye," he said. "I wouldn't be surprised if they're flanking us again. Although we've killed a lot of them already."

Teona nodded. "Trueman, cover that broken window. Ota, you cover the fire escape." The two soldiers obeyed with quick nods and quicker feet.

"Did anyone see what kind of artillery they had?" Rhys asked.

"Grenades, shotguns, assault rifles, that sort of thing," Teona answered nonchalantly, like this was a normal morning for her.

"Great," Rhys muttered. "And we have what? Four rifles and five handguns, all of which are running low on ammo."

"Fuck me, you're optimistic, aren't you?" Teona rolled her eyes. "Listen up, people, as soon as they get back with the food, we leave out the back door and get the fuck out of here down the river."

"Oh, is that all?" Rhys said sarcastically.

"No," Jennifer said. Everyone turned to look at her. "We aren't leaving Heather. God knows what he's going to do to her, we *can't* leave her here."

Teona sighed. "Okay, how about this. The first part still stands, we get out and go down the river, then some of us double back and—"

The rest of what she was going to say was drowned

out by loud gunfire coming from Anthony's direction. *Fuck, we're out of time.* Not a second later, Hiran and Danny barrelled out of the kitchen carrying backpacks that were full to bursting.

Jennifer grabbed Dan, keeping him close as she moved nearer to Alexia. She didn't have time to say anything as a shock ripped through the room. The next thing Jennifer knew she was picking herself up off the ground. Smoke and dust were everywhere, and she couldn't hear anything over the ringing in her ears. She shook her head to try to clear the roaring and saw people piling in through the breach in the wall where the door used to be.

They've blown up their own building? Brendon is a fucking madman. Bedlam reigned as bullets and blows were traded. Jennifer saw a short man prowling forward, eyes squinting against the dust, and without thinking she lurched forward and bit into his exposed forearm. He dropped his gun as he yelped in shock. Jennifer's own gun lay forgotten on the floor.

The whites of his eyes stood out in his grey face. "I didn't sign up for this." He moved to run, but a bullet from Alexia caught him square in the chest. Jennifer watched as the red stain spread over his white top. She spat out the blood in her mouth. *What a waste. This could have all been avoided.*

Alexia grabbed Jennifer and started hauling her away. She caught glimpses of fighting shadows shifting in the smoke, and the odd burst of bright light from discharging muzzles. Chaos ruled in the Red Lion, and Jennifer felt like a deer in headlights, terror filling up every crevice of her mind as she followed in Alexia's wake.

Chapter Thirty-Five

"You *can't* be serious."

Heather thought that was a redundant statement considering Frankie had already pulled the pin and thrown the grenade.

The resulting blast was one Heather wouldn't forget for a long time. She detested the Red Lion and the people who called it home, but its walls had offered her protection from the death and turmoil that raged all around. Seeing those walls tumble as if they were paper made her stomach drop to her feet. Judging from the looks of the people around her, they felt the same. *Maybe now he's gone one step too far for them.* It was fine when Brendon's cruelty didn't affect them, but now they couldn't turn a blind eye to his brutality, his special brand of madness.

"Brendon, you've *blown up* our home," Lucy said in a voice whispery with incredulousness.

"*Shut up,*" Brendon snarled, before collecting himself and turning up the wattage on his smile. Heather almost snorted. *Too late for that.* "We can rebuild. But right now, we need to rid the place of vermin, even if it means burning it to the ground."

"What about the zombies?" Steve asked. Sweet, dim Steve, asking the question Brendon clearly hadn't thought about. *Maybe he doesn't care.*

"*Enough.*" The gun that had been held to Heather's head was pointed at Steve's. The poor boy's eyes went comically wide.

Heather didn't wait around to see what happened next. As soon as the cold metal was off her skin she bolted, not knowing where this newfound courage came from and not caring in the slightest. As long as it got her away from Brendon. All the heartache and horror came bubbling up into her throat and she knew she was screaming but she didn't know how to stop. She didn't know if she was going to live or die, and it didn't seem to matter. She knew Kallie would be proud. She'd finally made her escape. Maybe that was what pushed her on. If her wife saw her then, Heather knew she would be cheering her on.

She ran as fast as her legs could carry her. She heard distant shouting, and she almost tripped over her feet when the gun went off, but she wasn't hit, so she kept running.

She ran toward the fighting. She could get her gear in the chaos and escape around the back of the pub. *As if it would be that easy.* Heather mentally kicked herself for dashing toward death, but if she could help the people who offered to take her away from hell then she would damn well help them.

She jumped straight through the hole in the building with no hesitation. It had nothing to do with fearlessness—she'd screamed herself hoarse. Inside was as much of a mess as outside. Bodies littered the floor like discarded rubbish, unnaturally still in death, and Heather

gulped away the sudden emotion gripping her throat. There was Jonny, and Stacey, and wait. Was that one alive?

Heather rushed to the young man's side. He was part of Jennifer's group—Heather didn't know his name. The gunshot wound to his thigh was bad, really bad, and even when Heather applied pressure, she knew it wouldn't be enough.

"Please..." He reached for her. She grabbed his cold hand and held on hard, compassion blurring her vision as she watched him die. His grip slowly slackened, his eyes lost that *something*, and Heather knew he was gone.

She stood up, tears and blood soaking her skin. *Have to keep going.* She'd barely stepped forward before she was yanked backward. Frankie. She looked into his brown eyes and saw nothing reflected back. No remorse, no familiarity. Just anger. "Frankie, please," she said as she struggled. He'd always been strong, and she was powerless against him as he dragged her back out into the sunlight.

"I'm sorry, Heather," he said without an ounce of apology in his voice. "But I can't let you get away. Brendon wants to make an example out of you."

Heather went cold all over. She knew what *that* entailed. She redoubled her efforts, but it had no effect. Heather was so focused on getting away that she didn't see another man come out of nowhere and tackle Frankie to the ground.

All three of them ended up in a heap on the floor. Heather struggled to get up as her breath left her in a rush. She rolled away from the grappling men, coughing as she pushed herself back up. As soon as she regained her feet

she was being hauled around, and a flash of fear pulsed through her. *Brendon!*

It wasn't Brendon. It was one of Jennifer's men, a tall man with kind eyes. Heather let herself be pulled away, not looking back as two loud gunshots reverberated through her and the sounds of struggle ceased.

"Where are the others?" the man who'd been fighting with Frankie asked breathlessly. Frankie lay immobile on the ground. Heather turned away.

"Round the back, let's go."

Heather didn't look back. Not once.

*

One minute, Teona was talking, and the next James was on the floor, trying to orientate himself. His ears felt stuffed full of wool.

He wasted no time being dazed. With a heave that threatened to make him black out, he regained his feet as Brendon's people started pouring through the breach like a tidal wave of shite. James raised his weapon and fired indiscriminately, edging back all the while. He couldn't see a lot in the smoke, but he saw Coyne dragging Dan out of the back door. *Good man. Get the kids out.*

He emptied his clip into a man with wide, bloodshot eyes, and threw the gun at a woman who fired at someone else. He ducked down as she swung around to him, practically falling behind the bar as bullets embedded themselves into the wood. *No weapon, no way out. What can I do?* James spotted a solid length of wood lying on the ground next to his feet. It looked like a small, grey pillar. Maybe it had been decoration? He picked it up, swinging

it a few times to get a feel of the weight. *This'll do.*

He utilized it not a moment later. The woman he'd thrown his gun at stepped around the bar, cautious but clearly thinking she'd got him. More fool her. James rocketed the club into her knee and winced at the sickening snap. She went down with a scream. Not one to waste an opportunity, James stood up and smacked her over the head. The screaming stopped.

A man fought Elise on a small stage, and Ismay curled into herself in the corner. He hadn't seen James, who sidled up behind him and clobbered him over the head as well. *Who the* fuck *goes after kids? Fucking disgusting.*

He pulled Elise to her feet, and she nodded her thanks. "Jams!" Ismay attached herself to his legs, and Elise had to pry her off to pick her up.

"Get her out of here," James shouted, already turning away to deal with the next bastard. Elise didn't need telling twice. James watched as she scrambled around fights and fire, and he caught Ismay's eye as they ducked out the back door. She was crying. *You'll be all right, lass.*

James looked back around the pub. It was clear the Red Lion lot weren't trained soldiers. Aye, they had the advantage in numbers, and they'd *had* the advantage with weapons, but James saw how they were losing. Most of the weapons were out of ammo, and those that weren't had quickly been disarmed. He made sure to clock Teona and keep an eye on her. She winked at him as she dropped a man almost twice her size.

Ignoring his shoulder, James jumped back into the fray, swinging his club about with abandon. His shirt quickly became bloodstained as he broke bones and heads, but he didn't slow. These people looked the part

with their fancy grenades and shotguns, but they clearly didn't have a clue how to use them.

A broken arm, a broken nose, a smash to the stomach. James was a hurricane, blowing through them like they were made of nothing. He knew he had to disengage soon though—he was tiring, and he was pretty sure his shoulder was bleeding again.

Trueman and Ota dashed past him, but his eyes were drawn to someone else. Charlie. The lad lay prone on the floor, blood covering the ground around him. *Fuck, he was just a kid.* Rage fanned familiar flames in his stomach, and he laid into the remaining enemies with renewed vigour. Another broken head, another broken arm, another—

A loud bang set his ears ringing. *The fucking shotgun.* Victoria limped past, but James had to duck out of the way before he could go to her. *Where the fuck is Teona?* He'd lost sight of her.

There.

She was locked in a fist fight with a man. James felt cold all over. She couldn't see. She couldn't see. He pushed himself forward, running on tired legs. Running to the blond bastard with that fucking shotgun. That fucking shotgun that was aimed at Teona. His heart stuttered in his chest before pounding as fast as it ever had, spurring him on and on until—

Pain.

He was on the floor again. *Fuck.* He didn't know how long he lay there, breathing in smoke and sweat. *Have to get up. Have to check on Teona.* His thoughts were slow. Sluggish. He knew this was bad. *Have to get up.*

He moved slowly. He was fast losing feeling in his numb legs. His heart still beat, but it struggled. He wasn't able to prop himself up, and he stopped trying with a quiet sigh. He thought nothing could hurt more than the wound to his shoulder, but a shotgun blast to the gut was excruciating. He coughed, and the tangy taste of blood left a foul residue in his mouth.

James looked desperately around the pub. Victoria had taken care of the blond bastard, and as he made eye contact with her, he knew. He knew. She wiped away tears as something behind James caught her attention, but he didn't turn to look. A grenade had rolled next to his knee, and as he reached for it, he coughed up even more blood. He lay painted in red.

"No. No, no, no, no."

Teona fell to his side hard, lacking her usual grace. She put pressure on his stomach and James almost passed out from the sudden rush of burning agony. "You need to get out of here, Teona," James muttered. He didn't seem capable of anything louder. He couldn't feel his legs any more.

"What the fuck, James? Why'd you go and get yourself shot?" She was crying. She shouldn't be crying. James reached up and wiped the tears away, but more fell in their place.

He tried to laugh, but more blood came up instead. "Sorry, but he was going to shoot you. Couldn't let that happen."

"You idiot," she said. "It's going to be okay, James. We'll get you out of here. Heather and Riya can stitch you up good as new."

"Hey." James cradled her wet cheek, running his thumb under her eyes to catch her tears. "You're going to be okay, but you have to leave, Teona, please. Get out and live. Keep the others alive too, aye?"

Victoria appeared behind Teona, her top splattered with so much blood James wouldn't have known it was white if he'd hadn't seen it earlier. "We have to leave. They're regrouping. The others are already out the back."

Contentment rushed through him. The others had gotten out. Charlie was the only one he'd seen who hadn't made it. Well, and himself. "See? Go, Teona, they need you. I'll delay them as much as I can so you can have a good head start." He coughed again. More blood. "If they come through the pub, I'll kill them so you don't have to worry." He held out the grenade for them to see.

"I'm not leaving you," Teona said ferociously. "No fucking way."

"Teona, please."

"We have to go *now*," Victoria said, grabbing Teona's arm and pulling. Teona yanked it out of her grip.

"*No.*"

"Wait," James suddenly remembered the antibiotics. "My pocket, take them."

Victoria frowned and reached into his pockets when it became clear Teona wasn't going to move. She pulled the packet out and nodded, clutching the medicine in a bloody fist.

"Teona," James pleaded. "If you get killed here then I'll have died for nothing. Please go."

"*Teona.*" Victoria fired the shotgun somewhat

awkwardly with the antibiotics, but the warning shot had the desired effect. James flinched at the sound. With a sob, Teona pressed a hard kiss to his forehead, causing warmth to spread through his numb body. She was gone a moment later, both women dashing out of the back door.

He thought of his parents then, and their meaningless deaths. His was going to be different. He had saved Teona's life, and he was going to give the group precious time to get away. Tears trickled free, and he closed his eyes to slits as Brendon walked into the room with only six other people. The rage still burned in his chest, and he tightened his grip on the grenade.

"They've completely destroyed the pub," a redheaded man was saying, his jaw slack with disbelief. "There's only us left, Brendon. What are we going to do?"

That was all James needed to know. They picked their way slowly over the bodies and blood, inching ever closer to his position. His heart thudded dully and his hands were clammy, but he'd be damned if he didn't stay alive long enough to pull the pin out.

Brendon stopped at his feet. James couldn't believe his luck. He was going to get them all, and the group could get away safely. "We rebuild," the bastard said in a weak voice, like he couldn't believe his eyes. "We...keep going."

James could make out the blue of the sky through the blown-out wall. He was glad it was a bright day.

"No, Brendon," another man spat. "I came here for safety from the zombies, and I stayed because it was safe, not to play soldier for your fucked-up ego. Look at what you've done. They're all dead."

James imagined it was warm. He was beyond feeling

temperature, but he didn't want to think it was cold.

"We have to go after them," Brendon said in that same soft voice. "We can't let them get away with this."

James thought about winter, and all the shite that had happened to him during that season. It struck him that it had been mild lately. Maybe spring had arrived.

"Are you even listening to us?" A woman spoke for the first time. "It's *over*."

He was going to die in spring, as the flowers bloomed bright and life started anew. He had helped the group escape, and no one else would have to die for him to live. Peace settled over him.

"Hey, Brendon," James said, making his voice as loud as he could. His vision was dark around the edges, but he saw everyone turn to look at him with varying degrees of horror. "Fuck you."

James pulled the pin out.

Chapter Thirty-Six

Victoria heard the blast before she felt it. A deafening roar followed by a physical anguish. She and Teona stumbled to a halt a little way down the path, and Victoria lifted her eyes to the sky as Teona sank to her knees. Bright blue greeted her gaze. *Not a cloud in sight. Such cheerful weather for such a dreadful day.*

As much as she was loath to push Teona, she knew they couldn't linger. The others couldn't be far. *Bloody hell, I hope no one else has—*she couldn't finish the thought. Her throat felt raw. Her eyes were dry. *Grieve later. Keep going.*

"Teona," she started, but Teona was already up and moving again.

They found the group not much farther up the river. Victoria did a frantic headcount. Everyone was there. Everyone except...

Charlie.

Danny.

James.

Victoria blew out a breath as Jennifer rose to meet them, her smile so bright Victoria could barely look at it.

"Oh my God."

Victoria found herself in a tight embrace, and she clutched just as hard as Jennifer. She finally felt wet on her cheeks. Everything that had happened that morning surged through her, and Victoria was helpless as all her fear and adrenaline and fury poured out through her eyes.

It felt like an age before she pulled away. Tears still squeezed their way down her face, but Victoria was more in control. Jennifer looked at her, compassion shining in her hopeful smile.

"Are James and the others on their way?"

And just like that, her control slipped away. She shook her head in a silent no and dropped her gaze as her eyes burned again. "That explosion was James. He said he'd help us get away." She heard Jennifer take several deep breaths and watched as her blurry hands clenched and unclenched. When she looked back up, Jennifer's watery gaze was fixed on Teona.

Teona sat by the water, her arms wrapped loosely around her drawn-up knees. Teona could have been a fort with how closed off she was, her back to everyone and a brittle kind of tension thrumming through her slack body. Victoria blinked. She looked fragile and unbreakable simultaneously.

Jennifer gulped down a large breath of air as she braced herself. "Today has been…"

Everyone, bar Teona, looked at her. Heather and Riya checked people over and dealt with injuries. Dan had the worst one she could see, a nasty-looking slice on his arm, blood flowing freely. The cut on Victoria's leg hurt, but she knew it was minor and wouldn't cause any lasting

damage.

"God, it's not even midday." Jennifer gave a wet-sounding laugh. "I'm sorry. I'm sorry. I promised you all I'd get you to safety and now..." Fresh tears slid down her face. "James and Danny and Charlie were good people. They died fighting. I wish they hadn't died at all." Jennifer stopped again to compose herself. Victoria held more tears at bay as best she could—after months of barely crying at anything, she hadn't thought it possible any more.

"We're going to carry on for them," Jennifer continued. "They'd want us to be safe. I know you're all feeling like shit right now, I know you're all wondering what the point is. Why bother, right? The world is dark and dangerous, and it feels like the moment we catch our breath something comes along to snatch it away. Believe me, I know. But we have to keep going. For them. For us. Remember Danny and Charlie splashing around yesterday in the water. Remember how patient James was with Ismay and how he got her to smile again. Remember how they all brought us friendship and family in this crazy world. We keep going for one another. I *need* you all to keep going for one another."

Victoria nodded to herself. She would keep going. She remembered her conversation with James back at the castle, what felt like a million years ago.

She'd do him proud.

*

"Okay," Jennifer said. She wanted to scream her grief out for everyone to hear, she wanted to rage and cry and curl up, but she reined it all in. God, when would the pain end? "As much as I'm sure you all want to get as far away from

here as possible, we need supplies before we can leave." She gestured for Anthony and Edward. "Can you two please go back and salvage anything we can use? See if you can find any of our own bags as well." Jennifer hoped they could find the one with the tampons and pads, otherwise she was in for a horribly bloody week. "And be careful. We don't know if James managed to get everyone."

"Can you try to find my first aid kit as well?" Heather asked in a quiet voice, like she wasn't sure she was allowed to speak or not. *God, Brendon really did a number on her.*

Oh shit. "Can you please look for my camera as well?" Jennifer couldn't mask the desperation in her voice. How the fuck had she forgotten that? What if it was destroyed? Damaged beyond repair? Jennifer sucked in a deep breath, trying to keep a lid on the rising panic. Losing the camera would be the icing on the worst cake ever.

Anthony and Edward nodded and jogged off. Jennifer turned back to her little group of survivors. They were bloodied and bruised and tired, but they were carrying on. She pushed aside her own melancholy and stepped forward to talk to them all individually, even Aarav, if he'd speak to her. She'd make sure they were all okay even as she herself struggled to stay afloat in a sea of numbness.

The two soldiers returned ten minutes later according to the gold hands on Dan's watch. Jennifer had spoken to everyone bar Aarav, reiterating her "don't give up" rhetoric. James, Danny, and Charlie. She'd never really gotten the chance to know Charlie, but his death still hurt. Pushing down regrets, Jennifer rose to greet Anthony and Edward.

"What did you manage to get?" They were carrying two backpacks each, and all four were bursting at the

seams. "Was there anyone left alive?"

"Your camera," Anthony said, holding it out for her to take. Jennifer did so quickly, barely refraining from snatching it out of his hand. It didn't look any worse for wear. She switched it on, stunned to discover it worked fine. Jennifer closed her eyes against a wave of emotion. "It survived the damage without a scratch." Anthony smiled. "That's a good piece of equipment right there."

"A lot of the building was damaged from the grenade blast," Edward said, placing his two bags on the ground. "No one was left alive. We managed to get back one of ours—Victoria, I think this is the one you were carrying. There's a lot of, erm, women's products in here."

Victoria snorted. "You can say the word tampon, it's not going to bite you."

Edward looked uncomfortable until she stepped forward and relieved him of the bag. He cleared his throat. "Right. We also managed to salvage some extra clothes and underwear, so if you want to change just pick your size." He gestured at his remaining bag.

Anthony took over. "Here is the first aid kit." Heather took the bag silently. "We managed to salvage more weapons as well." He handed out handguns and rifles to the soldiers. Jennifer was happy to see them. She never thought she'd be glad to see heralds of death and pain, but there she was. "We found one of the food bags as well, but not the other."

Jennifer nodded. They'd brought back more than she could have hoped for. "You've done well, thank you both." The two men nodded. "Right then, we need to start moving. I want to be as far away from here as possible when we camp for the night."

"I have a suggestion," Edward said. "We thought about it scouting the pub out. Why don't we take the bus? The one on the roundabout, not the bridge, obviously."

"Does it have fuel?" Teona spoke up for the first time, her voice flat.

"There's no harm in trying," Jennifer said. It would be amazing if it did—just the thing to take them away from this devastating day. "Let's avoid the pub on the way around."

They quickly washed in the freezing water and changed out of their stained clothes. Jennifer took some dark-grey jeans and a navy button-up shirt, then Heather led the way around the blown-up building. Jennifer couldn't look too closely at it. James, Danny, Charlie. That husk of a building housed their bodies. There was nothing Jennifer could do, and it hurt like hell. When they came around to the front of the building, she took a quick picture of the destruction, the camera perfectly preserving all the loss and heartache permeating the atmosphere. The bright sky, marred by wisps of smoke. The crumbled red of the bricks, the charred remains of the beams. Her camera felt heavy in her hands. She tried to regulate her breathing as her throat began to burn.

They walked a couple more steps when a little voice threatened to tear down all her carefully constructed barriers.

"Jams?"

Ismay's frizzy hair bounced around as she looked every which way, high in Elise's arms. The burn in Jennifer's throat became unbearable.

"Jams?"

"James isn't coming, kiddo," Teona answered. Her voice sounded raw, like she too, fought tears. "I'm sorry."

"Jams?" Ismay's voice was quieter, a watery quality taking over as her lip began to quiver. Elise started singing softly, rocking her in her arms as fat tears rolled down Ismay's cheeks. She even cried silently.

Jennifer hastily wiped her own eyes and glimpsed Dan and Riya doing the same. *We need this struggle to be over. God, let there be somewhere out there we can just live in peace.* Jennifer was tired. She'd said goodbye to her parents before their time, her friends, her life. And now her second family was in danger of being torn apart.

Fuck this day.

Chapter Thirty-Seven

Anthony turned the key in the ignition and the bus rumbled to life. Jennifer's knees buckled with relief.

"It's good they left the key in," she said. *About time we had some good luck.*

"I kind of knew," Edward said as he passed her. Everyone piled on, dumping the bags on the shelf at the front and moving down the aisle to claim a seat. "I overheard some of them talking yesterday about how the key was in the ignition ready to go. It could have been any one of the vehicles, but I assumed this one in case they needed to move everyone at once."

"Well, thank fuck they were prepared," Jennifer sighed. Anthony pulled away, and Jennifer held on to the bar as the bus carried them from death and heartache.

She glanced at Anthony. His face was relaxed as he manoeuvred the bus down the road. His soft eyes held a melancholy she hadn't seen there before, and she hoped it wasn't permanent. He'd exchanged his old clothes for clean new ones, and the baby-blue polo shirt and grey pants were better suited on a well-off businessman enjoying a golf trip than a battle-worn soldier who had survived hell. He still had his army boots on—they all did—which

made the outfit even more bizarre. The image was jarring, and Jennifer blinked away tears as everything threatened to overwhelm her again. Anthony was a good man. He didn't deserve all the shit that had happened to them.

She turned and looked down the bus as she regained her equilibrium.

Edward sat with his head propped up on his fist, his eyes closed. A peaceful look adorned his face, but his body told another story. The weapon on his lap was anything but peaceful. His black T-shirt was clean, but blood seeped through a couple of the bandages on his arms, and his jeans—which he hadn't changed—were ripped above the knee. Looking at those bandages now, Jennifer was glad she'd made the decision to stop using hers. They wouldn't have had enough for everyone otherwise. Jennifer didn't really know Edward that well, but he'd proven himself time and again.

Elise and Ismay were across the aisle from Edward. Elise had Ismay wrapped in a tight hug on her knee, and the poor girl looked all cried out. Her little round face was blotchy, and she closed her red eyes as Elise tucked her head under her chin. Jennifer hoped she wouldn't remember much of this when she got older. She was still in her clothes from the castle. They'd been washed, but Jennifer made a note to find her new ones soon. Her top was more grey than white, and her leggings had more holes in them than Swiss cheese.

Elise gazed out of the window, her face pulled into sharp focus by her severe ponytail. She wore a black tank top and black jeans above her black army boots, and everything about her looked hard. But she gently rocked Ismay as the girl fell asleep. Jennifer hadn't thought Elise

capable of such softness. Her steel eyes briefly met Jennifer's as she glanced her way, and what Jennifer saw there made her think Elise didn't have that death wish any more.

Behind them sat Hiran. Jennifer had only known him for about a week, but she trusted him. He'd been nothing but helpful, fitting into their group like he'd been there from the beginning. His short black hair was damp from the river, and he looked fresh, like he hadn't been involved in a massive shootout where three of their group had died. He didn't have any injuries beyond the expected cuts and bruises, and his white pinstriped shirt and neat trousers made him look like he was on his morning commute to work in an office. His gaze fixed on his lap, and a sadness etched itself around his eyes. Jennifer hoped it would ease with time.

Across the aisle from him and behind Edward sat Riya and Aarav. Jennifer's emotions were all in turmoil when she looked at the young couple.

Sweet, caring Riya. Sitting next to her husband in soft black pants and a red top that was much too big for her. Jennifer couldn't wrap her head around how someone as lovely as Riya would be with someone as horrible as Aarav. She considered her a friend, but Jennifer knew she'd never see Aarav as such. She and Riya talked about India and culture and anything and everything, yet she couldn't say more than a few words to Aarav without it devolving into an argument. His white tennis top was also too big for him, but Jennifer couldn't care less.

Heather slouched behind the newlyweds. Her mouth was open slightly as she stared out of the window, and Jennifer allowed herself a little smile at the sight. Saving

her was the one good thing that had come out of the Red Lion. Heather hadn't changed out of her baggy grey joggers and her white tank top under a pink checked shirt, opting to dress people's wounds instead. She and Riya would make a good team. Jennifer felt safe knowing the two women were good at what they did.

Behind Heather were Rhys and Dan, sitting next to each other on the group of four seats. They both had their feet up on the opposite chair, their big army boots no doubt tracking mud all over them. Rhys wore a pink polo top similar to Anthony's that looked a size too small, with grey pants that also seemed a tad too tight to be comfortable. Together with the boots the outfit looked ridiculous. His eyes were closed and Jennifer wasn't sure if he was asleep or not. He'd shaved at the pub, and he looked a bit more like the old Rhys, albeit with longer hair, and guilt stirred in her chest as she looked at him. They still hadn't caught up. Jennifer had kept putting it off, citing different things, but she knew it was because she didn't want to relive all the shit that happened in London. Still, it wasn't fair on them both. She sighed and resolved to sit down with him one evening and let it all out. It would be nice to have him back as a proper friend again.

Dan, like Heather, stared out of the window. He was wearing black ripped jeans and a black bomber jacket, and it would have looked quite stylish if not for the gaudy orange gym top underneath. Jennifer had been craving somewhere safe since this whole mess began, but she hoped they'd find somewhere soon for him more than anything. He'd started to open up at the castle, without the constant threat of death, and to see him retreat back into himself had been heartbreaking. They needed somewhere secure so he could flourish.

Across the aisle from them was Alexia. Strong, kind Alexia. Jennifer couldn't believe she was interested in her. Those butterflies still fluttered at the sight of her, and Jennifer didn't think they'd leave anytime soon. She let her eyes rake over Alexia's form, clad in soft leggings and an oversized T-shirt that had a picture of a glittering Eiffel Tower stamped across it. Alexia had snatched it up with a smirk as soon as she'd seen it. Jennifer couldn't wait to learn everything there was to know about her. Meeting her was one of the few good things to happen in the past couple of months.

At the back of the bus were Victoria and Teona, both seated at either end next to the windows. They gazed out at the passing scenery, frowns marring their faces, and both wore identical dark-blue tank tops. Victoria's weapon was propped up in her lap, her hand holding it in a loose grip, while Teona had abandoned hers across the seats next to her.

Jennifer couldn't get a read on Teona's emotions, but she had to be all over the place. Her growing relationship with James had been cut so cruelly short, yet none of it showed on her face bar the slight frown. If she'd learned anything about the woman since they'd met, however, it was that she could tackle anything. Jennifer was confident she'd come out of this fighting.

She rolled up her sleeves and lined up her camera, snapping several shots of everyone down the bus, and two of Anthony at the wheel, one where he was oblivious to her presence and the other as he smiled after he'd spotted her. She stood at the front fiddling with the settings for a while, letting her mind get lost in the creative process. A welcome distraction. When she was happy with the

results, she switched it off and moved to sit next to Alexia.

She was asleep—Jennifer envied Alexia's ability to fall asleep wherever—so chatting for a bit was off the table. Not that she would have been a good conversationalist after the day they'd had.

Instead of sleeping, Jennifer's mind turned to thoughts of grief and loss. The two emotions weighed heavy in her heart, and she felt almost sick at the thought of pushing everyone on when she herself struggled too. She'd hit rock bottom in London but had managed to push herself back up. Finding Rhys, meeting Alexia, building a new family. She'd been knocked back down again, grief squeezing the air from her lungs and loss making it difficult to see the good still left in the world.

She hadn't known Charlie. He'd been a quiet person, and Jennifer had only spoken to him properly once. He'd helped Ismay, and Teona with the helicopter before that. He'd been brave to help.

She hadn't known Danny for that long either, but he'd been kind and earnest, and so positive even in this shitty world. Jennifer would miss him. He'd saved her in Paris. She hated that she hadn't been able to do the same for him.

James. She would miss him the most. She would keep going for him. He'd want her to get everyone somewhere safe. Gruff, grouchy, and serious, she knew he'd cared for them all, and she'd do her best for him. She almost started crying again.

She sighed, settling further into her seat. Outside the bus trees and fields passed silently as Anthony weaved their way north. Propping her feet up on the seats opposite, Jennifer let her head fall onto Alexia's shoulder. She

needed to help everyone, give them a better life. She couldn't let her mind get stuck in a rut.

The scenery passed by in a blur, but Jennifer didn't take any of it in. She focused on all the good that had happened, all the good she'd done for people, all the good she could do for everyone. She focused on her family around her, on the will and strength they gave her, on how she knew they loved her.

She wouldn't let grief win.

Chapter Thirty-Eight

Five hours and six stops later—one toilet break and five road blockages—the bus finally ran out of fuel. It had managed to keep going for far longer than Jennifer had thought it would. They were somewhere in the North—they had passed signs for Leeds, then Newcastle—and when the bus rolled to a stop everyone let out a collective breath. They were a hundred miles away from the disaster. The air felt cleaner here.

And colder, Jennifer thought as she stepped off the bus, taking a deep breath of the crisp air. She rolled her sleeves down as a shiver swept through her. *I wish I had a coat.*

"More walking," Victoria grimaced. "Bloody brilliant."

"You mean you're not used to it already?"

Victoria shot her a glare. "I don't know about your feet, but mine are crying out for some tender love and care. A bit of moisturiser. A massage. One day's rest was nowhere near enough."

Jennifer shook her head, smiling to herself. Victoria could be so dramatic sometimes. Although in this case,

she did have a point. Jennifer's feet hated her.

They were in the middle of the motorway, with tall, bare trees lining either side of the road, creating a sort of tunnel effect and making everything feel narrow and closed in. Jennifer lifted her gaze to the sky, only to be greeted by steel grey as cloud covered up any trace of blue.

"Right then, everyone knows the drill," Jennifer said. "Supreme Commander?" She wanted to keep Teona as involved as possible and hoped her joking-but-real title would help drag her into the conversation—she hadn't said anything for hours. It was unnerving.

Teona gave her a flat look before sighing. "Trueman and Ota take point, Rhys, Victoria, and Alexia at the rear, Hiran and myself on the left and right, respectively. Elise, you stay in the middle with Ismay and everyone else. Let's get this show on the road."

They set off without further ado. Jennifer fell into step next to Teona, making sure she kept an eye on her surroundings as she tried to subtly watch her too. Teona's eye roll told her how successful she was. "I don't need a fucking babysitter," she muttered, clenching her jaw as she glared at the trees.

"I never said you did." Jennifer shrugged. They continued walking in silence, and Jennifer resolved not to pester Teona. Grief was a solitary process. Instead, she forced her mind to think about where they'd camp for the night, or what to do when the food ran out, or what to do if Scotland wasn't feasible. How would they sustain themselves? Even if they got the power on, they would still need food. James said there would be fresh water, which was good, but how were they supposed to grow food? They'd need seeds and stuff they didn't have. Jennifer began to

feel overwhelmed, so she shut off that line of thinking.

Teona cleared her throat. "Look," she started then stopped, looking like she wanted to be talking about literally anything else. "It's shit. I... I really liked him, you know? And now he's gone, and there's fuck all any of us could have done about it. He saved us. I'm going to mourn, and I might even be a bitch if you lot bug me with your touchy-feely shit, but I'm going to be okay. I have to be okay. You were right—he would want us to continue, he'd want *me* to continue. I know you're worried but give me time. I'll be fine."

Jennifer's shoulders lost their tension. She hadn't realised how wound up she'd been over Teona's mental state. "Okay. I know this is probably the last thing you want to hear, but I'm here if you need to talk." Teona rolled her eyes and Jennifer rushed on in case she interrupted. "We all are. Mourn, take your time, do it in your own way, whatever, but know that we'll all be here for you. Hell, we're all right there with you."

They walked forward a few more steps in silence before Teona finally met her eyes. She nodded once, and Jennifer caught a brief glimpse of vulnerability there before the dark gaze moved away. It shook her. Teona had always been a pillar of confidence, solid and unbreakable. To see her struggling, even if only for a short time, was unsettling.

I'll be that pillar of strength. I can do this. She still thought she didn't have a clue what to do, but like Teona said, half the battle was looking the part. *Fake it till I make it. We can do this. We can survive.*

A new surge of energy sang in her blood, washing away some of her tiredness.

We will *survive.*

*

They'd been walking for about an hour when Hiran suddenly stopped, causing the whole group to halt and look around. Jennifer's eyes darted about, trying to locate the danger. Victoria fingered her gun and glared about the place like she expected infected to come streaming over the hills. All Jennifer could see was a six-car pileup further down the road, and trees, trees, and more trees. No movement.

"What is it, Hiran?" Jennifer asked in a quiet voice.

"I think I remember..." He frowned at nothing.

"Spit it out," Teona all but growled.

"Erm," Hiran said, doing his best impression of Dan. "I'm sure I remember something about a safe zone being built up in Northumberland. We might not be far from it. If we found it, we could stay there for the night."

"That's not a bad idea," Edward said slowly. "I remember something like that as well. It would offer good shelter."

Jennifer had heard the soldiers talking about these "safe zones" in the past, but they'd always dismissed them. "From the way you all talked about safe zones I got the impression they weren't worth our time."

Anthony sighed. "They were supposed to be these great, secure places that the military built as a safeguard against, well, this. In the event of a catastrophic failure—basically exactly what happened—we were supposed to take any and every uninfected civilian to the nearest safe zone where they could ride out the worst of it. Food and

water were stockpiled, generators were there to provide electricity, the facilities were all either fenced or walled off."

Jennifer couldn't believe her ears. "That sounds *incredible*."

Teona snorted. "We were originally taking you all to one. Remember Thorney Island? We converted Baker Barracks into a safe zone, but when we got there it had been gutted and burned."

"Most reports said they were either overrun or they never got the chance to get going," Anthony continued. "I imagine by now the majority have been ransacked. Although a lot were in remote locations, like Northumberland. There's a good chance stuff will still be there."

"It is the same in France," Alexia said. "The Commandant wanted to start supply runs to them but the one closest to the castle had already been looted."

Hope tightened Jennifer's throat, causing it to burn like she was holding back tears. Maybe she was. This was *fantastic* news. Maybe they wouldn't have to go to Scotland after all. This could solve their food and power issues. They could get it up and running, secure it, maybe even broadcast to other survivors. Jennifer took a deep breath and reined in her excited thoughts.

"Do any of you know its exact location?" The idea had taken root in her head, and it wasn't going to be shaken free easily.

"Well, we're already past Alnwick," Hiran said, still frowning. "It was north of Alnwick, wasn't it?" He looked around at the other soldiers.

"Don't look at me, I haven't got a fucking clue." Teona

held a hand up as she continued scanning the treeline.

"Was it near Bamburgh?" Edward asked no one in particular.

"I think so," Anthony said, screwing his face up as he tried to remember. "That castle does ring a bell."

Irritation trickled through her, even though she knew they were doing their best. Hell, it was probably a miracle Hiran had remembered it existed in the first place. "We can't just wander through Northumberland aimlessly," she said, managing to keep the snap out of her tone. "We need something more than that to go on."

"We should keep walking while you think," Victoria said. She was right—they'd been in one place for too long.

Hiran joined Anthony and Edward at the front as the group set off again, and Alexia came around to cover the side. The clouds overhead thickened as the day crawled on, and the temperature, while still better than it had been, dropped to the point where Jennifer seriously contemplated jogging to work some warmth back into her body.

They must have walked for another few hours at least, only stopping once for food and another toilet break. Jennifer had never felt as unclean as she did when she skulked into the trees and bushes lining the road to pee and change her tampon. The sooner they found somewhere with working toilets the better.

The three men at the front eventually led them off the road, skirting around small towns until they were deep in the country. Evening chased the daylight away, and the temperature dropped yet again, leaving everyone shivering. Jennifer was about to call a halt and set up camp

where they stood when she saw it. The faint shimmer of light in the distance. It could have been anything really, but the soldiers up front stopped and turned around, wearing matching grins. Jennifer sagged with relief.

"I *knew* it was around here," Hiran exclaimed, looking moments away from dancing with happiness.

Edward clapped him on the back. "Good job remembering that."

Jennifer smiled at the group. "We did it. Just a few more minutes walking and we can rest safe for the night." It was good timing—the sky had darkened to a blue bordering black, and soon the remnants of daylight would be gone completely.

"The lights are on," Alexia said slowly.

"Shit, yeah," Rhys chimed in, the first he'd spoken in hours. "Someone's already there."

Relief fled as anxiety rushed in. Jennifer turned to Hiran. "Is there any possibility they could have been left on from the start of the outbreak?"

His throat bobbed as he swallowed. "The generators running constantly for over two months? No way. They would need to be topped up."

Fuck, Jennifer thought. They did *not* need another Red Lion. Maybe it would be like the castle, but she wasn't willing to take that chance. *No one* else was going to die. *No one else.* "How much ammo do we have?"

Teona snorted. "You want to storm that place?"

"Of course not," Jennifer snapped. "I want to know if we have enough bullets to cover us if we need to make a hasty retreat. If that happens, we can easily get lost in the

darkness, right?"

"Yeah," Rhys said. "The light would work to our advantage, blinding them. We'd have to be careful not to lose each other."

"They might be good, though," Riya said hopefully. "Like the castle?"

"Plan for the worst," Victoria said firmly. "Anything else that happens will only be good for us."

"Okay, people," Teona started, gathering everyone around. She seemed more focused now they had a mission. The melancholy in her eyes had been replaced with determination, and Jennifer was glad to see it. The last thing they needed was their Supreme Commander going off the rails.

"They'll have lookouts who should spot us from far out if they're worth their salt. We walk forward slowly and calmly, with our hands and weapons in the air—"

Victoria cut her off. "What if they start firing? I don't like this; it feels too exposed."

"You're good with your weapon, Victoria, but you still have a lot to learn," Teona chastised. "If we go running up with our weapons ready to fire, they'll cut us down faster than you can even think of pulling the trigger. We walk slowly, to show them we aren't a threat. We know jack shit about this place. Those people in there could be trigger happy. This way we won't panic them into making stupid decisions."

"We'll be staying here," Aarav said, his chin lifting as he glared at Jennifer. She felt anger burn hot again at his contrariness and closed her eyes as she pinched the top of her nose.

"Aarav—" Riya started, but Jennifer cut over her.

"I don't give a *fuck* what you think of me, or if you want to follow me," Jennifer growled, her patience at an end. "You want to stay here, fine, be my guest, but when the rest of us are all nice and cosy in that safe zone, don't think for *one second* that I'm letting you in. So, you can either stay out here, or you can stop being a *fucking arse-hole* and come with us. Your choice."

They glared at each other for a couple of seconds. She knew the fury in his face was mirrored on her own. She was sick of putting up with his bullshit, sick of playing nice and trying to reason with him.

He broke eye contact first, and a rush of satisfaction filled her up at the small victory. She watched as his jaw clenched and his lip curled, but he didn't say anything.

"We'll come with you," Riya said in a small voice. "I'm sorry. It is a difficult thing, overcoming things that have been engrained since childhood."

Jennifer wasn't willing to feel sorry for him. "And yet you don't seem to be having as much trouble as him." She turned away before she could properly lose her temper. She took a deep breath, the cool air filling her lungs and calming her down. "Look, we'll sit down and talk about it later, when we're settled in the zone." She needed to be diplomatic, even when the thought of sitting down and hearing his disgusting views made her skin crawl. Maybe she could change his mind.

"Right, well, now that that's sorted." Teona clapped her hands together. "Let's get a move on."

They walked toward the light, and Jennifer's palms became sweaty as her heart started to race. What if they

opened fire? What if she got shot? What if the others did? Dan? Alexia? She didn't think she could forgive herself if anything happened to them. The guilt of James and Danny and Charlie was already eating her up—she couldn't add more fuel to that fire. *She* had decided to stay at the Red Lion, *she* had decided to let Heather steal the food. Their deaths were on her. Jennifer didn't think she could take it if anyone else died.

As they got closer to the fence Jennifer couldn't see any movement, couldn't hear any sounds other than their own. Where was everyone? They made it right up to the gate, and found it open enough for people to slip through individually. Jennifer exchanged a suspicious look with Victoria before turning to Teona. God, she'd hoped this place would live up to its name, but who knew what lay beyond in the gathering darkness?

There was a pause as no one spoke, then Teona shuffled forward. "Trueman, Ota, with me. The rest of you stay here."

"Wait—"

Victoria barely got the word out before Teona snapped at her. "Shut up and obey your orders, soldier. You've not been trained for this. The three of us can clear this place quicker without you." Victoria looked like she'd been slapped. "Let's go."

Without another word, the soldiers crept through the gate and disappeared into the gloom. Anthony shot Victoria a parting shrug, and she huffed as they vanished.

"Come on," Alexia said. "Let's settle a little way away from here and wait for them to return." The group followed Alexia and Rhys to a spot not too far away, one that was out of reach of the lights in case something went

wrong. Jennifer hoped not. This day couldn't possibly get any worse.

They sat waiting for what felt like forever, and Jennifer ended up shivering uncontrollably as the sun finally fell below the horizon and night blanketed the hills. The soldiers stood guarding them, and they didn't seem affected by the temperature. Jennifer didn't know how they did it.

Rhys spotted them first. Jennifer pushed her frozen limbs up, squinting, and eventually saw them strolling toward them, looking like they didn't have a care in the world. Jennifer hadn't heard any gunfire, but that didn't mean anything. They could have killed people silently. She frantically searched them for blood or wounds but couldn't see anything in the dark.

Teona wasted no time. "Six people, all dead. All infected. Maybe they were infected before they found this place or maybe infected got in," she shrugged. "There's no breaks in the fence that we could see, but I'd like to double check in the morning. Let's get in, it's fucking freezing."

Jennifer made sure she was the last person through the gate. She turned to look out over the open expanse, but only blackness greeted her. Still, she could feel the weight of it pressing down, and as Hiran shut the gate she breathed in deeply, her airways expanding as the pressure lifted. *In.*

And out.

Epilogue

Jennifer stretched, her back muscles pulling pleasantly as she lifted her arms over her head. Her camera caught her eye from the table across the room. She smiled softly at it, thoughts of the people and lives it contained filling up her mind. *You'd all be happy we made it here.* She'd almost deleted Brendon but hadn't been able to in the end. The future needed to know that evil had a face, and that face smiled so easily. Bright sunlight streamed in through the flimsy curtains, and Jennifer's smile widened, the last vestiges of sleep falling away as she pulled a top on and moved to the window.

Down in the courtyard were three figures, framed by the rising sun. Jennifer watched as their breath steamed in the cold air, two heavy and hard, one calm and even. Edward sat on a crate, bundled up in a large coat as he wrote, and Anthony and Victoria moved around each other in an intricate way that looked less like fighting and more like dancing. Anthony had told her the other day that it wouldn't be long before he could no longer teach Victoria, and watching them, even with her limited knowledge, Jennifer had to agree. *The student surpasses the teacher.* She snorted. Of course Victoria would be a teacher's pet.

Edward and Anthony were like each other's shadows. Jennifer hadn't thought much of it at first, until Anthony had haltingly come out to her a couple of days after they'd arrived at the safe zone. *My gaydar really is terrible.* She'd ended up being Anthony's wing woman and judging from his and Edward's smiles the next morning, she'd done her job well.

Jennifer didn't hear Alexia come up behind her. She almost jumped when strong arms wrapped around her waist, and she smothered a laugh at herself. She was getting better, but she still startled far too easily for her liking.

"You're up early," Alexia murmured into her hair.

Jennifer shrugged one shoulder. "Sorry, I didn't mean to wake you. I said I'd meet with Elise this morning, and then Teona." It seemed she'd never stood still since they'd arrived three weeks ago. "Believe me, I would much rather stay in bed with you all day."

She turned in Alexia's arms and kissed her soundly, her hands coming up to tangle in her hair. She really did love her hair. She'd finally seen her tattoo, and now she couldn't imagine waking up without Alexia. Everything was moving so fast, but Jennifer wouldn't have it any other way.

She stopped the kiss before she would be *really* late. Alexia laughed as Jennifer pouted, throwing her clothes at her and telling her to get a move on.

"Say hi to Dan for me."

"I will." Alexia smiled. She'd been taking Dan on her guard shift, teaching him the tools of the trade. Anthony had picked up his combat training as well. Dan was

becoming quite the little badass. A *shy* badass, but a badass, nonetheless. "He's picking it all up well. And yesterday he even told me a story of his old school."

"Yeah?" Jennifer beamed. She couldn't wait for him to come properly out of his shell. She didn't like that he'd chosen to train to become a soldier, but she couldn't control his actions, and if it helped him build his confidence Jennifer was all for it.

They quickly washed, and parted ways outside the building. Alexia gave her a lingering kiss and a wink as she sauntered off to the guard post near the gate. Jennifer stood watching her for a few seconds before she shook herself and moved off in the opposite direction.

The compound was a maze, but Jennifer had quickly acclimatised. She had pictures of the entire place. The sleeping quarters were like a hotel, four stories high with a multitude of rooms that included a bedroom, bathroom, and living room. Jennifer had almost cried at the working toilets and showers. She'd let out an embarrassing shout of joy upon seeing a toothbrush. Teona still teased her about it.

The mess hall was her first stop, and she quickly grabbed an apple from the kitchens. The place was huge, clearly designed to house a lot more people than it currently did. Round tables littered the floor, and the kitchens were massive, with a large stockpile of food ready and waiting to be cooked and eaten. Jennifer had been cautious about the food—the virus could be in any of it, but there wasn't a lot they could do about that. They all had to eat, after all. They kept a chart of who ate what and when. It was a constant source of anxiety for Jennifer.

She made her way back out into the sunlight, and

stood for a moment, feeling the cold rays on her skin. She kicked a bit of snow with her foot as she set off again, feeling a shiver work its way under her coat. The warm weather had deserted them, and it had snowed over the last few days. Heavily, in the middle of March. Ismay loved it, running around with Dan and Elise, making snow angels and building snowmen. That had been a good day. Jennifer only wished James had been alive to hear her laugh.

She worked her way up to the building Elise waited at. She knew what Elise wanted to talk to her about. She'd given up her soldier's mantle, opting instead to be with the children, which so far consisted of Dan and Ismay. Victoria and Elise seemed to have swapped roles. Victoria took to being a soldier like a duck to water, and Elise had a way with kids that Jennifer hadn't expected.

She wanted to turn the building toward the middle of the compound into a school. Its original purpose was vague—Hiran had thought it was supposed to be some sort of meeting hall, and it had several rooms that could be used as classrooms—and it stood empty and unused. Jennifer didn't see any issue with it being turned into a school, except for the glaringly obvious lack of children. They'd started broadcasting last week—Edward, Rhys, and Alexia had worked hard to get the radio operational— but so far no one had made it to them. They *were* in the middle of nowhere. Jennifer pushed down the voice that said everyone else was dead or infected. That was too horrible to contemplate. People would start arriving soon.

She knew Teona wanted to speak to her about soldiers going out and bringing back supplies like fuel and food. It was a good idea, and they also needed

information. About the world, about anything they heard. If everywhere was as devastated as she thought, they were going to be here for the rest of their lives, and Jennifer wanted to build a proper little settlement. She didn't want all the knowledge of the old world lost. Teona had already mentioned bringing back books, phones, anything they could use to educate themselves. Humanity wasn't going to fall back to the dark ages.

She waved to Elise as she walked up to her, and she was about to say hi when she heard running footsteps behind her. She turned, dread churning her stomach into a maelstrom.

"Jennifer!" It was Rhys, panting from running across the compound.

"What's happened?"

"People at the gates."

Fluttering excitement tickled her stomach. Jennifer apologised to Elise and started jogging through the snow. Rhys kept pace next to her, and she could tell from his laboured breathing that he was excited. Could this be it? The beginning of the rest of their lives?

She slowed to a walk as they reached the gate to the zone, and Jennifer took a deep, calming breath. These would be the first survivors they'd found. She had to make a good first impression.

Riya was searching them for bites, and she said Heather was on her way. Teona stood in front of them all, her gun held calmly in her arms. Jennifer made her way over to her, standing tall as they observed the newcomers. There were seven people in total, two men, three women, and two children, a boy and a girl, around ten Jennifer

guessed. She took in their shivering forms, their wide eyes that held both wonder and hesitation, and smiled. She knew that feeling.

"What do you think?" Jennifer quietly asked Teona. The boy had an open wound on his arm, and one of the women favoured her left leg, but other than that they seemed to be in good condition.

"Ragtag bunch of sorry bastards." Teona shrugged. "But they made it this far, so they must be either incredibly lucky or damn good at surviving."

Teona seemed fine, but Jennifer had once caught her staring at a chocolate bar, of all things, and when she'd asked about it, Teona had snapped at her and stormed off. Jennifer hadn't brought it up again.

"My name is Jennifer," she said as Riya finished their checks. She saw Heather making her way over. The paramedic was teaching everyone advanced first aid. The world was brutal, but they would have the skills to handle it. "And I want to offer you all a massive welcome. You'll be safe here. Your time running for your lives is over. But while you don't have to worry about infected here, please don't let yourself get too lax. It's still dangerous out there."

Heather had said the infected should be dying off anyway, but that didn't diminish the threat just yet. People were still out there getting bitten.

A chorus of *thank-yous* reached Jennifer's ears, and the gratitude in their watery eyes made her swallow roughly.

"I'd like to talk to you all if that's okay. I have a camera, and I want to show you my story, and then I want to hear yours." Jennifer had thought hard about how she

wanted to record the outbreak, and she'd decided first-hand accounts was the only way to do it justice. "I want everyone who makes it here to be as informed as possible, so the future generations don't repeat the mistakes of the past." She took in their overwhelmed wide eyes. "I won't bombard you all just yet." She smiled. "You're in good hands with Commander Wright here, she looks after us all."

"Damn right I do," Teona said.

Heather finally arrived, only to stop dead. "Kallie?"

The woman with the injured leg let out a sob as her eyes landed on Heather, and before Jennifer could even blink the two women embraced each other so tightly Jennifer couldn't see where one ended and the other began.

They began talking over each other, their voices stained with tears.

"I thought I'd lost you—"

"—I've missed you so much—"

"—Are you okay—"

"—What happened—"

They both cut off with a laugh, and leaned back, their eyes drinking each other in. Jennifer almost cried at the relief she saw between them, and she didn't know what was going on.

Heather gestured to the woman she'd called Kallie's leg. "Is that okay?"

Kallie grimaced. "I cut it on a tree branch, of all things. It's infected."

Heather nodded. "You'll be all right. We have antibiotics." She turned to Jennifer and Teona. "This is Kallie,

my wife." Fresh tears slipped down her face as she turned back to Kallie. "I never thought I'd see you again."

Jennifer's face strained as a wide grin spread. "This is amazing. I'm so happy you made it. All of you."

Teona took over as Heather and Kallie continued holding on to each other like they never intended to let go. "Okay, people, listen up and follow me. We're going to the mess hall, where you can have warm food and drinks and we can get you changed out of those clothes. No offense but you all reek something terrible. After that I'll give you a quick tour and show you to rooms…"

Teona's voice drifted off as they moved away, and Jennifer watched their retreating backs, her grin still firmly in place. Hopefully this group was the first of many. They would help people, make them feel safe and secure again. They would get Elise's school up and running, and they would gather information as they built a life for themselves. Dan would grow into a good man. Jennifer would laugh and joke with Rhys again. Maybe she'd even get to grow old with Alexia by her side.

"We're going to be okay, aren't we, Jen?" Rhys's voice was soft, and when she looked at him his eyes shone bright.

She smiled. "We're going to be okay."